Adobe® PhotoDeluxe® 4 For Dummies®

Cheat Sheet

D0567553

File Menu Shortcuts

To Do This	Use This Shortcut
Open, Close an existing image	Press Ctrl+O, Ctrl+W
Open the PhotoDeluxe clip art	Press Ctrl+\
Save the active image in the PhotoDeluxe format (PDD)	Press Ctrl+S
Print the active image	Press Ctrl+P
Preview an image before printing	Press Ctrl+/
Open the Cursors dialog box	Press Ctrl+K
Shut down PhotoDeluxe	Press Ctrl+Q

Image-Viewing Shortcuts

To Do This	Use This Shortcut
Zoom in on the image	Press Ctrl+Plus Key or Ctrl+Shift+Plus Key
Zoom out	Press Ctrl+Minus Key
Scroll image in the image window	Hold down the spacebar and drag
Show/hide the rulers	Press Ctrl+R

Selection Shortcuts

To Do This	Use This Shortcut
Select the active layer	Press Ctrl+A
Remove a selection outline	Press Ctrl+D
Invert the existing selection outline	Press Ctrl+I
Select the Trace selection tool	Press Ctrl+L
Select the Rectangle selection tool	Press Ctrl+M
Select the Color Wand selection tool	Press Ctrl+F
Select the Move tool	Press Ctrl+G
Move a selection outline	Ctrl+Alt+Drag with Move tool

Copyright © 2000 IDG Books Worldwide, Inc.
All rights reserved.

Cheat Sheet $2.95 value. Item 0708-7.

For more information about IDG Books,
call 1-800-762-2974.

IDG BOOKS WORLDWIDE

For Dummies®: Bestselling Book Series for Beginners

FOR DUMMIES™

BESTSELLING
BOOK SERIES

Adobe® PhotoDeluxe® 4 For Dummies®

Cheat Sheet

Painting Shortcuts

To Do This	Use This Shortcut
Select the Brush tool	Press Ctrl+J
Select the Text tool	Press Ctrl+T
Select the Eraser tool	Press Ctrl+E
Adjust opacity of Brush, Line, Clone, or Eraser tool	Press a number key
Adjust pressure of Smudge tool	Press a number key
Open the Selection Fill dialog box	Press Ctrl+9
Open the Gradient Fill dialog box	Press Ctrl+8
Fill a selection with the foreground color	Press Alt+Backspace
Paint a horizontal or vertical stroke	Shift+Drag with the Brush tool
Constrain a line to 45-degree angles	Shift+Drag with the Line tool

Color Correction Shortcuts

To Do This	Use This Shortcut
Adjust color balance	Ctrl+Y
Adjust contrast/brightness	Ctrl+B
Adjust hue/saturation	Ctrl+U
Convert to a grayscale image	Ctrl+0

Basic Editing Shortcuts

To Do This	Use This Shortcut
Undo last edit	Press Ctrl+Z or click Undo button
Select Trim tool and crop an image	Press Ctrl+7+Drag with Trim tool
Cut, Copy selection to the Clipboard	Ctrl+X, Ctrl+C
Paste Clipboard contents into open image	Ctrl+V
Move a selection	Drag with Move tool
Copy selection and move the copy	Alt+Drag with Move tool
Rotate selection 90° degrees clockwise/counteclockwise	Press Ctrl+>, Press Ctrl+<
Display resize handles	Press Ctrl+6

The IDG Books Worldwide logo is a registered trademark under exclusive license to IDG Books Worldwide, Inc., from International Data Group, Inc. The ...For Dummies logo is a trademark, and For Dummies is a registered trademark of IDG Books Worldwide, Inc. All other trademarks are the property of their respective owners.

For Dummies®: Bestselling Book Series for Beginners

 TM

References for the Rest of Us! ®

BESTSELLING BOOK SERIES

Are you intimidated and confused by computers? Do you find that traditional manuals are overloaded with technical details you'll never use? Do your friends and family always call you to fix simple problems on their PCs? Then the *...For Dummies*® computer book series from IDG Books Worldwide is for you.

...For Dummies books are written for those frustrated computer users who know they aren't really dumb but find that PC hardware, software, and indeed the unique vocabulary of computing make them feel helpless. *...For Dummies* books use a lighthearted approach, a down-to-earth style, and even cartoons and humorous icons to dispel computer novices' fears and build their confidence. Lighthearted but not lightweight, these books are a perfect survival guide for anyone forced to use a computer.

> *"I like my copy so much I told friends; now they bought copies."*
>
> — *Irene C., Orwell, Ohio*

> *"Quick, concise, nontechnical, and humorous."*
>
> — *Jay A., Elburn, Illinois*

> *"Thanks, I needed this book. Now I can sleep at night."*
>
> — *Robin F., British Columbia, Canada*

Already, millions of satisfied readers agree. They have made *...For Dummies* books the #1 introductory level computer book series and have written asking for more. So, if you're looking for the most fun and easy way to learn about computers, look to *...For Dummies* books to give you a helping hand.

IDG BOOKS WORLDWIDE ®

1/99

Adobe® PhotoDeluxe® 4

FOR

DUMMIES®

Adobe® PhotoDeluxe® 4 FOR DUMMIES®

by Julie Adair King

IDG Books Worldwide, Inc.
An International Data Group Company

Foster City, CA ◆ Chicago, IL ◆ Indianapolis, IN ◆ New York, NY

Adobe® PhotoDeluxe® 4 For Dummies®

Published by
IDG Books Worldwide, Inc.
An International Data Group Company
919 E. Hillsdale Blvd.
Suite 400
Foster City, CA 94404
www.idgbooks.com (IDG Books Worldwide Web site)
www.dummies.com (Dummies Press Web site)

Copyright © 2000 IDG Books Worldwide, Inc. All rights reserved. No part of this book, including interior design, cover design, and icons, may be reproduced or transmitted in any form, by any means (electronic, photocopying, recording, or otherwise) without the prior written permission of the publisher.

Library of Congress Catalog Card No.: 00-100126

ISBN: 0-7645-0708-7

Printed in the United States of America

10 9 8 7 6 5 4 3 2 1

1B/RU/QU/QQ/IN

Distributed in the United States by IDG Books Worldwide, Inc.

Distributed by CDG Books Canada Inc. for Canada; by Transworld Publishers Limited in the United Kingdom; by IDG Norge Books for Norway; by IDG Sweden Books for Sweden; by IDG Books Australia Publishing Corporation Pty. Ltd. for Australia and New Zealand; by TransQuest Publishers Pte Ltd. for Singapore, Malaysia, Thailand, Indonesia, and Hong Kong; by Gotop Information Inc. for Taiwan; by ICG Muse, Inc. for Japan; by Intersoft for South Africa; by Eyrolles for France; by International Thomson Publishing for Germany, Austria and Switzerland; by Distribuidora Cuspide for Argentina; by LR International for Brazil; by Galileo Libros for Chile; by Ediciones ZETA S.C.R. Ltda. for Peru; by WS Computer Publishing Corporation, Inc., for the Philippines; by Contemporanea de Ediciones for Venezuela; by Express Computer Distributors for the Caribbean and West Indies; by Micronesia Media Distributor, Inc. for Micronesia; by Chips Computadoras S.A. de C.V. for Mexico; by Editorial Norma de Panama S.A. for Panama; by American Bookshops for Finland.

For general information on IDG Books Worldwide's books in the U.S., please call our Consumer Customer Service department at 800-762-2974. For reseller information, including discounts and premium sales, please call our Reseller Customer Service department at 800-434-3422.

For information on where to purchase IDG Books Worldwide's books outside the U.S., please contact our International Sales department at 317-596-5530 or fax 317-572-4002.

For consumer information on foreign language translations, please contact our Customer Service department at 1-800-434-3422, fax 317-572-4002, or e-mail rights@idgbooks.com.

For information on licensing foreign or domestic rights, please phone +1-650-653-7098.

For sales inquiries and special prices for bulk quantities, please contact our Order Services department at 800-434-3422 or write to the address above.

For information on using IDG Books Worldwide's books in the classroom or for ordering examination copies, please contact our Educational Sales department at 800-434-2086 or fax 317-572-4005.

For press review copies, author interviews, or other publicity information, please contact our Public Relations department at 650-653-7000 or fax 650-653-7500.

For authorization to photocopy items for corporate, personal, or educational use, please contact Copyright Clearance Center, 222 Rosewood Drive, Danvers, MA 01923, or fax 978-750-4470.

LIMIT OF LIABILITY/DISCLAIMER OF WARRANTY: THE PUBLISHER AND AUTHOR HAVE USED THEIR BEST EFFORTS IN PREPARING THIS BOOK. THE PUBLISHER AND AUTHOR MAKE NO REPRESENTATIONS OR WARRANTIES WITH RESPECT TO THE ACCURACY OR COMPLETENESS OF THE CONTENTS OF THIS BOOK AND SPECIFICALLY DISCLAIM ANY IMPLIED WARRANTIES OF MERCHANTABILITY OR FITNESS FOR A PARTICULAR PURPOSE. THERE ARE NO WARRANTIES WHICH EXTEND BEYOND THE DESCRIPTIONS CONTAINED IN THIS PARAGRAPH. NO WARRANTY MAY BE CREATED OR EXTENDED BY SALES REPRESENTATIVES OR WRITTEN SALES MATERIALS. THE ACCURACY AND COMPLETENESS OF THE INFORMATION PROVIDED HEREIN AND THE OPINIONS STATED HEREIN ARE NOT GUARANTEED OR WARRANTED TO PRODUCE ANY PARTICULAR RESULTS, AND THE ADVICE AND STRATEGIES CONTAINED HEREIN MAY NOT BE SUITABLE FOR EVERY INDIVIDUAL. NEITHER THE PUBLISHER NOR AUTHOR SHALL BE LIABLE FOR ANY LOSS OF PROFIT OR ANY OTHER COMMERCIAL DAMAGES, INCLUDING BUT NOT LIMITED TO SPECIAL, INCIDENTAL, CONSEQUENTIAL, OR OTHER DAMAGES. FULFILLMENT OF EACH COUPON OFFER IS THE RESPONSIBILITY OF THE OFFEROR.

Trademarks: Adobe and PhotoDeluxe are registered trademarks of Adobe Systems, Inc. For Dummies, Dummies Man, A Reference for the Rest of Us!, The Dummies Way, Dummies Daily, and related trade dress are registered trademarks or trademarks of IDG Books Worldwide, Inc. in the United States and other countries, and may not be used without written permission. All other trademarks are the property of their respective owners. IDG Books Worldwide is not associated with any product or vendor mentioned in this book.

 is a registered trademark under exclusive license to IDG Books Worldwide, Inc. from International Data Group, Inc.

About the Author

Julie Adair King is the author of *Digital Photography For Dummies* and *Microsoft PhotoDraw 2000 For Dummies.* She has contributed to several other books on digital imaging and computer graphics, including *Photoshop 4 Bible, Photoshop 4 For Dummies, CorelDRAW! 7 For Dummies,* and *PageMaker 6 For Dummies.* She is also the author of *WordPerfect Suite 7/8 For Dummies* and *WordPerfect Office 2000 For Dummies.*

Photo Credits

All images in this book are © 2000 Julie King Creative, Inc., with the exception of the following:

Image	Photographer/Source
Figures 4-5, 6-1, 6-4, 7-2, 9-2, 9-6,10-6, 10-7, 12-2, 13-1, 13-3, 15-1 through 15-12; Color Plates 3-1, 10-2, 10-3, 0-4, and 12-1	Adobe PhotoDeluxe (Adobe Systems, Inc.)
Figures 8-1, 8-2, 8-3, 9-9; Color Plates 8-4, 7-2, and 13-4	Linda S. Stark
Figure 10-4; Color Plate 10-1	George E. Harris
Figures 3-8 and 3-9	F. Dale King

All images are the property of the photographer/source and may not be reproduced without permission.

ABOUT IDG BOOKS WORLDWIDE

Welcome to the world of IDG Books Worldwide.

IDG Books Worldwide, Inc., is a subsidiary of International Data Group, the world's largest publisher of computer-related information and the leading global provider of information services on information technology. IDG was founded more than 30 years ago by Patrick J. McGovern and now employs more than 9,000 people worldwide. IDG publishes more than 290 computer publications in over 75 countries. More than 90 million people read one or more IDG publications each month.

Launched in 1990, IDG Books Worldwide is today the #1 publisher of best-selling computer books in the United States. We are proud to have received eight awards from the Computer Press Association in recognition of editorial excellence and three from Computer Currents' First Annual Readers' Choice Awards. Our best-selling ...*For Dummies*® series has more than 50 million copies in print with translations in 31 languages. IDG Books Worldwide, through a joint venture with IDG's Hi-Tech Beijing, became the first U.S. publisher to publish a computer book in the People's Republic of China. In record time, IDG Books Worldwide has become the first choice for millions of readers around the world who want to learn how to better manage their businesses.

Our mission is simple: Every one of our books is designed to bring extra value and skill-building instructions to the reader. Our books are written by experts who understand and care about our readers. The knowledge base of our editorial staff comes from years of experience in publishing, education, and journalism — experience we use to produce books to carry us into the new millennium. In short, we care about books, so we attract the best people. We devote special attention to details such as audience, interior design, use of icons, and illustrations. And because we use an efficient process of authoring, editing, and desktop publishing our books electronically, we can spend more time ensuring superior content and less time on the technicalities of making books.

You can count on our commitment to deliver high-quality books at competitive prices on topics you want to read about. At IDG Books Worldwide, we continue in the IDG tradition of delivering quality for more than 30 years. You'll find no better book on a subject than one from IDG Books Worldwide.

John J. Kilcullen
John Kilcullen
Chairman and CEO
IDG Books Worldwide, Inc.

VIII
WINNER

*Eighth Annual
Computer Press
Awards ≥1992*

IX
WINNER

*Ninth Annual
Computer Press
Awards ≥1993*

X
WINNER

*Tenth Annual
Computer Press
Awards ≥1994*

XI
WINNER

*Eleventh Annual
Computer Press
Awards ≥1995*

IDG is the world's leading IT media, research and exposition company. Founded in 1964, IDG had 1997 revenues of $2.05 billion and has more than 9,000 employees worldwide. IDG offers the widest range of media options that reach IT buyers in 75 countries representing 95% of worldwide IT spending. IDG's diverse product and services portfolio spans six key areas including print publishing, online publishing, expositions and conferences, market research, education and training, and global marketing services. More than 90 million people read one or more of IDG's 290 magazines and newspapers, including IDG's leading global brands — Computerworld, PC World, Network World, Macworld and the Channel World family of publications. IDG Books Worldwide is one of the fastest-growing computer book publishers in the world, with more than 700 titles in 36 languages. The "...For Dummies®" series alone has more than 50 million copies in print. IDG offers online users the largest network of technology-specific Web sites around the world through IDG.net (http://www.idg.net), which comprises more than 225 targeted Web sites in 55 countries worldwide. International Data Corporation (IDC) is the world's largest provider of information technology data, analysis and consulting, with research centers in over 41 countries and more than 400 research analysts worldwide. IDG World Expo is a leading producer of more than 168 globally branded conferences and expositions in 35 countries including E3 (Electronic Entertainment Expo), Macworld Expo, ComNet, Windows World Expo, ICE (Internet Commerce Expo), Agenda, DEMO, and Spotlight. IDG's training subsidiary, ExecuTrain, is the world's largest computer training company, with more than 230 locations worldwide and 785 training courses. IDG Marketing Services helps industry-leading IT companies build international brand recognition by developing global integrated marketing programs via IDG's print, online and exposition products worldwide. Further information about the company can be found at www.idg.com. 1/26/00

Dedication

This book is dedicated to the memory of George E. Harris, the best grand-father a girl could have.

Author's Acknowledgments

Like all books, this one would be languishing in a digital dustbin somewhere were it not for the efforts of a terrific team of editors and production professionals. I am fortunate to have on my side a wonderful group of people from IDG Books Worldwide, including project editor Nicole Haims, copy editor Tonya Maddox, acquisitions editor Steve Hayes, and production experts Shelley Lea, Emily Perkins, and Angie Hunckler.

I also want to thank technical editor Hew Hamilton, whose expertise added much to the quality of this book, and Linda Stark, who contributed some terrific photographs.

Finally, continued gratitude to my family for putting up with me all these years and especially to my nieces and nephews, Kristen, Matt, Adam, Brandon, and Laura, for posing patiently whenever I come around with camera in hand.

Publisher's Acknowledgments

We're proud of this book; please register your comments through our IDG Books Worldwide Online Registration Form located at http://my2cents.dummies.com.

Some of the people who helped bring this book to market include the following:

Acquisitions, Editorial, and Media Development

Project Editor: Nicole Haims

Acquisitions Editor: Steven H. Hayes

Copy Editor: Tonya Maddox

Proof Editor: Dwight Ramsey

Technical Editor: Hew Hamilton

Editorial Manager: Rev Mengle

Editorial Assistants: Candace Nicholson, Beth Parlon

Production

Project Coordinator: Emily Perkins

Layout and Graphics: Amy Adrian, Angela F. Hunckler, Barry Offringa, Jill Piscitelli

Proofreaders: John Greenough, Charles Spencer, York Production Services, Inc.

Indexer: York Production Services, Inc.

Special Help
Amanda Foxworth, Kristin Nash

General and Administrative

IDG Books Worldwide, Inc.: John Kilcullen, CEO

IDG Books Technology Publishing Group: Richard Swadley, Senior Vice President and Publisher; Walter R. Bruce III, Vice President and Publisher; Joseph Wikert, Vice President and Publisher; Mary Bednarek, Vice President and Director, Product Development; Andy Cummings, Publishing Director, General User Group; Mary C. Corder, Editorial Director; Barry Pruett, Publishing Director

IDG Books Consumer Publishing Group: Roland Elgey, Senior Vice President and Publisher; Kathleen A. Welton, Vice President and Publisher; Kevin Thornton, Acquisitions Manager; Kristin A. Cocks, Editorial Director

IDG Books Internet Publishing Group: Brenda McLaughlin, Senior Vice President and Publisher; Sofia Marchant, Online Marketing Manager

IDG Books Production for Branded Press: Debbie Stailey, Director of Production; Cindy L. Phipps, Manager of Project Coordination, Production Proofreading, and Indexing; Tony Augsburger, Manager of Prepress, Reprints, and Systems; Laura Carpenter, Production Control Manager; Shelley Lea, Supervisor of Graphics and Design; Debbie J. Gates, Production Systems Specialist; Robert Springer, Supervisor of Proofreading; Kathie Schutte, Production Supervisor

Packaging and Book Design: Patty Page, Manager, Promotions Marketing

◆

The publisher would like to give special thanks to Patrick J. McGovern, without whom this book would not have been possible.

◆

Contents at a Glance

Cartoons at a Glance

By Rich Tennant

"Hey- let's put scanned photos of ourselves through a ripple filter and see if we can make ourselves look weird."

page 7

"My God! I've gained 9 pixels!"

page 75

"SOFTWARE SUPPORT SAYS WHATEVER WE DO, DON'T ANYONE START TO RUN."

page 291

"...and here's me with Cindy Crawford. And this is me with Madonna and Celine Dion..."

page 217

"Okay, enlarge the chicken bone by 900 percent and attach it to an email to the museum saying, "Getting close...send more money.""

page 143

Fax: 978-546-7747
E-mail: richtennant@the5thwave.com
World Wide Web: www.the5thwave.com

Table of Contents

Introduction

*I*f you were to eavesdrop on a roomful of computer-industry marketing gurus, you'd hear the phrase *out-of-box experience* flung about on a regular basis. This buzzword — or, more accurately, buzz phrase — refers to how easily an ordinary mortal can get up and running with a new piece of software or hardware. In the ideal out-of-box scenario, you can install your new program or gadget and make it productive in minutes, without even having to (gasp!) read the instruction manual.

As computer programs go, Adobe PhotoDeluxe delivers a fairly decent out-of-box experience. Designed for those with little or no background in digital artistry, this entry-level program enables you to open a scanned photograph or image from a digital camera and perform a variety of retouching and special-effects maneuvers. Without exerting much mental energy at all, you can create some pretty cool pictures, and even put your photographic creations on calendars, greeting cards, business cards, and the like. PhotoDeluxe is stocked with templates and wizards, so all you have to do is follow the on-screen prompts and do as you're told.

Well — almost, anyway. Where the out-of-box experience breaks down is when you stop being dazzled by the colorful effects that you can produce in PhotoDeluxe and start looking closely at the *quality* of your digital art. The truth is that despite the generous amount of hand holding that PhotoDeluxe provides, image editing is still fairly complex stuff. Even when you use the PhotoDeluxe wizards to get things done, you have to make decisions about which way you want the program to implement your ideas. And unless you take a few moments here and there to acquire some fundamental image-editing knowledge, you can easily choose the wrong fork in the road. The result is images that look amateurish at best — and downright embarrassing at worst.

That's where *Adobe PhotoDeluxe 4 For Dummies* comes in. This book explains the science behind the art of PhotoDeluxe so that you can use the program to its fullest advantage. In simple, easy-to-read language, *Adobe PhotoDeluxe 4 For Dummies* helps you wrap your brain around such perplexing subjects as choosing the right image resolution, selecting a file format, and other topics that are essential to creating good-looking images.

Beyond that, you gain the information you need to venture past the program's surface level and explore its considerable hidden talents. Almost obscured by the consumer-friendly PhotoDeluxe interface lurk some very powerful image-editing tools — the kind that you may expect to find only in professional (read, *expensive*) graphics software. This book shows you how to exploit those tools and even how to work around some built-in limitations to get a bit more flexibility than the program's designers likely intended.

Finally, this book gives you the know-how to put your own personal, creative stamp on your images instead of relying solely on the prefab templates and wizards that PhotoDeluxe provides. The templates and wizards are great as a starting point, and they're very useful for those quick-and-dirty, everyday projects. But for those times when you really want your image to stand out — which is *always* if you're creating images for business use — you need to abandon the automatic, cookie-cutter approach and start wielding the editing tools with a bit more individuality. Let's face it: You can't create the kind of unique images that attract an audience to your company's Web page or product brochure if you're using the same design templates as millions of other PhotoDeluxe users.

In short, by heading out of the PhotoDeluxe box and into this book, you can get more from a $50 image-editing program than most people get from far more expensive software. You not only get tons of artistic ideas, but you also gain the technical background you need to make sure that the quality of your finished images is as impressive as your creative vision.

About This Book

PhotoDeluxe has evolved through several incarnations in its short life. This book covers Home Edition 4, while another edition covers Versions 2, Home Edition 3, and the Business Edition.

Available only for PC users, PhotoDeluxe 4 runs on Windows NT 4 (with Service Pack 5), Windows 98, and Windows 95. This book focuses on Windows 98 and does not specifically address Windows 95 and NT. If you're running Windows 95 or NT, you may find a few areas where things work differently than described here, but the majority of the information is absolutely the same no matter what flavor of Windows you fed your computer.

Finally, if you're wondering what level of digital-imaging experience you need to understand the goings-on in this book, the answer is none. The book is designed for those who are at the beginner or intermediate level when it comes to image editing. However, I do assume that you have a basic understanding of how to use your computer. For example, you know what it means to click and drag with a mouse; you understand how to move through file folders, hard drives, and the like; and you know just where to whack your computer when it misbehaves. If you need help with these fundamentals, pick up a copy of the *For Dummies* book for your specific operating system.

Sneak Preview

If I had to give a one-sentence synopsis of this book, I'd say "Everything you ever wanted to know about PhotoDeluxe — and then some." Fortunately, I'm not limited to one sentence; in fact, my editors graciously allotted me several paragraphs to give you a brief summary of the topics covered in each part of the book. As they say in those late-night infomercials, "Just look at all you get for one low, low price!"

Part I: It's a Brave New (Digital) World

This part of the book gives you a firm foundation for working with digital images and PhotoDeluxe, whether you want to create an attention-getting picture for your company's customer newsletter or simply apply goofy special effects to a photo of your pesky brother-in-law.

Chapters 1 and 2 familiarize you with the PhotoDeluxe *interface* (the on-screen components that you use to control the program), and Chapter 3 covers the inner workings of a digital image, explaining vital technical issues such as resolution and pixels.

Part II: Save, Print, Send!

Chapters 4 and 5 show you how to save and print your masterpieces, which seem as though they should be simple, painless tasks but sometimes are anything but. You get the lowdown on which file formats you should use when saving your pictures, how to get your on-screen colors to match your print colors, and more. Chapter 6 provides assistance with creating images for use on a Web page, sending pictures with an e-mail message, and taking advantage of the Adobe online picture-sharing service.

Part III: Editing Boot Camp

Don't be put off by the title of this part — you're not subjected to any grueling calisthenics or hard-nosed drill sergeants. This is boot camp *For Dummies*-style, where you acquire important image-editing skills in a fun, relaxed fashion.

Chapter 7 shows you how to do simple, everyday edits such as cropping an image and correcting brightness and contrast. Chapter 8 covers more complicated image-correction tasks, such as covering up photographic flaws and removing red-eye from snapshots. Chapter 9 explains how to use the PhotoDeluxe selection tools, which enable you to limit the effects of your edits to one portion of your image.

With the basic training provided in this part, you're well prepared for the rest of your image-editing life — and you don't even have to break a sweat to earn your stripes.

Part IV: Amazing Feats of Digital Trickery

If Part III is boot camp, Part IV is summer camp — a really great summer camp, not the kind where you sing dopey songs and make lame crafts out of sticks and yarn. Here, you find out about the really fun games you can play with digital images.

Chapter 10 shows you how to paint on your photographs and replace one image color with another. Chapter 11 introduces you to the wonderful world of image layers, which enable you to combine images into photographic collages and perform other neat tricks with surprising ease.

Chapter 12 explains how to add basic text to your image and also gives you a top-secret recipe for creating special text effects, such as text filled with an image. In Chapter 13, you experiment with more special effects, and Chapter 14 shows you tricks for adding clip art to your image and offers a few more ideas about putting the images you create to good use. Suffice it to say, you're going to be one happy camper exploring this part.

Part V: The Part of Tens

In the time-honored *For Dummies* tradition, this part of the book contains short chapters that follow the popular "Top Ten List" format. Turn here when you're in short-attention-span mode or just want a quick bit of information or inspiration.

Chapter 15 shows you ten ways to distort an image using the PhotoDeluxe distortion filters, which are always good for a laugh. Chapter 16 answers the ten most frequently asked questions — *FAQs (pronounced F-A-Q),* as they're known in Internet lingo — about image editing and PhotoDeluxe. To wrap things up, Chapter 17 helps you shave minutes off your image-editing projects by listing ten groups of keyboard shortcuts.

Appendix: Installing PhotoDeluxe

Of course, you need to install the PhotoDeluxe program on your computer before you can dive into all this image-editing stuff. If you haven't already done so and you want some advice about this chore, check out the appendix, which explains how to get started and which installation options to choose.

Conventions Used in This Book

As you probably already know, *For Dummies* books are anything but conventional. But this book, like others in the series, does follow a few conventions — stylistic guidelines, if you will — in how it presents information.

First, two or more words linked by an arrow represent a command or commands that you choose from a menu. The instruction "Choose File➪ Open," for example, means that you need to choose the Open command from the File menu.

Second, if you see words and letters joined by a plus sign — as in Ctrl+*A* — you're looking at a keyboard shortcut. Keyboard shortcuts enable you to select a command using your keyboard rather than a mouse. Pressing the Ctrl key and then the A key, for example, is the same as choosing the Select➪All command.

You can read more about both these subjects in Chapter 1, so don't worry about them now. I only mention them here so you don't freak out if you notice odd-looking bits of text as you flip through the book.

Icons Used in This Book

On just about every page in this book, you're likely to encounter an *icon* — a little circular graphic in the margin. Although icons certainly spice up the page from a design standpoint, they also have a practical purpose: to let you know that you're about to read something especially useful, important, or otherwise noteworthy.

The Tip icon flags information that you can use to get a job done faster, better, and easier. Don't read these paragraphs if you have way too much time on your hands or if you like doing things the long way.

Pay extra attention to paragraphs marked with a Remember icon. You'll need this information often during your image-editing adventures, so give it a prominent place in your memory bank.

This icon is akin to a "Danger Ahead!" road sign. When you see the Warning icon, slow down, hang up the cell phone, and read the corresponding paragraph carefully to avoid making a horrible, life-altering mistake. Well, a mistake you may live to regret, anyway.

If you want to be able to carry on a meaningful conversation with digital-imaging fanatics or impress the neighborhood computer geek, look for the Technical Stuff icon. This icon marks paragraphs that provide background information about technical concepts, as well as explanations of all those gobbledygook acronyms that the computer industry loves so much.

As you explore some image-editing projects presented in this book, you may encounter terms or need to use techniques that are covered in another chapter. This icon tells you where to look for details about those unfamiliar terms or techniques.

This icon highlights new features in Version 4 and changes from earlier versions of the program. Because some readers may be upgrading to Version 4 directly from Version 2, I point out major differences between that early edition of the program as well as between Version 3 and the Business Edition.

Where Do I Go from Here?

The answer to that question depends on you. If you're a neat, orderly, step-by-step sort of person who wants to find out about PhotoDeluxe in a neat, orderly, step-by-step sort of way, start with Chapter 1 and read straight through to the end of the book.

If, on the other hand, you have neither the time nor inclination to give this book a traditional read — or you're trying to solve a specific image-editing problem — simply turn to the section of the book that interests you. This book is designed so that it works both for those who want to take the beginning-to-end reading path and those who prefer the reference-book approach, where you can find out about a particular subject without having to read all the pages that come before.

Whichever route you choose,   leads you safely along the sometimes-rocky image-editing trail, gets you out of jams when necessary, and even offers you some entertainment along the way. In short, it's the perfect companion for your PhotoDeluxe journey.

Part I
It's a Brave New (Digital) World

The 5th Wave   By Rich Tennant

"Hey - let's put scanned photos of ourselves through a ripple filter and see if we can make ourselves look weird."

In this part . . .

Sometime during my childhood, a well-meaning teacher introduced the notion of the daily food pyramid. You know, the chart that prescribes how many servings of this and how many servings of that you should eat in order to maintain good health.

This theory has been completely wasted in the realm of my daily food intake. Not in this lifetime or in any other am I going to ingest the recommended amount of fruits and vegetables — unless, of course, you count microwave popcorn as a vegetable and grape suckers as fruit.

But the food pyramid concept does serve me well (hey, a pun!) as the perfect analogy for describing this part of the book. If this scintillating tome were a smorgasbord, this first part would be the fruit and vegetables. Like lima beans and brussels sprouts, the chapters in this part aren't the tastiest, most appetizing offerings on the menu. First, you find out how to open images and customize your PhotoDeluxe workspace. Following that, you get a thorough explanation of important technical issues such as pixels and image resolution.

Although I've done my best to sauce up these dissertations, they're hardly as mouthwatering as later chapters, which dish out such juicy topics as using special effects and creating photo collages. Without the information in this part, though, your images can never be healthy, well-balanced, or long-lived. In fact, they're going to be downright sickly. On top of that, PhotoDeluxe won't perform at peak capacity, either.

So skip ahead to the dessert section if you must, or make a run for the sushi bar. But at some point, come back and get your required portions of fruit and vegetables. This stuff may not be as fun to swallow as other parts of the book, but I guarantee that it can save you a major case of indigestion down the line.

Chapter 1

Cruising the Image-Editing Freeway

*R*emember the last time you bought a new car? After you maneuvered your pride and joy into the driveway, you spent a glorious hour inhaling that new car smell and exploring all the bells and whistles. You figured out how to boost the bass on the stereo, how to blast your horn at all those idiotic drivers, and, most important, how to work the cup holders.

This chapter and the one that follows offer you a similar get-acquainted session with PhotoDeluxe. You get a quick introduction to the PhotoDeluxe interface, including an explanation of the Guided Activities and other features designed to steer you through the sometimes-confusing world of image editing. You also find out how to open an image, which is an essential task if you plan on doing something more than staring at the PhotoDeluxe background screen all day long.

While this chapter familiarizes you with the PhotoDeluxe basics, Chapter 2 shows you how to customize the program's interface according to your preferences, just as you give a new car your personal touch. Sadly, PhotoDeluxe doesn't have an option that enables you to slip on a wooden-bead seatcover or hang fuzzy dice from the rearview mirror. But if you have a really big monitor, you can stick one of those stuffed animals with suction-cup feet to your screen if you want. Good taste has never been a requirement for driving on the image-editing highway, as a quick scan of any supermarket-aisle tabloid reveals.

Unlocking Your Image-Editing Vehicle

I trust that if you're advanced enough to venture into image editing, you're far enough down the technology highway to know how to start PhotoDeluxe. But just in case you're new to the whole computer thing, here's a quick review of your options:

- ✔ Click the Start button on the Windows taskbar. Then choose Programs⇨Adobe⇨PhotoDeluxe Home Edition 4.0⇨Adobe PhotoDeluxe Home Edition 4.0. Adobe wanted to be sure that you know what program you're using.

- ✔ Want to save yourself a few mouse clicks? PhotoDeluxe puts an icon on your Windows desktop during program installation. Just double-click the icon to shift the program into gear.

PhotoDeluxe requires plenty of memory (RAM) to maneuver. Version 4 insists on a minimum of 32MB RAM for both Windows 95 and 98. In my experience, you want more than the minimum; 64MB is good, more is even better. On systems with only 32MB RAM, PhotoDeluxe may slow to a frustrating crawl or refuse to budge altogether when you try to edit large images or apply complex special-effects filters. If you can't afford a memory upgrade, at least shut down any other open programs *before* launching PhotoDeluxe. That way, you allow the program to use as much of your available RAM as possible.

You also need a fair amount of empty space on your hard drive, because PhotoDeluxe writes some data to the hard drive when you process an image. For more on the subject of hard drive and RAM requirements, read Chapter 2.

After you launch PhotoDeluxe, you're greeted by the PhotoDeluxe *splash screen,* which names the people responsible for the program, sort of like the credits at the end of a movie. Then the splash screen disappears, and one of two things happens. If you're starting the program for the first time, you see the nearly empty PhotoDeluxe window, shown in Figure 1-1.

Menu bar ┌Guided Activities buttons

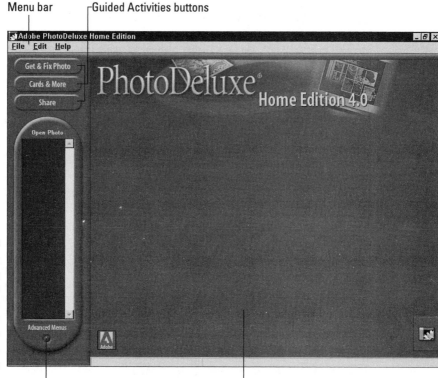

Figure 1-1:
You see this
window
when you
first fire up
Photo-
Deluxe.

Click to display hidden menus   Image-editing area

If you previously ran PhotoDeluxe, you may see a dialog box that asks
whether you want to install new Seasonal Activities or wallpaper designs. You
can read more about Seasonal Activities later in this chapter, in the section
"Trying out the Guided Activities." To find out about PhotoDeluxe wallpaper,
check out Chapter 2. Click Decide Later in the dialog box to ignore the whole
issue and to access the program window shown in Figure 1-1.

However you get there, the program window is pretty, but not too exciting. If
you want to explore the real action, you need to open an image, a process
that I explain in mind-numbing detail a little later in this chapter.

Working the Controls

You can access PhotoDeluxe tools, filters, and features three ways:

- ✔ You can choose commands from the menu bar, labeled in Figure 1-1. Click the menu name to display a list of commands and then click the desired command. In some cases, choosing a command results in a sub-menu of additional commands. Again, just click the command that you want to use.

- ✔ You can click the Guided Activities buttons, also labeled in Figure 1-1. The buttons access the PhotoDeluxe Guided Activities, which provide on-screen instructions that guide you through various editing projects. Computer gurus refer to these on-screen help functions as *wizards*.

- ✔ For some commands, you can use *keyboard shortcuts* — press one or two keys on your keyboard.

You can access some program features via the Guided Activities panel only. For other features, you must use menu commands or keyboard shortcuts. The following sections explain all three approaches of putting PhotoDeluxe to work.

Turning on hidden menus

By default, PhotoDeluxe displays only three menus: File, Edit, and Help, as shown in Figure 1-1. If you click the Advanced Menus button, labeled in the figure, the program presents a slew of other menu choices. You need to dig into these additional menus to take advantage of many PhotoDeluxe features, so go ahead and click that button now.

Frankly, I don't understand why Adobe hides some of your options in this fashion. Perhaps the program designers feared that you would be intimidated by so many menu choices. Well, ours is not to reason why, as they say. Just turn on the hidden menus and leave them on.

In Version 4, the extra menus remain visible until you click the Advanced Menus button again. PhotoDeluxe remembers this setting even when you shut the program down. You don't have to toggle the feature on and off in the Preferences menu as you did in earlier versions of the program.

Trying out the Guided Activities

Throughout this book, I explain how to do most things by using menus and keyboard shortcuts rather than Guided Activities. Choosing commands from the menus or via the keyboard is almost always faster than working your way through the Guided Activities. In addition, although many Guided Activities do provide valuable on-screen help, a fair share simply open a dialog box and leave you hanging. You don't get any advice on which options to select inside the dialog box.

Finally, getting to know the menu commands gives you a head start if you decide to move up to Adobe Photoshop, the professional image editor from which PhotoDeluxe was spawned, or Photoshop LE, the "lite" edition of Photoshop. Many commands work exactly the same in all three programs.

That said, you do need the Guided Activities if you want to create greeting cards, calendars, and other projects using the templates on the PhotoDeluxe CD-ROM. The templates offer fun ways to use your images, and I certainly urge you to explore them.

Using the Guided Activities is simple. The following steps give you a general overview of how the Guided Activities work; Chapter 14 provides an example that goes into more detail.

1. **Click the Guided Activities button for the task you want to do.**

   If you want to put a picture on a greeting card, for example, click the Cards & More button. You then see a row of icons representing different categories of projects — Cards, Calendars, Pages & Certificates, and so on, as shown at the top of Figure 1-2.

2. **Click an icon to display a list of options within each category.**

   In Figure 1-2, I clicked the Cards icon.

3. **Click the option that you want to use.**

   PhotoDeluxe replaces the strip of category icons with tabs that guide you through each step of the project, as shown in Figure 1-3.

4. **Click each tab, starting with number 1, and follow the prompts that the program gives you.**

   In the figure, I've completed the first two steps in the project and have moved on to the third tab of the wizard.

As you work through the tabs, PhotoDeluxe provides instructions on the project tabs. An additional help screen, known as the Assistant Drawer, slides out from the right side of the window. You can see the Assistant Drawer in Figure 1-3. If the Assistant Drawer gets in the way, click it to close it. Choose File⇨Preferences⇨Show Assistant Drawer to keep the thing from appearing at all. (Chapter 2 provides more details about the Preferences commands.)

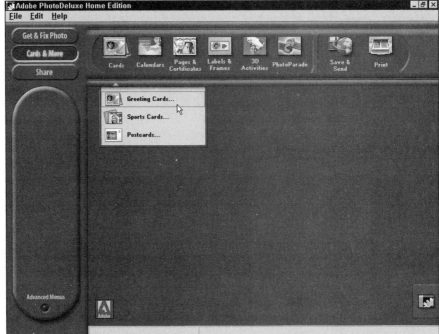

Figure 1-2:
Click an
icon to
display a list
of related
options.

If you decide to bail midway through a project, click the Done tab to exit the wizard. Depending on how many steps you completed, PhotoDeluxe may leave your work-in-progress open in the image window. You can continue to edit your picture or, if you don't want to keep it, just close the image window and click No when PhotoDeluxe asks whether you want to save the image.

Directing traffic from the keyboard

You can access many of the PhotoDeluxe commands and tools by using *keyboard shortcuts*. For example, if you want to open the Cursors dialog box to change your cursor's on-screen appearance, you can press the Ctrl key along with the K key instead of choosing File⇨Preferences⇨Cursors from the menu bar.

PhotoDeluxe lists the available keyboard shortcuts in the menus, to the right of the corresponding command. I also include shortcuts when I give you instructions in this book. For a list of my favorite shortcuts all in one place, flip to the Cheat Sheet at the front of this book and also to Chapter 17.

Project tab   Assistant Drawer

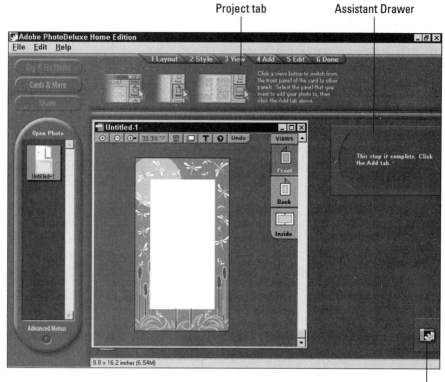

Figure 1-3:
Follow the
instructions
on each tab
to complete
a Guided
Activities
project.

Web links button

If no keyboard shortcut exists for a command, you can still use your keyboard to control PhotoDeluxe. The underlined letters that appear in command names on your computer screen represent *hot keys,* which you can press to trigger the commands.

To open a menu, press the Alt key along with the hot key. For example, to open the File menu, press Alt+F. After displaying the menu, press the hot key for the command you want to apply — you don't need to press Alt this time.

Pulling Out of the Driveway: Opening Images

Opening images in PhotoDeluxe is a fairly straightforward process, which is covered from several different angles in upcoming sections. But a few aspects of working with images in PhotoDeluxe may cause you some confusion, especially if you've used other image editors:

✔ **PhotoDeluxe converts all images to its native file format for editing.**
When you open an image that you saved in any file format other than
the PhotoDeluxe format (PDD), the program creates a copy of the image,
converts the copy to the PDD format, and opens that PDD copy for you
to edit.

PhotoDeluxe does this because the PDD format is optimized to take best
advantage of the program's features and to speed up editing operations.
For more information about file formats, see Chapter 4.

✔ **The image filename must include the three-letter extension associated
with the file format.** PhotoDeluxe can open files saved in many different
formats; for a full list, look in the Files of Type list in the Open dialog
box. (The "Opening images directly from disk" section explains the
dialog box later in this chapter.) However, if the name of the file doesn't
contain the standard three-letter extension associated with the file
format, PhotoDeluxe thinks that it can't open the image. For example,
PhotoDeluxe expects to see the extension .tif on files saved in the TIFF
format. If you name the file *Image.wow* instead of *Image.tif,* PhotoDeluxe
gets flustered and says that the image's file format is unsupported.

To fix the problem, rename the file or try using the File⇨Open
Special⇨Open As command to open the file. This command enables you
to assist PhotoDeluxe by specifying the format of the image. When
PhotoDeluxe displays the Open As dialog box, select your file and also
select the format from the Files of Type drop-down list.

✔ **PDD images are always 24-bit, 16-million-color images.** Even if you
open an 8-bit, 256-color or grayscale image, the PDD copy that
PhotoDeluxe creates is a full-color image. You have access to all 16 million colors for your painting and editing tools. For more about bit depth
and colors, read Chapter 3. If you're working with grayscale images, also
review Chapter 13.

✔ **PhotoDeluxe can't open images created in certain color models.** *Color
model* refers to how a device creates colors. Digital cameras, scanners,
and monitors use the RGB color model, which means that they create
colors by mixing *r*ed, *g*reen, and *b*lue light. Printers go by the CMYK
color model, mixing *c*yan, *m*agenta, *y*ellow, and blac*k* ink to produce the
colors on a printed page.

PhotoDeluxe, like other programs in its class, limits you to working with
RGB images. If you see a message saying that PhotoDeluxe can't open an
image because the image was stored in an unsupported format, but you
know that the format *is* accepted by PhotoDeluxe, the problem may be
the color model. Ask the person who gave you the file to convert it to
RGB for you.

Now that you've survived your initial driver training course, you're ready to
pull out of the driveway and onto the image-editing expressway. Well, maybe
not the expressway yet — how about exploring that nice farm road outside of

town? Come to think of it, maybe we should just do a few spins around the school parking lot and see how you do. We don't want any innocent bystanders to get hurt in the event of a crash, you know. (My, isn't the automobile metaphor holding up nicely?)

Opening the sample images and clip art

The PhotoDeluxe CD-ROM includes a slew of sample photographs and clip art graphics. The program also ships with a photo organizer that enables you to preview these and other pictures.

Version 4 provides a new photo organizer in place of the EasyPhoto organizer that shipped with earlier versions. The new organizer works much the same way as EasyPhoto, though, so you shouldn't have any trouble adapting if you're used to EasyPhoto. You can preview and open the sample photographs and clip art as follows:

1. **Put the PhotoDeluxe CD-ROM in your CD-ROM drive.**

   If your computer's autoplay feature is enabled, the PhotoDeluxe installation program may overtake your screen. Press the Esc key on your keyboard and then click the Quit button in the installer window to shut down the installer.

2. **To preview the clip art, choose File⇨Open Special⇨Clip Art.**

   To get the job done faster, press Ctrl+\ (backslash). PhotoDeluxe displays thumbnail previews of the clip art graphics inside the organizer window shown in Figure 1-4.

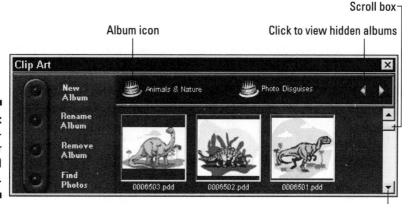

Figure 1-4: The thumbnail browser is simplified in Version 4.

Scroll box

Album icon

Click to view hidden albums

Scroll arrow

3. **To preview the sample photos, choose File⇨Open Special⇨Get Sample Photo.**

   PhotoDeluxe opens a second window displaying the sample photos.

4. **Find just the right image.**

   Along the top of the organizer window, you see a series of icons that represent different albums (refer to Figure 1-4). Each *album* stores a different category of pictures. To explore the possibilities, use these techniques:

   - Click an album icon to display thumbnails of pictures in that album.

   - Click the arrows at the end of the row of album icons to scroll through all the albums.

   - Scroll through the thumbnails using the scroll arrows and scroll box, just as you do in an ordinary program window.

   - Drag an edge of the window outward to enlarge the organizer so that you can see more thumbnails at a time. Drag an edge inward to shrink the organizer window.

5. **Double-click the thumbnail of the picture you want to open.**

   You also can drag the thumbnail onto an empty spot in the image-editing area. PhotoDeluxe opens the picture in a new image window. The photo organizer window remains open; to put the window away, click the close button (that little X in the upper-right corner of the window). Alternatively, drag the window by its title bar to move it out of the way.

   If you want to add a graphic to an existing image, drag the thumbnail from the organizer window into the existing image's window. PhotoDeluxe pastes the picture onto your image as a separate layer. Chapter 11 explains everything you need to know about layers.

Opening your own images using the photo organizer

You can use the new photo organizer to view thumbnails of your own photos as well as the PhotoDeluxe sample art. However, you first have to create thumbnails for your pictures. To get the step-by-step instructions, travel to Chapter 4.

After you create thumbnails, choose File⇨My Photos⇨Show My Photos to display them in the My Photos organizer window, which looks just like the one shown in Figure 1-4, except for the window title. Instead of showing thumbnails of the PhotoDeluxe sample art, the My Photos organizer displays your personal thumbnails.

You preview and open your images the same way you preview and open the PhotoDeluxe sample art. Steps 4 and 5 in the preceding section spell everything out, so I won't bore you by repeating the instructions here. I may bore you some other way, mind you, but not by droning on further about this topic.

Opening images directly from disk

You don't have to bother with the photo organizer if you know the exact name and location of the image file that you want to open. You can open the image file more efficiently by following these steps:

1. **Choose File⇨Open File.**

   Or press Ctrl+O (the letter *oh,* not zero). PhotoDeluxe responds by displaying the Open dialog box. Figure 1-5 shows the dialog box as it appears in Windows 98. If you're using Windows 95, the dialog box lacks a few of the Windows 98 buttons, but otherwise looks the same.

File list box   Up One Level

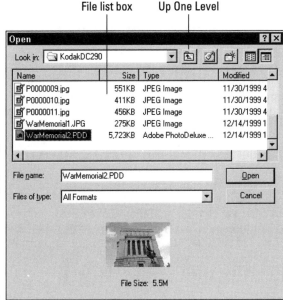

Figure 1-5: If you know the name of the image you want to open, go directly to the Open dialog box.

2. **Find the file that you want to open.**

   To track down a file, use these tactics: Choose a drive name from the Look In drop-down list. In the file list box, you see all folders and files on the drive you selected. Double-click a folder to display the contents of that folder. Click the Up One Level button (labeled in Figure 1-5) to move up one level in the folder/drive hierarchy. Be sure to select the All Formats option from the Files of Type drop-down list to display all available files in the file list box.

3. **Click the filename in the file list box.**

   If you previously opened and saved the image in PhotoDeluxe, you see a thumbnail preview of the image at the bottom of the dialog box, as shown in Figure 1-5.

4. **Click the Open button or double-click the filename.**

Want to work with several photos at the same time? You can open multiple images with only one trip to the Open dialog box. Inside the dialog box, click the first image that you want to open, Ctrl+Click any additional images you want to open, and then click Open. For more information about working with multiple pictures, see Chapter 2.

PhotoDeluxe uses the same Open dialog box as most Windows programs. If you need more help understanding how to navigate this dialog box, grab *Windows 95 For Dummies* or *Windows 98 For Dummies,* both by Andy Rathbone (IDG Books Worldwide, Inc.).

Scanning images into PhotoDeluxe

If you have a scanner, you can scan an image directly into PhotoDeluxe. In Version 4, PhotoDeluxe no longer supplies the scanning utility provided with some earlier versions of the program. Instead, PhotoDeluxe automatically launches your scanner's own software when you choose the scanning command (of course, you have to install the software first).

As with most other PhotoDeluxe operations, you can scan pictures either by choosing menu commands or by following the Guided Activities wizard. Both options require about the same amount of work — that is to say, not much. But you need to be aware of one catch: The first time you scan a picture into PhotoDeluxe, you must specify the *scanning source* — the scanner software that PhotoDeluxe should use to perform the scan. After you scan once, you don't have the option of selecting a different scanning source if you scan via the menu commands. If you need to change the scanning source, you must use the Guided Activities wizard.

The following steps include instructions for both approaches to scanning in Version 4.

1. **Choose File⇨Open Special⇨Scan Photo.**

   If you want to use the Guided Activities wizard, click the Get & Fix Photo button to display the Guided Activities icons. Click the Get Photo icon and then click the Scanners option to display the scanning wizard.

2. Select your scanning source.

You need to take this step only if you're scanning into PhotoDeluxe for the first time or want to select a different scanning source than you previously used. Otherwise, skip to Step 3.

If you choose Scan Photo from the File menu in Step 1, the program displays a dialog box that asks you to name your scanning source. Choose the option that your scanner's manual recommends, then click OK. PhotoDeluxe launches your scanner software.

If you're using the Guided Activities wizard, click the Scanner project tab and then click the Choose Scanner icon to get to the dialog box. After you select a source and click OK, PhotoDeluxe displays the Scan project tab. Click the Scan icon to launch your scanner software.

3. Perform your usual scanning routine.

Your scanner software works exactly as it does when you use it outside PhotoDeluxe. When the scanner finishes its gyrations, PhotoDeluxe displays the scanned image in a new image window.

For recommendations on the input resolution setting to use when scanning images, read Chapter 3.

4. Save your image right away.

If you upgraded to Version 4 from Version 2, you probably expect PhotoDeluxe to do the saving chores for you. But in Version 4, as in Version 3 and the Business Edition, PhotoDeluxe hands you the saving reins. This change gives you control over the location and file format you use when saving the scan; in Version 2, PhotoDeluxe always saved scans in the JPEG format in a particular folder on your hard drive.

Don't forget to take this step — if you close the image without saving, the image and any changes that you've made are history. For details about saving files, flip to Chapter 4.

Getting an image from a digital camera

Just as you can scan directly into PhotoDeluxe, you can download images from a digital camera into the program. However, getting your camera and PhotoDeluxe on speaking terms isn't always easy — not because either device doesn't work well, but because camera-to-computer connections require some system configurations that can be difficult to figure out.

I can't give you specific configuration settings — you need to consult your camera manual for that information. Also check the manual to find out how to plug the camera into the computer and what camera software you need to install before you can transfer images.

When you have your camera cabled to your computer, follow these steps:

1. **Click the Get & Fix Photos button.**

2. **Click the Get Photo icon and then click the Cameras option.**

   You also can choose File⇨Open Special⇨Get Digital Photo, but you have slightly less control over the process if you go that route.

   The Camera tab appears no matter which method you've chosen to use.

3. **Choose your camera or download software from the drop-down list and then click the Open Camera icon.**

   From there, everything works as it does when you download images outside of PhotoDeluxe.

4. **After you finish downloading images, click the Done tab and save each image to disk.**

   Chapter 4 tells you how to do this stuff.

Of course, if you own a Sony Digital Mavica camera that stores pictures on a floppy disk, you can just open your images from the floppy as you would any file. Likewise, if your camera stores images on a SmartMedia, CompactFlash, or Memory Stick media card, you can buy a card reader or adapter that enables you to open pictures directly from the card rather than hooking your camera to the computer. Trust me: The $70 or so you spend on the reader or adapter will be well spent. You'll be able to transfer pictures with much less hassle and in a fraction of the time it takes to send images through a cable.

Opening a Photo CD image

If you buy an image collection from a stock photo agency or have your own images scanned to CD at a professional image-processing lab, the images may be provided in the Kodak Photo CD file format. Photo CD images have the file-name extension .PCD. You and I can't save images in this format; it's strictly a professional imaging lab format. But PhotoDeluxe can open Photo CD files.

Don't confuse Kodak *Photo* CD with Kodak *Picture* CD. Picture CD, a new product offered by many photo-finishing services, enables you to drop off a roll of undeveloped film and get back both regular prints and a CD-ROM containing digital copies of the pictures. If you want to open an image from a Kodak Picture CD, check out the next section.

Now back to Photo CD: Every Photo CD image file actually contains several copies of the image, each of which provides a different number of image pixels. (See Chapter 3 if you need a pixel primer.) When you open the image, you select which copy you want to use. If you're putting an image on the Web, for example, you want minimal pixels, so you choose the smallest copy. If you want to create a high-quality print of the image, you select the copy that contains the most pixels.

Unlike previous editions of PhotoDeluxe, Version 4 does *not* offer built-in support for Photo CD files. If you want to open Photo CD images in PhotoDeluxe, you must install a special bit of software known as the Kodak Photo CD Acquire Module, which you can download for free from the Kodak Web site (www.kodak.com). The Acquire Module really was developed as a plug-in for Adobe Photoshop, but works swell with PhotoDeluxe, too.

Before you go the trouble of downloading the plug-in, choose File➪Open File to display the Open dialog box and look for the Photo CD format in the Files of Type drop-down list. If you've installed other digital imaging programs on your system, the plug-in may already be installed. Not there? Time to download. Be sure to read the directions for downloading and installing the software. When you install the Photo CD module, accept the default installation choices. You should then find Photo CD on the list of file formats available in the Files of Type list box in the Open dialog box.

To open a Photo CD image, press Ctrl+O or choose File➪Open File to display the Open dialog box, discussed in the section "Opening images directly from disk," earlier in this chapter. Track down your file in the normal fashion, click it, and click Open. PhotoDeluxe then shows you the impressive dialog box shown in Figure 1-6.

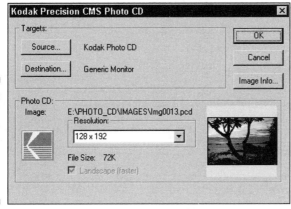

Figure 1-6:
Select an image size from the Resolution drop-down list.

The Source, Destination, and Image Info buttons enable you to fiddle with settings related to the type of film used to shoot the original image and the monitor on which you want to display the picture. If you know what you're doing, fiddle away. Otherwise, ignore all three buttons and head straight for the meat of the dialog box: the Resolution drop-down list.

In the Resolution list, you see five options: 128 x 192, 256 x 384, 512 x 768, 1024 x 1536, and 2048 x 3072. These values indicate the pixel *dimensions* — number of pixels wide by the number of pixels tall — for each of the copies in the image file. Some Photo CD images also provide a copy with a whopping 4096 x 6144 pixels, but PhotoDeluxe can't open these files.

When pondering which option you should select, keep the final destination of the image in mind. You don't want to wind up with too few pixels, but you don't want too many pixels, either. Chapter 3 can guide you in this regard. After you pick an option from the Resolution drop-down list, click OK to open the image.

Remember that each additional pixel adds to the size of the image file. And the larger the image file, the more memory (RAM) and empty hard disk space PhotoDeluxe needs to process your edits. If the program tells you that you don't have the system resources to open a Photo CD image, select the next smallest option and try again. Table 1-1 shows you the size of the image file generated by each of the five resolution options.

One more bit of news about Photo CD: Somebody, somewhere, assigned scientific-sounding names that involve the word *Base* to the sizes provided on a Photo CD. Table 1-1 provides the technical lingo so that you, too, can sound like a nerd when you speak of Photo CD images. Don't pronounce the slash — just say, "Base 4, Base 16," and so on.

Table 1-1	Photo CD Resolution Options	
Official Name	*Pixel Dimensions*	*File Size*
Base/16	128 x 192	72K
Base/4	256 x 384	288K
Base	512 x 768	1.13MB
4 Base	1024 x 1536	4.5MB
16 Base	2048 x 3072	18MB

Opening a FlashPix image

PhotoDeluxe can open images stored in the FlashPix file format, which Chapter 4 explains fully. Like the Photo CD format, FlashPix stores the same image at several different sizes. The different versions are stacked in a sort of pyramid inside the file, with the largest version sitting at the bottom of the pyramid.

In PhotoDeluxe Version 2, the program asked you to specify which image size you wanted to use, just as when you open a Photo CD image. In Version 4, as with Version 3 and the Business Edition, you don't have this option. PhotoDeluxe automatically makes the choice for you.

Why the change? To save you from yourself, essentially. If you open and edit the smallest version of a FlashPix image and resave the image under its original name, PhotoDeluxe rebuilds the FlashPix pyramid, using the open image as the bottom layer in the stack. Should you ever need the image at a larger size, you're sunk. (The same crisis can't occur with Photo CD images, because you can't save to the Photo CD format — which means that you can't overwrite the original image file with another version of the image.)

PhotoDeluxe now automatically opens all FlashPix images at the largest size, so you don't have to worry about screwing things up. Of course, if you resample your image (a subject Chapter 3 discusses) and want to retain a copy at the original size, you must give the edited version a new name when saving the file.

Opening Kodak Picture CD images

Had any film developed lately? If so, you've probably been offered the chance to take advantage of Kodak Picture CD. In exchange for a few additional dollars, you can have your pictures scanned onto a CD-ROM at the same time you order your regular prints.

The CD you receive contains some basic photo-editing software as well as some other goodies, which change depending on what promotion Kodak and its affiliates want to offer during a particular season. But you already have all the photo-editing tools you need in PhotoDeluxe, so you probably don't want to install the editing software.

Picture CD images get stored in the JPEG file format, a leading image file format that nearly every program, including PhotoDeluxe, supports. You can open your Picture CD images directly through the Open dialog box. If you need help, see "Opening images directly from disk" earlier in this chapter.

Creating an image from scratch

PhotoDeluxe, like other image editors, is designed primarily for editing existing images. The program doesn't offer many tools for painting an image from scratch because most folks don't have the need — or patience — for that kind of project. If you want to create a logo or some other piece of art from scratch, you're better off using a drawing program such as CorelDraw. (Read the sidebar "Can I edit drawings in PhotoDeluxe?" in Chapter 3 for more information on why drawing programs are typically better than image-editing programs for creating simple graphics.)

But on occasion, you may want to start with a blank image canvas. To do so, choose File⇨New or press Ctrl+N. PhotoDeluxe displays the New dialog box, shown in Figure 1-7. Here you can set the size and resolution of your new image. The Width, Height, and Resolution options work just as they do inside the Photo Size dialog box, which Chapter 3 covers fully.

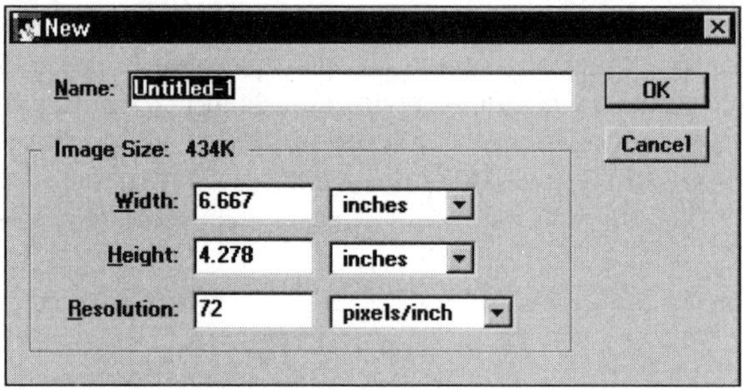

Figure 1-7:
Select the
size and
resolution of
new images
here.

New

Name: Untitled-1   OK

Image Size: 434K   Cancel

Width: 6.667   inches

Height: 4.278   inches

Resolution: 72   pixels/inch

Touring the Image Window

Regardless of which path you follow to open an image, the image appears inside its very own window. Figure 1-8 gives you a peek at the image window, while the following two bulleted lists explain the various window elements:

- The *title bar,* labeled in Figure 1-8, displays the name of the image. Until you save the image for the first time in the PhotoDeluxe file format (PDD), PhotoDeluxe assigns the image a meaningless name like *Untitled-1.* (See Chapter 4 for details on saving images.)

- The *File Information box,* located at the bottom of the program window, shows you two pieces of data. The first set of values indicates the current print size of your image. Following the print size, the value inside parentheses tells you how much RAM your computer is using to process the image. You can display some additional image information by clicking the box. For more about this feature, read Chapter 3.

- Like just about every other program on the planet, PhotoDeluxe offers a built-in *help system,* which is quite good compared to those offered by many programs. You can fire up the help system by clicking the Help button in the image window (labeled in Figure 1-8), by pressing F1, or by using the commands on the Help menu.

Title bar   Help   Maximize/Restore   Minimize⌐   ⌐Close

Figure 1-8:
A
PhotoDeluxe
image
window
works much
like any
other
document
window.

File Information box

Of course, with this book at your side, you're not likely to need the help system, but you may find it handy if you're away from home and didn't tote the book along with you. If you need an explanation for finding information in the help system, choose Help⇨How to Use Help.

You can manipulate the window itself as follows:

✔ To shrink or enlarge the image window, click the Minimize, Maximize/Restore, and Close buttons, all labeled in Figure 1-8. With the exception of the Minimize button, these buttons work just as they do in any program or document window.

✔ To enlarge the window so that it fills all the available space on the PhotoDeluxe screen, click the Maximize/Restore button. When you do this, the three window-control buttons jump to the right end of the program title bar, and the Restore button changes to show a picture of two tiny boxes instead of a single box. To reduce the window to its former size, click the button again. The buttons then jump back to the right end of the image window's title bar.

✔ In most programs, clicking the Minimize button shrinks the window so that only the title bar remains visible. PhotoDeluxe does things differently. When you click the button, the image window disappears altogether. To bring the window back, double-click the image thumbnail that appears on the left side of the program window. If you want to know more about using the thumbnails, see the next chapter.

✔ You can also resize the window by placing your cursor over a corner of the window until it becomes a two-headed arrow and then dragging. You can't use this method when the window is maximized, however.

✔ To move the window, drag its title bar. Again, you don't have this option when the window is maximized.

✔ To close an image, click the *Close button,* or choose File⇨Close, or press Ctrl+W. PhotoDeluxe may ask whether you want to save the image before you close.

Zooming in and out

When you first open an image, PhotoDeluxe displays the entire picture on-screen. To zoom in or out on the image, you can use the Zoom controls located at the top of the image window. Check out Figure 1-9 for a look at these controls. You can also use a few keyboard techniques that you may find even easier than working with the Zoom controls.

The following list details all your zooming options:

✔ The value in the Zoom menu (labeled in Figure 1-9) reflects the current level of magnification. At 100 percent, one screen pixel is used to display one image pixel. For an explanation of this pixel stuff, check out Chapters 3 and 6.

✔ Remember that the on-screen size of the image at 100 percent is *not* equal to the printed size of your image unless you set the image resolution in the Photo Size dialog box to match the resolution of your monitor. Again, see Chapters 3 and 6 for more information about screen resolution, image resolution, and image size.

✔ To zoom in on your image, choose a value higher than 100 percent from the Zoom menu or click the Zoom In button, labeled in Figure 1-9.

✔ To zoom out, choose a value lower than 100 percent from the Zoom menu or click the Zoom Out button, also labeled in the figure.

Zoom In

Zoom Out

Zoom tool   Zoom menu

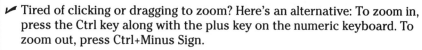

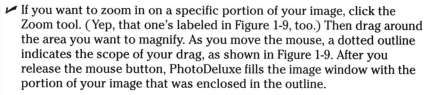

Figure 1-9:
PhotoDeluxe
offers you
several
ways to
zoom in and
out on your
image.

Zoom marquee   Scroll box   Scroll arrow

✔ If you want to zoom in on a specific portion of your image, click the Zoom tool. (Yep, that one's labeled in Figure 1-9, too.) Then drag around the area you want to magnify. As you move the mouse, a dotted outline indicates the scope of your drag, as shown in Figure 1-9. After you release the mouse button, PhotoDeluxe fills the image window with the portion of your image that was enclosed in the outline.

✔ Tired of clicking or dragging to zoom? Here's an alternative: To zoom in, press the Ctrl key along with the plus key on the numeric keyboard. To zoom out, press Ctrl+Minus Sign.

You can also use the plus and minus keys that lie above all your letter keys. If you do, you may need to press Ctrl+Shift along with the plus key to make the zoom-in shortcut work. (Pressing Shift activates the plus key on most keyboards.) You don't need to press Shift to use the zoom-out shortcut.

Viewing hidden areas of the image

When you zoom in on an image or work with a very large image, portions of the image may be hidden from view. To scroll the display so that you can see the hidden areas, you can do any of the following:

- Drag the scroll boxes (labeled in Figure 1-9) along the bottom and right side of the window.

- To scroll in smaller increments, click the scroll arrows, also labeled in the figure.

- Using the scroll boxes and arrows can be a little clumsy. To move quickly to a certain part of your image, try this method instead: Place your mouse cursor inside the image window and then press and hold the spacebar on your keyboard. The cursor turns into a little hand. While keeping the spacebar depressed, drag inside your image to pull into view the area you want to see.

Changing the image orientation

If your image opens up lying on its side, you can rotate it to the proper orientation by choosing Orientation⇨Rotate Right or Orientation⇨Rotate Left, depending on which way you want to spin the picture.

Should you need to flip the image from left to right or top to bottom, choose the Flip Horizontal or Flip Vertical commands, also found on the Orientation menu.

If you find yourself rotating or flipping lots of images, you may want to commit these keyboard shortcuts to memory:

- Rotate Left: Ctrl+<

- Rotate Right: Ctrl+>

- Flip Horizontal: Ctrl+[

- Flip Vertical: Ctrl+]

For the first two shortcuts to work, you must press the Shift key. (The greater than and less than symbols are accessible by pressing the comma and period keys along with the Shift key.)

For additional ways to rotate an entire image or a portion of an image, read Chapter 9.

Communicating via a Dialog Box

When you choose some PhotoDeluxe commands the program responds by displaying a dialog box. Inside the dialog box, you can specify how you want PhotoDeluxe to apply that command.

For the most part, a PhotoDeluxe dialog box works like any other dialog box. But some PhotoDeluxe dialog boxes, like the one shown in Figure 1-10, offer special features that you can use to make your editing easier.

Hand cursor

Preview box   Option box

Figure 1-10:
PhotoDeluxe
dialog boxes
contain
some
special
features that
make life
easier.

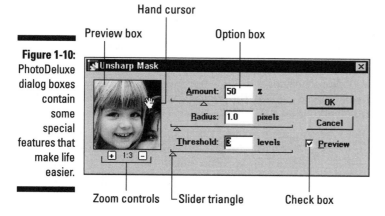

Zoom controls   └Slider triangle   Check box

The following list offers the insider's guide to these dialog boxes:

- ✔ In many cases, you can change the value for a particular option several ways. You can drag a slider triangle, labeled in Figure 1-10, or you can double-click the corresponding option box and type in a value.

  After you double-click an option box to make it active, you can press the up- or down-arrow keys on your keyboard to raise or lower the value by 1, .1, or .001 (depending on the values permitted for the option). Press Shift+↑ or Shift+↓ to raise or lower the value by 10, 1, or .1 (again, depending on the parameters of the particular value). For example, if the option allows only whole number values, pressing the up-arrow key once raises the value by 1; pressing Shift with the arrow key raises the value by 10.

- ✔ Click a check box to turn the corresponding option on or off. A check mark in the box means that the option is turned on.

- ✔ The preview box shows you how the values you select will affect your image. If you select the Preview check box in the lower-right corner of the dialog box, you can also see the effects of your changes in the main image window. A blinking line appears underneath the check box while PhotoDeluxe updates the previews.

To magnify or reduce the view shown in the preview box, click the zoom controls underneath the box. Click the plus button to zoom in and the minus button to zoom out.

Use the two preview options to display both a close-up view and a big-picture view at the same time. Before you open the dialog box, zoom out on your image so that you can see the entire picture in the image window; then magnify the view shown in the dialog box to see small details.

✔ To display a different portion of your image in the preview box move your cursor into the box. The cursor changes into a hand, as shown in Figure 1-10. Drag to pull a hidden area of the image into view.

Alternatively, move your cursor into the image window. The cursor takes on a square shape. If you click the mouse button, the preview box changes to show the portion of the image that you clicked.

✔ To compare how the image looks now and how it will look if you apply the command, click the Preview check box and watch the image window. With the check box off, you see the "before" version of the image; with the check box on, you see the "after" version.

Another way to accomplish the same thing is to place the cursor in the preview box. Press and hold on the box to display the "before" view. Let up on the mouse button to see the "after" view.

✔ If you press and hold the Alt key, the Cancel button transforms itself into a Reset button. You can then click the Reset button to return all values to the settings that were in place when you first opened the dialog box.

Parking PhotoDeluxe

To shut down PhotoDeluxe, choose File➪Exit, press Ctrl+Q, or click the Close button in the upper-right corner of the program window.

If you have an image open and you haven't yet saved it to disk in the PhotoDeluxe file format (PDD), PhotoDeluxe asks whether you want to do so, even if you didn't make any edits to the image. If you do want to save the picture in the PDD format, click Yes and follow the saving instructions outlined in Chapter 4. To save the image in some other file format, choose the File➪Export➪File Format command, which Chapter 4 also explains. If you don't care to save any of your work, click No and say good riddance to bad rubbish.

Before PhotoDeluxe curtsies and exits the room for good, it may tell you that the Clipboard contains image data and ask whether you want that data to be available to other programs. For more about this tantalizing offer, read Chapter 2. But in short, if you want to paste the Clipboard contents into a document that you're creating in another program, click the Yes button when PhotoDeluxe prompts you. Otherwise, click No.

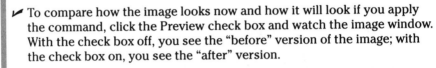

Chapter 2

Customizing Your Darkroom

. . . .

In This Chapter

▶ Displaying more than one image on-screen at a time

▶ Changing your cursor's size and shape

▶ Turning the rulers on and off

▶ Setting your preferred unit of measurement

▶ Changing the image canvas color and size

▶ Itching the scratch disk and managing memory

▶ Getting rid of the Assistant Drawer

▶ Setting other obscure preferences

. . . .

*A*lmost every computer program these days gives you the option of customizing the interface to suit your own taste. PhotoDeluxe is no exception. You can change several aspects of how the program looks and behaves, if you like.

This chapter explains all your options and offers advice on which ones are best in certain situations. Don't you wish it were this easy to make the rest of the world conform to your whims?

Opening Multiple Images at a Time

You can open as many as 30 images at a time — assuming that your computer's resources can handle the load. PhotoDeluxe needs a good deal of system memory (RAM) as well as empty hard disk space to process each open picture. If you're working with minimal system resources, PhotoDeluxe may throw a tantrum if you try to keep more than one image open.

Assuming that you're working on a souped-up machine that's the envy of all your nerdiest friends, use the following tricks to manipulate all the open windows simultaneously:

✔ To see all your open images side by side, choose Window⇨Tile.

✔ To stack the image windows vertically, choose Window⇨Cascade. (If you don't see a Window menu, click the Advanced Menus button in the lower-left region of the PhotoDeluxe program window. Chapter 1 offers more advice on this option.)

✔ To move an individual window, drag its title bar.

✔ To close all open windows with one swift motion, choose Window⇨Close All.

Although you can keep several images open, only one image is *active* — affected by your edits — at a time. The title bars on the inactive image windows are *grayed out* (dimmed). In Figure 2-1, for example, the image Untitled-2 is active; image Untitled-1 is inactive. Click in an image window to make that image active.

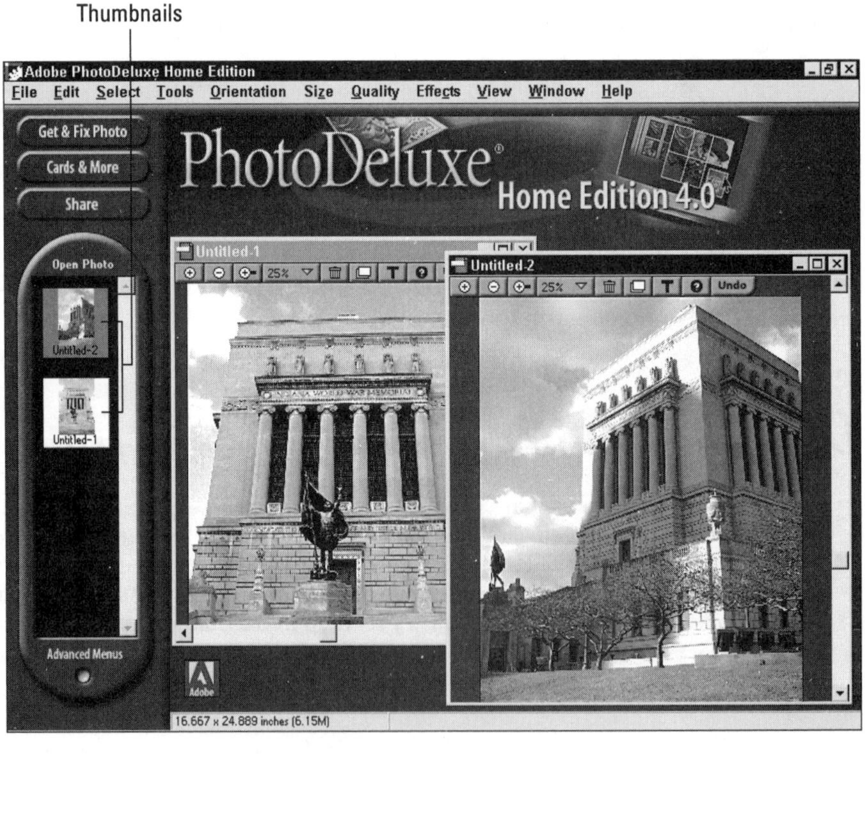

Thumbnails

Figure 2-1:
You can activate an image by choosing the image name from the bottom of the Window menu.

The Open Photo area on the left side of the image window displays a thumb-nail view of every open image, as shown in Figure 2-1. (If you're upgrading to Version 4 from Version 2, this thumbnail display replaces the Hold Photos fea-ture.) You can double-click a thumbnail to activate that image. This feature comes in handy when you have one of the open windows maximized, which prevents you from clicking any other open windows. Another option is to choose the image name from the Window menu.

For more information on opening, closing, and resizing image windows, head back to Chapter 1.

Changing the Cursor Style

PhotoDeluxe offers you a choice of cursor designs, which you select in the Cursors dialog box shown in Figure 2-2. To open the dialog box, press Ctrl+K. If you like doing things the long way, choose File⇨Preferences⇨Cursors instead.

Figure 2-2:
Choices
that you
make here
determine
how your
cursor
looks.

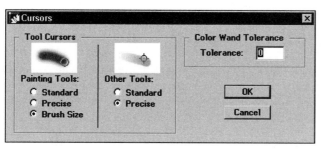

In this dialog box, you select one of the Painting Tools options to change how the cursor looks when you use the Eraser, Line, Brush, Clone, and Smudge tools. The Other Tools options control the cursor's appearance when you use the Color Change tool and all the selection tools. (You can find out about all of these tools in later chapters.) The options result in different sizes and shapes of cursors, as follows:

- ✔ **Standard:** If you click this option, your cursor resembles a tiny replica of the tool. If you select the Brush tool, for example, your cursor looks like a paintbrush. Folks who tend to forget what tool they're using may find this option helpful.

- ✔ **Precise:** Choose this option, and you get a simple crosshair cursor regardless of what tool you use. The crosshair cursor is best for making precise edits (hence the name), when the larger, standard cursors can obscure your view.

✔ **Brush Size:** If you choose this option, you get a round cursor that reflects the actual size of the brush you select for a painting tool. (Changing brush sizes is discussed in Chapter 10.) Except for those times when I'm doing precise close-up work, I prefer this option because it enables me to see how much territory the next swipe of the tool will cover. You can choose this option only when working with the painting tools (the Eraser, Line, Brush, Clone, and Smudge tools).

You can press the Caps Lock key to toggle between two cursors without opening the Cursors dialog box. The cursors you can select by pressing Caps Lock vary depending on the tool you're using and the cursor style currently selected in the dialog box.

✔ If you selected the Standard or Brush Size option in the Cursors dialog box, pressing Caps Lock switches you to the Precise (crosshairs) cursor.

✔ If you selected Precise as the Painting Tools option, Caps Lock turns on the Brush Size cursor when you're working with a painting tool.

✔ Turn off Caps Lock to return to the cursor option that you selected in the Cursors dialog box.

Turning Rulers On and Off

You may find it helpful to display rulers in the image window, as shown in Figure 2-3, if you want to place an image element at a specific position in your image — for example, to put a line of text exactly 2 inches from the top of the picture.

The rulers appear along the left and top sides of the image window when you choose View➪Show Rulers or press Ctrl+R. To turn the rulers off, choose View➪Hide Rulers or press Ctrl+R again. (If the View menu doesn't appear on your screen, click the Advanced Menus button, located at the bottom of the Open Photos area, along the left edge of the program window.)

By default, PhotoDeluxe aligns the rulers so that the zero point is at the top left corner of your image. The *zero point* is the point at which the zero tick mark on the horizontal ruler intersects with the zero tick mark on the vertical ruler. You can relocate the zero point by dragging the zero point marker, which is labeled in Figure 2-3. As you drag, dotted lines extend from each ruler to indicate the new position of the zero point, as shown in the figure. (I added the arrow for emphasis.) When you let up on the mouse button, the rulers reflect the new zero point.

Zero point marker   Ruler

Figure 2-3:
Turning on
the rulers
helps you
position
elements
precisely.

Why would you want to move the zero point? Take a look at Figure 2-3 as an example. Say that you wanted to crop the picture to 5 inches tall and 7 inches wide. You want to include all of that lizardy thing in the scene. You could find out where to place the crop boundary by eyeballing the ruler and then adding seven inches to the position of the left edge of the creature and five inches to the position of the top edge. But chances are, you'd wind up with a photo that's not precisely 5 x 7 inches — not to mention eye strain from counting all those tiny tick marks. To get the job done more accurately and more quickly, just drag the zero point to the top-left corner of the image area you want to keep. Then align your crop boundary with the 5-inch mark on the vertical ruler and the 7-inch mark on the horizontal ruler.

The ruler uses inches as the unit of measurement by default, but you can change the unit by heading for the Unit Preferences dialog box, whose exploration begins just inches from here.

Choosing Your Measuring Stick

Do you prefer to size things up in terms of inches? Picas? Pixels? PhotoDeluxe, ever so accommodating, offers you all these options and a few more.

Inside the Unit Preferences dialog box, shown in Figure 2-4, you specify the default unit of measurement that PhotoDeluxe uses in the Photo Size and Canvas Size dialog boxes, as well as on the rulers in the image window. To open the dialog box, choose File⇨Preferences⇨Units.

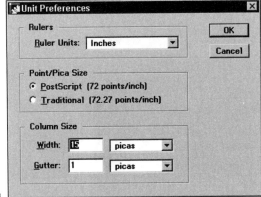

Figure 2-4:
Set your preferred unit of measure in this dialog box.

The following list explains your measuring options:

- ✔ **Select a measurement unit from the Ruler Units drop-down list.** If you plan to print most of your images, you probably want to choose a traditional print measure, such as inches, centimeters, points, or picas. If you're going to create images primarily for on-screen display, select Pixels as your measurement unit, for reasons that Chapter 3 explains.

- ✔ **Specify the number of points in a pica by clicking a Point/Pica Size radio button.** *Points* and *picas* are units of measure used in the commercial printing world; 12 points equal 1 pica, just as 12 inches equal 1 foot. The old-world school of publishing says that 72.27 points equal 1 inch. But the new-world school of publishing — that is, the one that uses PostScript printing devices — crams only 72 points into each inch. (Dealing with that extra 0.27 of a point is just too cumbersome, you know.) If you're printing to a PostScript device, make sure that the PostScript option in the Unit Preferences dialog box is selected. Otherwise, use whatever points-to-inches conversion makes you feel good about yourself.

- ✔ **Set column width and gutter width in the Column Size option boxes.** This option comes in handy if you regularly create images for use in a newsletter or other publication that features a columnar layout. You can size your images to match precisely the width of a column (or to span several columns, if you really want to get wild and crazy).

First, specify the width of the column in the Width option box. Enter the width of the *gutter* (the space between columns) in the Gutter option box. You can choose from several units of measurement from the adjacent drop-down lists.

When you set your image size, a topic that Chapter 3 explains, choose Columns as the unit of measurement for the Width option in the Photo Size dialog box. Enter the number of columns that you want the image to occupy as the Width value. For example, if you want the image to stretch across three columns, enter 3 as the Width value. You can also use the same approach when sizing your image canvas in the Canvas Size dialog box or creating a new image via the New dialog box. For the lowdown on the Canvas Size dialog box, see Chapter 7; for information about creating new images, go back to Chapter 1.

Exporting the Clipboard

One of the more obscure options on the File⇨Preferences submenu, the Export Clipboard command enables you to copy and paste an image or part of an image from PhotoDeluxe into another program.

PhotoDeluxe sends any data that you delete or copy using the Cut and Copy commands (both covered in Chapter 9) to the *Clipboard,* a temporary holding tank for data. If you turn the Export Clipboard option off, PhotoDeluxe eradicates the contents of the Clipboard when you shut down the program. If you turn the option on, PhotoDeluxe converts the image data into a format that enables you to paste it into a document that you're creating in another program.

Each time you shut down PhotoDeluxe, the program asks whether you want the Clipboard information to be retained, even though you have the Export Clipboard option turned on. Because you always get the option to keep or discard the Clipboard contents, I recommend that you leave the option turned on — especially if you use Windows and switch back and forth between applications frequently. Turning off the Export Clipboard option can speed things up a bit, however, because the computer doesn't have to process the Clipboard information.

Export Clipboard is one of those options that you toggle on and off simply by clicking the option name in the menu. A check mark next to the option name means that the feature is turned on.

Getting Helpful Hints

When you first install and start PhotoDeluxe, little panels offering helpful information slide out from the right side of the program window, as shown in Figure 2-5. PhotoDeluxe calls this feature the Assistant Drawer, presumably because the panels slide in and out like file drawers.

Assistant Drawer

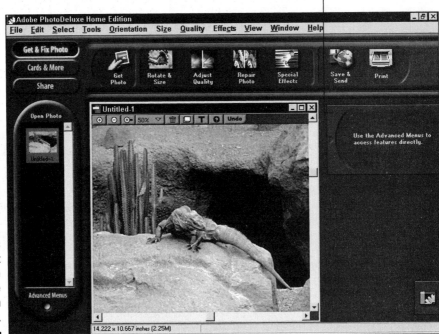

Figure 2-5: If you turn on the Assistant Drawer option, helpful tips slide out from the side of the program window.

After you read the tip on the Assistant Drawer panel, click anywhere on the panel to slide the drawer back into its digital filing cabinet. If the Assistant Drawer becomes tiresome, choose File⇨Preferences⇨Show Assistant Drawer. Choose the command again to turn the feature back on if you're so inclined. (A check mark next to the option name means that the option is turned on.)

Changing the Background Display

Every image in PhotoDeluxe rests atop a transparent background known as the image *canvas*. Normally, the canvas is completely hidden from view, and you needn't think a thing about it. But when you're creating a photo collage, cutting and pasting the elements of several images together, you may want to enlarge the canvas. (Chapter 7 covers that maneuver.) When you enlarge the canvas, portions of it may become visible, as shown in Figure 2-6. In the figure, the gray and white checkerboard area is the canvas.

Figure 2-6: Every image rests on a transparent canvas, represented here by the checkerboard area.

The canvas is white by default, but you can set the canvas to appear as a checkerboard pattern, as I did in Figure 2-6. Displaying the checkerboard pattern can be helpful in some editing projects. For example, if you have an image with a white border and you enlarge the canvas, you can easily see where the image ends and the empty canvas begins — something you can't easily do if you have the canvas color set to solid white.

PhotoDeluxe uses the background pattern you select to represent transparent areas of image layers as well as the image canvas. (Chapter 11 discusses layers, in case you're not sure what I mean by the term.) Again, switching to the checkerboard area enables you to more easily distinguish transparent portions of a layer.

The following steps explain how to change the canvas display from the default setting — solid white — to a checkerboard pattern:

1. **Choose File⇨Preferences⇨Image Background.**

   The Background Options dialog box, shown in Figure 2-7, rushes onto the scene.

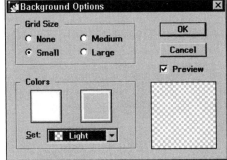

Figure 2-7:
You can
change the
look of the
background
canvas to
set it apart
from the
image itself.

2. Choose a Grid Size option.

Choose Small to make your checkerboard squares, er, small. Choose Medium or Large if you want the squares to be bigger than small. (Aren't you glad you have me to decipher these high-tech options?)

3. Set your checkerboard colors.

You can select one of the predefined color patterns from the Set drop-down list, as I did in Figure 2-7, or you can create a custom pattern. (Fussy, fussy.) Choose Custom from the Set drop-down list and then click one of the color swatches above the drop-down list. PhotoDeluxe opens the Color Picker dialog box, where you can choose a new color. (See Chapter 10 if you need help.) Click the other color swatch to set the second color in the grid.

If you select the Preview option, PhotoDeluxe displays your grid design in your on-screen image as well as in the dialog box. If the dialog box obscures the image window, you can drag the dialog box title bar to move the box aside. If you don't check the Preview option, you have to rely on the preview inside the dialog box.

4. Click OK.

To revert to the default solid-white canvas, head back to the Background Options dialog box, select None as your Grid Size option, and click OK.

Even though the canvas is transparent inside PhotoDeluxe, it always appears solid white when you open the image in other programs. For example, if you place the image on a Web page, any visible canvas areas appear white. Ditto for images that you place into a page-layout program. If you want the canvas to be some other color when you export the image, you must fill the empty canvas area with the color, as explained in Chapter 10. You may also want to explore the option of saving the image in the GIF file format, which enables you to make part of your image transparent when placed on a Web page. For details on that intriguing offer, check out Chapter 6.

Telling PhotoDeluxe Where to Scratch

PhotoDeluxe needs lots of computer memory — known as RAM — in order to carry out your image-editing requests. At times, the program needs more RAM than is available, even on computers that have gigantic memory banks. To get around this limitation, PhotoDeluxe uses virtual memory.

Despite the intimidating name, *virtual memory* is nothing more than empty hard drive space. When PhotoDeluxe runs out of memory to store image data, it puts that data temporarily in some empty portion of your computer's hard drive. Just to confuse you thoroughly, PhotoDeluxe (and other image-editing programs) refers to the drive used for virtual memory as the *scratch disk.*

To specify what drive you want to use as your scratch disk, choose File↝ Preferences↝Memory Preferences. Choosing the command displays the Memory Preferences dialog box, as shown in Figure 2-8.

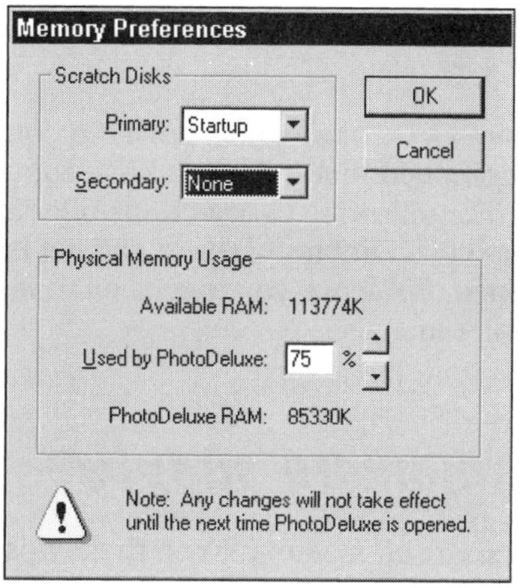

Figure 2-8: Changing the scratch disk and memory settings can improve the program's performance.

> **Memory Preferences**
>
> Scratch Disks
> Primary: Startup ▼   OK
> Secondary: None ▼   Cancel
>
> Physical Memory Usage
> Available RAM: 113774K
> Used by PhotoDeluxe: 75 %
> PhotoDeluxe RAM: 85330K
>
> ⚠ Note: Any changes will not take effect until the next time PhotoDeluxe is opened.

Here's my advice about making your scratch disk assignments:

✔ You have the opportunity to choose both a primary and secondary scratch disk. PhotoDeluxe turns to the secondary scratch disk only if your primary scratch disk is full.

✔ If you have only one hard drive, choose Startup from the Primary drop-down list and choose None from the Secondary drop-down list. Chances are, PhotoDeluxe made these choices automatically for you when you installed the program.

> ✔ If you have more than one hard drive, choose the drive that offers the best combination of empty space and access speed as your primary scratch disk. You want the computer to be able to read from and write to the disk as quickly as possible to cut down the time PhotoDeluxe needs to carry out your editing commands.
>
> ✔ Even if you have only one physical hard drive, it may be partitioned into several virtual drives on your system. For example, one of my computers has a 4GB hard drive, but Windows 95 separates those 4GB into three drives named C, E, and F. Again, select the drive that has the most free space. (The speed of the drives is the same in this case.)

When PhotoDeluxe can't find any empty scratch disk space, it announces that your scratch disk is full and refuses to do anything else until you free up some disk space. Unfortunately, I can't offer you a magic bullet for fixing this problem — you simply have to dump some of the data that's living on your hard drive.

Boosting Your Memory

If you work with very large image files — or an underpowered computer — PhotoDeluxe may occasionally complain that it doesn't have enough memory to complete certain operations. The following two sections offer a few techniques that you can try in order to placate PhotoDeluxe and get on with your work. If you continue to experience problems, you may need to install more memory or be content with smaller images.

Managing a tight memory supply

Your computer, like me, may be short on memory. Keep these tips in mind to get the most out of your available RAM:

> ✔ **Defragment the computer's memory by restarting your machine.** Each program that you're using consumes a portion of the system's RAM. So if PhotoDeluxe says that you're having a memory shortage, you simply shut down all the other open programs, right? Maybe. Maybe not.
>
> If you start and shut down several programs during a computer session, the system RAM can become fragmented. Instead of having a large, uninterrupted block of RAM, you can get little bits of RAM scattered here and there. PhotoDeluxe requires uninterrupted RAM to do its thing, which is why closing all other programs often doesn't satisfy PhotoDeluxe when it demands more memory.

To correct the situation, close down all programs — including PhotoDeluxe — and restart your computer. Then open PhotoDeluxe again to see whether you've resolved your memory crisis.

✔ **Turn off background applications.** Even small utilities that run in the background may eat up RAM that PhotoDeluxe needs.

✔ **Merge image layers.** If you're creating a layered image, use the Merge Layers command to flatten all the layers into one. (Chapter 11 explains this process in detail.) Images with layers require more RAM to process than flattened ones. Of course, you don't want to use this approach unless you're sure that you no longer need the layered version of the image.

Assigning memory to PhotoDeluxe

By default, PhotoDeluxe restricts itself to using a certain portion of your computer's memory, graciously leaving some RAM untouched for things like, oh, running Windows. You have the option of telling PhotoDeluxe that it can use more or less of the available RAM.

In all likelihood, you want to increase the RAM allocation rather than decrease it. But if you're having trouble running other applications at the same time as PhotoDeluxe and your image-editing projects typically involve small images that don't require huge amounts of RAM, you may want to trim back the PhotoDeluxe memory usage. If you do, however, PhotoDeluxe may run more slowly and balk at some memory-intensive commands.

You can allot a maximum of 75 percent of the system RAM to PhotoDeluxe. If you try to give PhotoDeluxe more RAM than 75 percent, you actually hinder the program instead of helping it.

 To set the RAM allocation, choose File⇨Preferences⇨Memory Preferences. PhotoDeluxe unfurls the Memory Preferences dialog box. (Refer to Figure 2-8, earlier in this chapter.) Raise or lower the Used by PhotoDeluxe value by clicking the arrows next to the option box or by typing in a new value. Your changes take effect the next time you start PhotoDeluxe.

Setting the Plug-Ins Directory

Many companies create filters and special-effects routines that work with PhotoDeluxe. Collectively, these add-ons are known as *plug-ins*. When you install plug-ins, the installation program usually asks where you want to store the plug-ins. Be sure to put any plug-ins in the appropriately named Plugins folder, which is inside the Program Files\Adobe\PhotoDeluxe folder on the hard drive where you installed the program. If you don't, PhotoDeluxe can't access or run the plug-ins.

If you choose the File⇨Preferences⇨Plug-Ins command in PhotoDeluxe, the program displays a dialog box in which you can specify the location of all your plug-ins. Don't change the location from the default setting (the Plugins folder) unless you actually move your plug-ins to some other folder or drive.

Keep in mind that PhotoDeluxe stores files that are necessary to run many of its own filters and effects in the Plugins folder. If you decide to move your plug-ins, be sure to move *all* the files in the Plugins folder, not just the third-party add-ons you've installed.

Many, but not all, plug-ins created for Adobe Photoshop also work with PhotoDeluxe. You can find tons of Photoshop-compatible plug-ins on the Internet as well as on the shelves of your local software store. Some of my favorite plug-ins come from Ulead Systems, which offers plug-ins for creating a number of special effects and stylized text. (You can find out more about these plug-ins at www.Ulead.com.) Extensis also sells several good plug-ins; the Intellihance filter provided on the PhotoDeluxe Quality menu is but one of the available plug-ins from Extensis (www.Extensis.com).

Dumping Your Custom Preferences

If you decide that you want to return all the settings in PhotoDeluxe to the defaults that were in force when you installed the program, you need to delete the PhotoDeluxe *preferences file*. PhotoDeluxe stores all your program settings in this file.

To delete your preferences file and start fresh with PhotoDeluxe, follow these steps:

1. **Shut down PhotoDeluxe.**

2. **In Windows Explorer, find the Pd20.psp file.**

   To launch Explorer, right-click the My Computer icon on your Windows desktop and then select Explore from the pop-up menu. Now track down the main PhotoDeluxe folder. Unless you changed the default installation settings, you can find the folder in the Program Files\Adobe folder on your hard drive. Open the PhotoDeluxe folder, which contains a Prefs folder. The PhotoDeluxe preferences file, named Pd20.psp, is located inside that Prefs folder.

3. **Delete the file.**

    You heard me — trash the thing. Don't worry, I know what I'm doing — or what you're doing, actually. This process doesn't touch any of your picture files, any PhotoDeluxe program files, or anything else except the preferences file.

4. **Restart PhotoDeluxe.**

    The program reappears in its original, untouched state. When you shut down the program, PhotoDeluxe creates a new preferences file in which it stores all the program settings that were in place at the time you exited the program.

If PhotoDeluxe starts behaving strangely, if you start getting a slew of disk error messages, or if you can't get the program to launch at all, try deleting the preferences file. Sometimes the file gets corrupted and causes problems. Of course, you have to reset all your custom preferences when you get the program up and running again, but doing that is better than not being able to use the program at all, right? Unless, of course, you're looking for a good excuse to skip out on that screwy image-editing project your manager wants you to do.

Displaying the Surfboard

In the lower-right corner of the image window, you see a square icon that looks just like the PhotoDeluxe program icon. Click the icon, and a panel full of other icons slides out, as shown in Figure 2-9. These icons serve as clickable links to different Web sites. If you connect to the Internet and then click an icon, you're taken directly to the corresponding Web site.

The icons connect you to the Adobe Web site home page, the Adobe ActiveShare home page, the technical support page, and to other companies that provide products related to PhotoDeluxe. To scroll through the available links, click the scroll arrows at either end of the row of link icons. If you like, you can keep the Web-surfing links displayed as you work on your pictures. To hide them, click the leftmost icon on the row (the one you clicked to display the row in the first place).

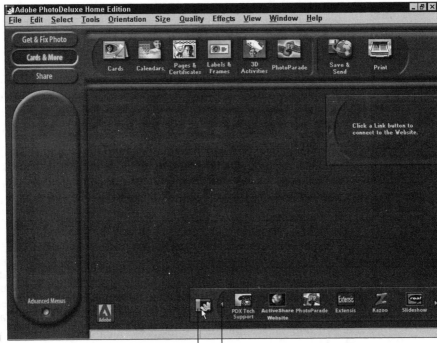

Figure 2-9:
Click an
icon to
connect to a
Web site
related to
Photo-Deluxe.

Click to display Web link icons ⌐   └Scroll arrow

Changing the PhotoDeluxe background

See that Adobe logo in the bottom-left corner of the program window? On
first glance, it looks just like an ordinary company graphic, but if you click
the logo, the dialog box shown in Figure 2-10 appears. The dialog box contains icons that represent different designs that you can display as the
window background in the image-editing area. By default, you get a plain,
dark background, but you can pick something more interesting — a beach
scene, for example, if you're easily bored. Just click an icon in the dialog box
and click OK. You can even install additional wallpaper designs via the
Seasonal Activities feature, which you can read about in the next section.

Although being able to change the appearance of the image-editing area adds
some entertainment to a dull day, you may be more interested in changing
the size of the image-editing area, which can feel pretty limited when you
work on large images. Unfortunately, Adobe doesn't provide this option in
PhotoDeluxe. You can't get rid of the Guided Activities portion of the window,
for example, to expand the height of the image-editing area. Nor can you hide
the Open Pictures panel that runs down the left side of the window. Sorry to
be the bearer of bad tidings, but at least you got the news without having to
search every nook and cranny of the program looking for a way to dedicate
more screen space to the image-editing window.

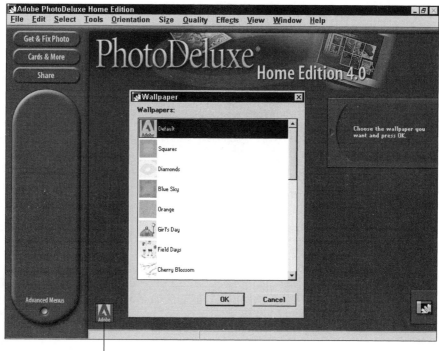

Figure 2-10:
Change the
window
background
by clicking a
different
wallpaper
icon.

Click to change PhotoDeluxe wallpaper

Turning off Seasonal Activities

PhotoDeluxe Version 4, like Version 3, offers a feature called Seasonal
Activities, which provide templates for creating projects related to the time
of year. When fall comes around, for example, you're presented with activities
related to autumn events. PhotoDeluxe can automatically offer the activities
according to the date on your computer's system clock.

In order for PhotoDeluxe to bring the seasonal templates to your attention,
however, you must turn on the Allow Seasonal Sharing option in the
File➪Preferences submenu. A check mark next to the option name means
that the option is turned on. Click the option name to toggle the option on
and off. When you first install PhotoDeluxe, the option is enabled.

Assuming that you don't immediately turn off the Allow Seasonal Sharing
option, PhotoDeluxe presents the Seasonal Activities dialog box shown in
Figure 2-11 the second time you start the program (after you install the program, open it for the first time, shut it down, and then reopen it). Choose the
activities that you want to install and then click Install. You can also choose

to install additional wallpaper for the program window if you like. (See the preceding section for more on this topic.) You must put the PhotoDeluxe program CD in your CD-ROM drive to complete the installation.

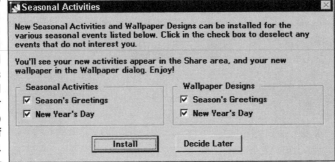

Figure 2-11:
You can install additional activities and wallpaper related to the time of year.

To use the activities that you install, click the Share Guided Activities button and then click the Seasonal Sharing icon. You then see icons representing the activities to the right of the Seasonal Sharing icon; click the icon for the activity you want to do.

If you don't care to add any Seasonal Activities at the time PhotoDeluxe presents the installation dialog box to you, click the Decide Later button at the bottom of the dialog box. PhotoDeluxe continues to present the dialog box each time you start the program unless you turn off the Allow Seasonal Sharing option.

Chapter 3

Putting Pixels into Perspective

● ●

In This Chapter

▶ Putting digital images under the microscope

▶ Shaking hands with a pixel

▶ Getting a grasp on resolution

▶ Understanding the difference between ppi and dpi

▶ Choosing the right input and output resolution

▶ Sizing images for print and on-screen use

▶ Working inside the Photo Size dialog box

▶ Resizing your images without turning them to muck

▶ Adding and subtracting pixels (resampling)

● ●

*I*f you're wired to the Internet, you may have discovered the world of online *newsgroups,* also known as *discussion groups* and *forums.* For the uninitiated, newsgroups serve as digital bulletin boards where people exchange information about a common interest. If you have a question about which digital camera to buy, for example, you can post a message asking for advice in the `rec.photo.digital` newsgroup. Within a few hours, helpful folks from all over the world reply with their recommendations.

I read several newsgroups every morning, including the aforementioned `rec.photo.digital` newsgroup. One reason I adopted this practice is that it gives me a legitimate excuse to enjoy another cup of coffee and put off doing anything really productive for 30 minutes or so. But reading the digital imaging newsgroups also gives me a clue as to what kind of problems people are having with their image-editing projects.

At any rate, my unofficial tally of newsgroup postings suggests that the top questions baffling image-editing newcomers are

- Why does my image look fine on-screen but like garbage when I print it?
- Why does my snapshot-size image get all fuzzy and yucky when I blow it up to an 8 x 10-inch print?
- What image resolution do I choose when scanning? When printing? When creating images for a Web page?

To understand the answers to these questions, you need a bit of knowledge about how digital images work, which is what you find in this chapter. You come face to face with the essential building block of every digital image, the *pixel.* You also get acquainted with a bunch of other important techie terms, including *resolution, ppi,* and *dpi,* all of which are critical to predicting whether your images will look sharp and beautiful or soft and cruddy when you display or print them.

I'll warn you straightaway, this stuff can be a little perplexing and, compared with the topics covered in the rest of the book, pretty dry and scientific. You even have to do some math here and there. But trust me, if you don't take some time to explore this information, you're going to be disappointed with the quality of your images. Not only that, but you'll be exposed as a naive, uninformed newbie when you post messages in your digital imaging newsgroup, which can only lead to deep feelings of inadequacy and shame. And really, don't we all have enough of those already?

Pixels Exposed

All digital images, whether they come from a scanner, digital camera, or some other device, are made up of tiny colored squares known as *pixels.* Pixel is shorthand for *picture element,* if you care, which you probably shouldn't. What you *do* need to know is how pixels operate.

Pixels work like the tiles in a mosaic. If you stand far away from a mosaic, you can't distinguish the individual tiles, and the image appears seamless. Only when you move closer can you see that the picture is indeed composed of tiles. The same thing is true with a digital image. If you print the picture at a relatively small size, as in the left image in Figure 3-1, the pixels blend together into a seamless photograph. But when you enlarge the picture, as I did with the eye in the upper-right portion of Figure 3-1, you can see the individual pixels.

Figure 3-1:
Zooming in
on a digital
image
reveals that
it's nothing
more than a
bunch of
colored
squares.

To see this phenomenon in action, follow these steps:

1. **Fire up PhotoDeluxe and open an image.**

   Chapter 1 provides detailed information about opening images.

2. **Click the Zoom In button.**

   The Zoom In button is the leftmost button on the toolbar at the top of
   the image window. (The button looks like a plus sign inside a circle.)
   PhotoDeluxe magnifies the view of your image.

3. **Click, click, and click again.**

   Keep clicking that button until you can make out the individual pixels in
   your image, as you can see in the upper-right portion of Figure 3-1.

   Another way to zoom in is by pressing the Ctrl key simultaneously with
   the plus key on your numeric keyboard (or Ctrl+Shift+Plus Sign on the
   regular number keys). To zoom out, press Ctrl+Minus Sign.

Having earlier made an analogy between a digital image and a mosaic, I should point out two subtle but important differences between the two:

✔ In a mosaic, the dimensions of individual tiles may vary. One tile may be slightly larger or have corners that are slightly more round, for example. All pixels in a digital image are perfectly square and exactly the same size.

✔ Although you may see some color variations within a single tile in a mosaic, each pixel in a digital image can represent only one specific color. A pixel can't be half red and half blue, for example. Nor can a pixel be dark blue in one area and light blue in another. You get exactly one hue and brightness level per pixel.

Of course, you can change the color of any pixel by using an image-editing program such as PhotoDeluxe. You also can change the number of pixels in your image and alter the size of all the pixels. You're the master of your pixel domain, as it were.

Can I edit drawings in PhotoDeluxe?

Computer artwork comes in two forms. *Digital images,* also referred to as *bitmap images, paintings,* or simply *images,* are composed of pixels. (This is explained in "Pixels Exposed," earlier in this chapter.) PhotoDeluxe and its big brother, Adobe Photoshop, are designed to edit this kind of picture, as are competing image-editing programs such as Corel Photo-Paint.

Other programs, including CorelDraw and Adobe Illustrator, enable you to create and edit vector graphics, often referred to as *drawings. Vector graphics* are made up of lines and curves that can be defined by mathematical equations. (Drawing software is sometimes called *object-oriented software* because every shape is considered a mathematical object.) You draw a line, for example, and the computer translates the distance and angle between the beginning and end points of the line into an equation. When you print the drawing, the drawing software sends the equation to the printer, which renders the line on paper as the equation dictates.

Because of the way vector graphics work, you can enlarge or reduce them as much as you want without any loss in print quality. This feature makes drawing software ideal for creating text, logos, and similar graphics that you need to output at several different sizes. But drawing programs don't do a good job of re-creating photographic images; for that task, pixel-based programs such as PhotoDeluxe offer a much better solution. The downside to pixel-based graphics is that they deteriorate in quality when you enlarge them. (See "Higher resolution = Better image quality" in this chapter for an explanation.)

Although PhotoDeluxe can open some types of vector drawings, it automatically converts them to bitmap images in the process. So if you want to retain the ability to scale your vector graphics to any size, don't try editing them in PhotoDeluxe.

Pixel Math

One of my favorite mottoes is "Friends don't let friends do math." To say that I am numerically challenged is an understatement. Unfortunately, working with digital images requires that you remember a few critical equations, which the next few sections explain in detail. If you're a math-hater like me, don't worry too much — if I can grasp this stuff, you surely can, as well.

Pixels ÷ image size = Resolution

Every digital image begins life with a specified number of pixels. Entry-level digital cameras, for example, typically create images that are 640 pixels wide by 480 pixels tall, for a total of 307,200 pixels. Higher-priced cameras create *megapixel* images, which are images with 1 million or more pixels. Table 3-1 presents some of the terms you need to know.

Table 3-1		Imagespeak	
Term	*Meaning*	*Example*	*Note*
Image size	The printed width and height of a picture.	You print an image that is 4 inches wide and 3 inches tall.	Some people inter change the term *pixel dimensions* with the term *image* size. I use *image size* when referring to the output size of the picture.
Image resolution	Indicates the number of pixels used to represent a specific area of the picture when you print it or display it on-screen. Resolution is usually measured in *pixels per linear inch,* or *ppi* for short.	An image may have an onscreen resolution of 75 ppi.	Image resolution is con stant throughout the entire image; in other words, you never have more pixels per inch in one area of your image than in another.
Pixel dimensions	Number of pixels in the image.	An image that is 307,200 pixels has pixel dimensions that are 640 pixels wide and 480 pixels tall.	Some people interchange the term *pixel dimensions* with the term *image size.* I use *pixel dimensions* when I mean the number of pixels in the photo.

(continued)

Table 3-1 *(continued)*

Term	Meaning	Example	Note
Pixels per linear inch (ppi)	Used to measure *image resolution,* the number of pixels in a linear inch is the number of pixels that goes *either* across the image *or* down the image — but not both.	An image may have an onscreen resolution of 75 ppi.	Do not confuse with *pixel dimensions,* which is a measurement of the total number of pixels in an image, not a specific area of an image shown on-screen or in print.

Some people use the phrase *image size* when discussing the number of pixels in the image, while other folks use the same words to mean the printed width and height of the picture. To avoid confusion, I use the term *pixel dimensions* when I mean the number of pixels in the photo and *image size* when referring to the output size of the picture.

Image resolution indicates the number of pixels used to represent a specific area of the picture when you print it or display it on-screen. Resolution is usually measured in pixels per linear inch, or *ppi* for short. Note that I said *linear inch* — you count the number of pixels across or down, but not both. The image resolution is constant throughout the entire image; in other words, you never have more pixels per inch in one area of your image than in another.

To determine the image resolution, you divide the number of horizontal pixels by the width of the picture, or you divide the number of vertical pixels by the picture height. For example, if your image is 640 pixels across by 480 pixels high, and you set the print size to 4 inches wide by 3 inches tall, the resolution is 160 ppi. (640 ÷ 4 = 160 or 480 ÷ 3 = 160)

Now that you know how to calculate the resolution of your image, you're no doubt wondering why you want to do so. The answer is that resolution determines whether your image looks lovely or lousy, as explained in the next section.

Higher resolution = Better image quality

Generally speaking, the higher the resolution, the better the quality of your images, especially for printed images. Figures 3-2 through 3-4 illustrate this point. The first figure has a resolution of 300 ppi; the second, 150 ppi; and the third, 75 ppi.

Figure 3-2:
A 300-ppi image looks smooth and detailed.

Figure 3-3:
When the resolution is cut in half, to 150 ppi, image quality suffers.

Figure 3-4:
A resolution
of 75 ppi
is fine for
on-screen
display, but
inadequate
for printing.

Why does the 75-ppi image look so much worse than the others? For one thing, with only 75 pixels per inch, you have fewer distinctly colored squares to represent the scene, which means that small details get lost. In Figure 3-4, the effect is particularly noticeable in the center of the daisy.

In addition, when you reduce the number of pixels per inch, the pixels have to grow in order to cover the same image ground. The bigger the pixel, the easier it is for the eye to distinguish the individual tiles, and the more the image looks like a bunch of squares rather than a continuous scene. Compare the edges of the petals around the bottom of the flower in Figure 3-2 with the same petals in Figure 3-4, and you can see how smooth, seamless edges turn to jagged, stair-step edges when printed at a lower resolution. In image-editing lingo, the image in Figure 3-4 suffers from *the jaggies,* or, in more technical terms, *pixelation.*

For another illustration of how resolution affects pixel size, take a look at the black borders around Figures 3-2 through 3-4. I applied the borders using the Outline command in PhotoDeluxe; you can find out how in Chapter 7. The border around Figure 3-2 is 2 pixels wide, as is the border around Figure 3-3. But the border in Figure 3-3 appears twice as thick because at 150 ppi, the pixels are twice as big as those in Figure 3-2, which has a resolution of 300 ppi. In Figure 3-4 (the 75-ppi image), I applied a 1-pixel border to create a border that's roughly the same size as the 2-pixel border in Figure 3-3 (the 150-ppi image).

As you can see, packing lots of pixels into your image can greatly improve how they look on the printed page. But *too many* pixels can spoil the image broth. For on-screen images, anything more than 96 ppi is overkill, and 72 ppi is usually adequate. Why? Because most computer monitors aren't set up to display more pixels than that, anyway. Too many pixels can also confuse some printers, which are designed to handle a certain number of pixels and no more. In fact, PhotoDeluxe protects you from this pitfall by limiting the number of pixels you can send to the printer. For more on the thorny question of how many pixels are enough, check out the section "So How Many Pixels Do I Need?" later in this chapter. For more on other printing issues, read Chapter 5.

More pixels = Bigger files

Your image file contains a certain amount of computer data for every pixel in the picture. The more pixels you have the bigger the image file, and the more room you need to save the image on your computer's hard drive or a removable storage disk (such as a floppy disk or Zip disk).

Just to give you a frame of reference, the 300-ppi image in Figure 3-2 contains more than a million pixels and consumes 2.5 megabytes (MB) on disk. The 150-ppi version in Figure 3-3 contains roughly 340,000 pixels and eats up 221K. Figure 3-4, at 75 ppi, contains approximately 84,700 pixels and requires a mere 170K of disk space. The number of pixels doesn't completely control file size — other characteristics of an image come into play, too. Pixel count is, however, a major contributor to file size.

Image file size is most important when you're creating images for the Internet, whether you want to place them on a Web page or e-mail them to a friend. The bigger the file, the longer the viewer's computer takes to download and display the image.

File size is also important from an everyday storage and file-transfer point of view. After you create that mondo-resolution, poster-size image, where are you going to keep it? Is your hard drive really so big that you can afford to fill it up with dozens of 20MB images? If you decide to have your image professionally printed, how are you going to get the image to the print shop? Your old floppy disk drive isn't going to cut it — a floppy holds less than 1.5MB of data. You're going to need a Zip drive or some other larger storage device for those big image files.

Additionally, large image files tax your computer's mental resources. The larger the file, the more memory (RAM) you need to open and edit the file. If you're working with less than 32MB RAM, applying a filter to or performing other editing tricks on a large image file can take a *loooonnng* time. Your computer may even refuse to carry out your instructions altogether.

Even an image file that doesn't consume a huge amount of storage space on disk can give your computer fits. That's because the amount of memory required to open and edit an image is greater than the size of the file on disk. For example, Figure 3-2 occupies 2.5MB on disk, but when opened in PhotoDeluxe, it uses 4MB of memory.

Finally, the bigger the image file, the longer it takes to print. Most home-office printers use the computer's memory in order to print images, which means that you can't do anything else while your image prints. Printers that come with their own stash of memory instead of relying on system resources may not have enough memory to handle really big image files.

The moral of this whole story: Before you crank up the pixel machine, be sure that you really need all those little squares and that your system can handle the strain. For a review of how many pixels are enough, see "So How Many Pixels Do I Need?" later in this chapter.

Adding pixels ≠ Better pictures

Some image-editing programs, including PhotoDeluxe, enable you to add or subtract pixels from your image. This process is known as *resampling*. The idea is that if you need more pixels, the software can simply add them. Similarly, if you want to reduce the number of pixels, PhotoDeluxe can weed out the excess for you. (For specifics on how to add or subtract pixels, see "Resampling your image," later in this chapter.)

Resampling *sounds* like a good idea. But in practice, resampling can turn your image to mud. When you add pixels, the image-editing program makes a calculated guess at the color and brightness of the new pixels. The results are usually poor, whether you're using an entry-level image editor such as PhotoDeluxe or a professional program such as Photoshop.

For proof, take a look at Figure 3-5. On the left is a 150-ppi image. At this resolution, the image is okay — but not great. But when I add pixels in PhotoDeluxe to increase the resolution to 300 ppi, the image doesn't get any better. In fact, the resampled image looks slightly less sharp than the original.

Downsampling — the techie term for tossing away unwanted pixels — is generally safer than *upsampling* (adding pixels). But any time you delete pixels, you're deleting image information. Throw away too many pixels, and you can lose important image details and reduce image quality.

Figure 3-5:
Resampling
a 150-ppi
image (left)
up to 300 ppi
results in an
even fuzzier
image
(right).

Whenever possible, avoid downsampling by more than 25 percent and avoid upsampling altogether. If you need to raise the image resolution, the only good way to do it is to reduce the image size, as explained in "Sizing an image for printing," later in this chapter.

Some image-editing gurus say that you can safely upsample by as much as 25 percent, too, but that figure depends on the image subject matter. Large expanses of color look better after upsampling than areas of intricate detail, and an image that's exceptionally sharp doesn't suffer as much from a pixel infusion as one that's already a little soft in the focus department.

For specifics on how to add or subtract pixels, see "Resampling your image," later in this chapter.

ppi ≠ dpi

If you've shopped for a printer, you've no doubt encountered the term *dpi, which stands for dots per inch.*

Many people assume that dpi and ppi mean the same thing, and the terms are often used interchangeably. Dots per inch is *not* the same as pixels per inch, however, so don't confuse the two. The term *ppi* refers to the number of pixels in the image; *dpi* refers to the number of ink dots a printer uses to reproduce one inch of the image on paper. Most printers create dots that are smaller than pixels, which means that the printer lays down several dots to reproduce each pixel. Each printer has an optimum pixel-to-dot ratio. Most 600-dpi inkjet printers, for example, do their best work when the image resolution is set to 250 to 300 ppi.

Sometimes dpi is used to describe the capabilities of monitors, scanners, and digital cameras, too. In all three cases, the term is a misnomer because these devices create images by using pixels, not printer dots.

For more on this issue, read "So How Many Pixels Do I Need?" and "Input Resolution," both of which are just around the bend. Chapter 5 offers more advice about printers and printing

So How Many Pixels Do I Need?

Ah, the $64,000 question. The answer depends on what you want to do with your finished image — print it or view it on-screen? You need far more pixels for the former than the latter, as explained in the sections about to jump out and grab you by the collar.

Satisfying a printer's pixel cravings

For best results when printing, check your printer's manual for information about the ideal image resolution (pixels per inch) to use. If you're having your image professionally printed at a copy shop or commercial printer, ask the printer's sales rep for the correct resolution. Each printer is engineered to deliver its best prints at a certain image resolution.

Don't confuse the printer's resolution, stated in dpi (dots per inch) with the image resolution you need to specify in PhotoDeluxe. If you have a 600-dpi inkjet, for example, don't assume that you should set your image resolution to 600 ppi. (For more on this subject, see "ppi _ dpi," earlier in this chapter.)

Consumer-level color inkjets typically deliver the best prints when the image resolution is in the 250–300-ppi neighborhood. A resolution of 300 ppi is also the norm for color images that are printed commercially, like the ones in this book. These same values apply for grayscale images as well, although you can often get away with a lower resolution for screen shots such as the ones you see in this book. (Most of my screen shots have a resolution of about 100 to 170 ppi.)

If you snapped your image with a digital camera, you may not have enough pixels to get both the print size and the image resolution that you want. In this case, you have to make a decision: Which is more important, size or quality? Strike the balance that's most suited to your printing project.

If you scanned your image or are working with an image from a commercial image collection, you may have *more* pixels than you need. You may think that if 300 ppi is required for a good printout, 450 ppi should be even better. The truth is that when the printer gets more pixels than it's designed to handle, it just dumps the excess. Your image doesn't look any better than it would at 300 ppi, and it may even look worse because the printer may not pick the best pixels to eliminate. For instructions on how to rid yourself of pixel overpopulation, see "Resampling your image," later in this chapter.

Meeting a monitor's meager pixel needs

If you're preparing an image for use on a Web page, in a multimedia presentation, or for some other on-screen use, your pixel needs are much lower than for printed images.

Screen displays, like digital images, are pixel-based. Your monitor displays everything you see on-screen, whether you're looking at a photo, a text document, or the latest computer game, by generating rows and rows of pixels.

Most monitors enable the user to choose between several display settings, each of which generates a different pixel population. Typically, you can select from the following options: 640 x 480 pixels, 800 x 600 pixels, 1024 x 768 pixels, and 1280 x 1024 pixels. The first number represents the number of pixels displayed across the screen, and the second number indicates the number of pixels displayed vertically.

The resolution of the monitor depends on the actual screen size. A 15-inch monitor set to display 640 x 480 pixels has a resolution of about 57 ppi, for example, whereas a 21-inch monitor has a resolution of around 41 ppi at the same setting. (If you're doing the math, remember that the actual screen space of monitors is much less than the stated monitor size. I based my resolution numbers on a screen size of 111/4 inches for the 15-inch monitor and 153/4 inches for the 17-inch monitor.)

I could provide you with a chart of all the possible monitor sizes and available screen resolutions, but that would only confound you and send me straight to the nuthouse. So instead, I'll just give you a general rule regarding screen resolutions: When they are shipped from the factory, most PC monitors are set to a screen resolution of 96 ppi, and most Macintosh monitors are set to 72 ppi. Of course, some people do change the monitor settings from the factory default. But even when set to the highest display setting, screen resolution rarely exceeds 100 ppi, and a 72-ppi image usually looks just fine at that resolution.

Many people in the image-editing world prepare their screen images using the 72 to 96-ppi rule, which is the only reason I mention it at all. The fact is, though, that you don't need to concern yourself with pixels per inch when you prepare images for the screen. No matter what the monitor size or display setting, the monitor devotes one screen pixel to each image pixel. So you can just set the pixel dimensions of your image according to how much of the screen you want the image to cover. To fill the entire screen of a monitor that's set to display 640 x 480 pixels, for example, you make your image 640 pixels wide by 480 pixels tall. For more on this topic, see "Sizing images for the screen," later in this chapter.

The Top-Secret File Information Box

The File Information box, near the bottom-left corner of the PhotoDeluxe program window, displays two values: the current print size and the amount of memory that PhotoDeluxe is using to process the image. If you place your cursor on the box and hold down the left mouse button, a second, bigger box appears out of nowhere, as shown in Figure 3-6. The box lists the pixel dimensions and resolution as well as the print size.

You can safely ignore the Channels data in the box. Like many other controls in PhotoDeluxe, this information is a carryover from Adobe Photoshop. In that program, you can view and edit the independent color channels in an image and convert an image from one color model to another, which makes the Channels information useful. You can't do either in PhotoDeluxe, though. For more on color models, see Chapter 5.

Figure 3-6:
This box
displays
information
about the
image size.

Press and hold to display file information

Field Guide to the Photo Size Dialog Box

If you want to make changes to your image size (width and height), pixel
dimensions (pixels across by pixels down), or resolution (pixels per inch),
head for the Photo Size dialog box, shown in Figure 3-7. To open the dialog
box, choose Size⇨Photo Size. Figure 3-7 shows the photo size data for the
daisy image in Figure 3-2, shown earlier in this chapter.

Upcoming sections provide details about using the dialog box to accomplish
various tasks. Here's a general overview of the dialog box options:

✔ The top section of the dialog box shows the image's current dimensions
and resolution.

✔ The Current Size and New Size values indicate how much room the
image consumes in your computer's memory *while the image is open for
editing in PhotoDeluxe.* This value is not the same thing as how much
space the image consumes on disk when you save it to your hard drive
or to a removable disk. For example, the daisy image in Figure 3-2 consumes 2.5MB when saved to disk but requires 4MB of memory to edit.

✔ You alter the image size and resolution by entering new values into the Width, Height, or Resolution option box. To replace an existing value, double-click the value and type a new number.

After you double-click, you also can press the up- and down-arrow keys on your keyboard to raise and lower the value. Depending on what unit of measurement is being used, each press of an arrow key changes the value by 1, 0.1, or 0.001. Press Shift along with the up- or down-arrow key to raise or lower the value in increments of 10.

✔ You can select from several units of measurement by using the pop-up menus beside the Width and Height option boxes. Choose Pixels to display the pixel dimensions of your image.

✔ To change the unit of measurement that appears by default when you open the Photo Size dialog box, choose File⇔Preferences⇔Units. Select the unit that you want to use from the Ruler Units pop-up menu and click OK. Bear in mind that your choice affects the rulers running along the top and left side of your image window. (Turn the rulers on and off by pressing Ctrl+R.)

✔ Select the Pixels/inch option from the Resolution pop-up menu unless you're working with an output device (printer or monitor) that requires you to set resolution in terms of pixels per centimeter. In that case, choose Pixels/centimeter.

✔ If you press and hold the Alt key, the Cancel button changes into a Reset button. Click the Reset button to return to the values that were in place when you first opened the Photo Size dialog box.

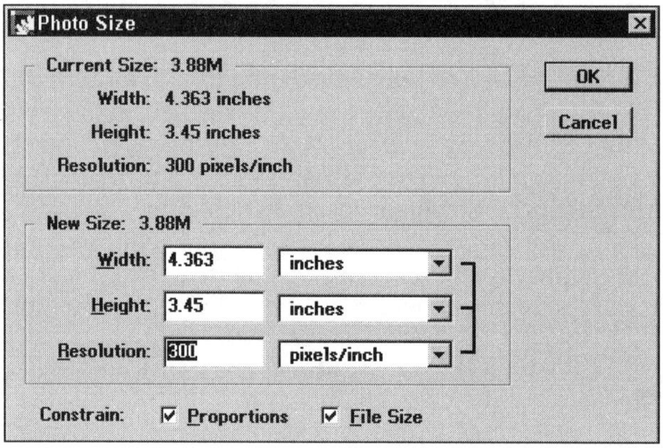

Figure 3-7:
To size or resample your image, crack open the Photo Size dialog box.

Photo Size	☒
Current Size: 3.88M	
Width: 4.363 inches	OK
Height: 3.45 inches	Cancel
Resolution: 300 pixels/inch	
New Size: 3.88M	
Width: 4.363 inches ▾	
Height: 3.45 inches ▾	
Resolution: 300 pixels/inch ▾	
Constrain: ☑ Proportions ☑ File Size	

Sizing an image for printing

PhotoDeluxe displays your image on-screen at the size you specify with the zoom controls, discussed in Chapter 1. To find out what size your image will be if printed, just glance at the File Information box in the bottom-left corner of the program window.

Alternatively, check the rulers along the top and left side of your image. (Press Ctrl+R to turn the rulers on and off quickly.) No matter what view size you choose using the zoom controls, the rulers always reflect the print size of your image.

If you're not happy with the print size of the image, you have two resizing options:

✔ **Keep the pixel count the same and change the resolution and pixel size.** If you enlarge the picture, the resolution goes down and pixels get bigger. If you reduce the picture, the resolution goes up and pixels get smaller. (Remember that image size divided by the pixel dimensions equals the resolution, so when the image size changes, resolution and pixel size has to change if the number of pixels doesn't.)

✔ **Keep the resolution and pixel size the same by adding or deleting pixels (*resampling*).** If you enlarge the image, the software creates new pixels to fill in the new image area. If you reduce the image, the software tosses out the extra pixels.

As discussed earlier, in "Adding pixels ≠ Better pictures," resampling can be a dangerous move. You can generally delete about 25 percent of your pixels without much change in image quality, and you may even be add a few pixels and not notice a huge difference. But for best image quality, avoid adding pixels and limit the number of pixels you subtract.

For information on how to resample your image, see "I Took on the Mob and Won!" later in this chapter. Er, hold that — got distracted by my *National Enquirer* for a moment. The section you want is the much more dull-sounding "Resampling your image."

The following steps explain how to change your print size *without* resampling:

1. **Choose Size⇨Photo Size.**

   The Photo Size dialog box appears, as shown in Figure 3-7.

2. **Select the Proportions check box.**

   This option, when turned on, ensures that your image is resized proportionately. If you change the Width value, the Height value changes, too.

3. **Check the File Size check box.**

   When File Size is turned on, the number of pixels in your image can't be changed. If you raise the Width and Height values, the Resolution value goes down automatically. If you decrease the Width and Height values, the Resolution value goes up. To indicate the link, PhotoDeluxe displays a line connecting the Width, Height, and Resolution options. You can see the line to the right of the option boxes in Figure 3-7.

4. **Set the Width and Height values as desired.**

Before you change the values, select any unit of measurement but Pixels or Percent from the adjacent pop-up menu. You then can double-click inside the Width or Height option box and either type in the new dimensions or press the up- and down-arrow keys to raise or lower the values.

When you select Pixels or Percent as the unit of measurement, PhotoDeluxe automatically resamples your image when you enter new values in the Width or Height option box. Select Pixels or Percent only when sizing images for on-screen display or when you want to resample your image, as discussed later in this chapter.

5. **Click OK.**

Don't be alarmed that the on-screen size of your image doesn't change. Remember, the on-screen display size is determined by the zoom level you set with the PhotoDeluxe zoom controls, not by the size you set in the Photo Size dialog box. To verify that your image is indeed the correct size, turn on the rulers (Ctrl+R) or check the File Information box, as shown in Figure 3-6. Now you can see that PhotoDeluxe did indeed resize your image as requested.

If your image *did* change size on-screen, you didn't select the File Size option box as instructed in Step 3. Press Ctrl+Z to undo the resizing and try again.

For more information on printing, take a spin through Chapter 5, which is devoted entirely to that subject.

Sizing images for the screen

If you're sizing an image for use on a Web page, a multimedia show, or some other on-screen use, you need to take an approach that's a little different than you take when printing your picture.

When you size an image for printing, you think in terms of inches, picas, or whatever other traditional unit of measurement you may use. But when sizing an image for the screen, you should think in terms of pixels instead.

Before diving into an explanation of exactly how to size images for the screen, I want to recap two important pieces of information presented earlier in this chapter:

✔ A one-to-one relationship exists between image pixels and *screen pixels* — the pixels that your monitor generates to display everything you see on-screen. A monitor uses one screen pixel to display one image pixel, in other words. (This rule doesn't apply when you're viewing pictures at a magnified zoom size in PhotoDeluxe; in that case, the monitor may use several screen pixels to reproduce one image pixel.)

✔ Most monitors can be set to several different screen display settings: 640 x 480 pixels, 800 x 600 pixels, 1024 x 768 pixels, and 1280 x 1024 pixels, for example. That one-to-one relationship between screen and image pixels, however, remains constant, no matter what the display setting or the size of the monitor.

To size an image for on-screen display, you simply figure out how much of the screen you want to cover and set your pixel dimensions accordingly. If you want to fill the whole screen on a monitor that's set to display 640 x 480 pixels, change the pixel dimensions of your image to 640 x 480 pixels. If you want to fill half the screen on that same monitor, change the pixel dimensions to 320 x 240.

The one difficulty you face when sizing images for on-screen display — especially Web images — is that you have no way to know what size monitors and display settings people will use when they view your image. You may create a 640 x 480 image, expecting it to fill the viewers' screens, but for viewers running their monitors at 1024 x 768, your image occupies a much smaller screen area. Figures 3-8 and 3-9 illustrate this dilemma. Figure 3-8 shows a 640 x 480 image displayed on a 17-inch monitor set to the 640-x-480-pixel display option. Figure 3-9 shows the same image when the display setting is changed to 1024 x 768.

Figure 3-8: A 640 x 480-pixel image consumes the entire screen when the monitor display is set to 640 x 480.

Figure 3-9:
When the monitor setting is 1024 x 768, the 640 x 480-pixel image consumes only a portion of the screen real estate.

Because you can't predict the monitor situation for all your viewers, the best idea is to go with the lowest common denominator and size your images for a 640 x 480-pixel screen.

Now that you have the background scoop, the following steps give you the 1-2-3, or, in this case, the 1-2-3-4-5, for resizing your images for screen display.

Before you take these steps, save a backup copy of your image in case you ever need all your original image pixels.

1. **Choose Size⇨Photo Size.**

   PhotoDeluxe displays the Photo Size dialog box, which you can see in Figure 3-7.

2. **Select the Proportions check box.**

   When selected, this option maintains the current image proportions. If you change the Height value, the Width value changes accordingly. A check mark in the box indicates that the option is turned on. If you don't see the check mark, click the box.

3. **Choose Pixels as the unit of measurement for both the Width and Height option boxes.**

4. Change the pixel dimensions as desired.

When you begin typing a new value in the Width or Height option box, PhotoDeluxe automatically deselects the File Size check box, enabling you to add or delete pixels.

If you increase the Width and Height values, you may not like the results. You're adding pixels, which usually doesn't work very well. For an explanation, see "Adding pixels ≠ Better pictures," earlier in this chapter.

5. Click OK.

As an alternative, you can choose Percent as your unit of measurement from the Width and Height pop-up menus and resize the image by a percentage of its current size. For example, setting the Width and Height values to 50 dumps exactly half of the image pixels.

"But what about resolution?" you ask. "Don't I have to worry about that value?" The answer is no. As long as you size your image using Pixels or Percent as your unit of measurement, you don't have to worry about resolution. Only if you can't think in terms of pixels and want to use inches or picas or whatever as your unit of measurement, do you need to adjust the resolution for screen display. In that case, deselect the File Size check box, set the desired Width and Height values, and set the Resolution value to match your monitor's screen resolution, if you know it. Otherwise, a resolution in the range of 72–96 ppi is appropriate. Flip back to "Meeting a monitor's meager pixel needs," earlier in this chapter, for more details on this subject.

Changing the image resolution

If you want to raise or lower the *image resolution* — the number of pixels per inch — you have two choices. You can add or delete pixels to the image, also known as *resampling.* Adding pixels *(upsampling)* isn't recommended, for reasons explained earlier in this chapter. If you want to try to it anyway or need to *downsample* the image (delete pixels), see the next section for instructions.

Alternatively, you can change the image size and retain the current number of pixels. As you enlarge the image, the resolution goes down; as you reduce the image, the resolution goes up. Reducing the size of the image is the only good way to raise the image resolution, by the way.

To walk the safer, better, resolution-changing path, follow the steps given in "Sizing an image for printing," earlier in this chapter, but change the Resolution value instead of changing the Width and Height values. PhotoDeluxe automatically adjusts the width and height of your image as needed.

Be sure that the File Size option is checked! Otherwise, PhotoDeluxe adds or deletes pixels to achieve the Resolution value that you specify.

Resampling your image

Resampling an image means adding or deleting pixels — also known as changing the pixel dimensions. You may need to resample your image to change the size at which an image is displayed on a Web page, or you may want to trim excess pixels to lower the image resolution and reduce file size.

As mentioned ad nauseam throughout this chapter, adding pixels *(upsampling)* is seldom a good idea. If your image is very sharp and contains mostly large areas of flat color, you may be able to get away with a small amount of upsampling. Otherwise, you're likely to do your image more harm than good.

Downsampling — deleting pixels — can also destroy an image when done to excess. For best results, don't downsample more than 25 percent. And before you resample an image at all, be sure to save a backup copy of the original. You may need the image at its original pixel count some day.

Now that the important legal disclaimers are out of the way, here's how to resample an image:

1. Choose Size⇨Photo Size.

The Photo Size dialog box appears. Refer to Figure 3-7.

2. Select the Proportions check box.

This option ensures that when you change the image height, the image width changes proportionately. A check in the box means that the option is turned on.

3. Deselect the File Size check box.

If this option is selected, PhotoDeluxe doesn't let you change the number of image pixels.

4. Change the Width/Height or Resolution values.

You're free to change the Width/Height values independently of the Resolution value, and vice versa. If you want to dump pixels, choose a print unit of measurement (inches, picas, and so on) and lower the Resolution value. Alternatively, choose Pixels or Percent as your unit of measurement and lower the Width or Height value.

To add pixels — and don't say I didn't warn you against it — raise the Resolution value while using a print unit of measurement for the Width and Height values. You also can increase the Width and Height values while using Pixels or Percent as your unit of measurement.

5. Click OK.

If you don't like the results — I *told* you so — press Ctrl+Z or click the Undo button in the image window to undo the resampling.

Applying the Unsharp Mask filter can sometimes improve the appearance of a resampled image. For how-to's, chart a course to Chapter 8

Input Resolution

Before I put the topic of resolution to rest for good, I want to add a few final tips about *input resolution* — which is a fancy way of referring to the resolution used when you scan an image, capture it with a digital camera, or open it from a Photo CD. The general guidelines are as follows:

✔ **Scanning:** When you set the image resolution in your scanning software, consider the final use of the image. If you're going to print the image, set the scan resolution to match the optimum resolution for the printer. (See "Satisfying a printer's pixel craving" and "Sizing an image for print," earlier in this chapter, for more information.) Likewise, if the image is destined for stardom as a Web image or as part of a multimedia presentation, set the scan resolution in the neighborhood of 72 to 96 ppi. Unfortunately, most scanner software doesn't enable you to set the scan size in pixels, which is the best way to size images for screen use. You may need to adjust the pixel dimensions slightly in PhotoDeluxe after you scan. (Check out "Meeting a monitor's meager pixel needs" and "Sizing images for the screen," also earlier in this chapter, for more details on screen images.)

✔ **Capturing with a digital camera:** Always use the highest resolution setting on your digital camera unless you're sure that you'll never use the image for anything other than on-screen display. Even then, you may want to capture the image at the highest setting to give yourself the most flexibility when you size the image. You can always go back and get rid of extra pixels if needed, but you can't add them after the fact with any degree of success.

✔ **Opening a Photo CD image:** Commercial collections of images on CD-ROM are usually stored in the Kodak Photo CD format, which provides you with the same image at several different pixel dimensions. (Don't confuse this format with Kodak Picture CD, which is a different animal entirely.) A standard Photo CD includes an image at 128 x 192 pixels, 256 x 384 pixels, 512 x 768 pixels, 1024 x 1536 pixels, and 2048 x 3072 pixels. Again, select the image size that's appropriate for the printer or monitor you're going to use to print or display your image.

From smallest to largest, the five sizing options are known in techie terms as Base/16, Base/4, Base, 4 Base, and 16 Base. This kind of information can be helpful when you want to get away from someone at a party. Launch into a heartfelt discourse on the merits of the various Base options, and you can bore almost anyone into a hasty retreat. (Chapter 1 includes a table listing the dimensions for each of the Base options in case you want a handy reference to stick in your pocket protector.)

How deep are your bits?

You may occasionally hear people referring to image bit depth. Well, not if you keep company with sane, normal people, of course. But if you lurk in Internet image-editing newsgroups or hang around the coffee shops where all the hippest digital artists gather, you'll definitely catch wind of the term.

Just so that you don't feel like a total outsider, *bit depth* is a measure of how many colors an image can contain. Bit depth is sometimes also called *pixel depth* or *color depth.*

Common bit-depth values range from 1-bit to 24-bit. Each bit can represent two colors. A 1-bit image puts two colors at your disposal (black and white). A bit depth of 8 translates to 256 colors ($2^8 = 256$); 16 bits gives you about 32,000 colors; and 24 bits delivers a whopping 16 million colors.

A higher bit depth translates to a more vibrant, natural-looking image. (See Color Plate 3-1 for a look at the difference between an 8-bit color image and a 24-bit color image.) On the downside, higher bit depth also means a larger image file, because all those extra bits mean more data for your computer to store.

Part II
Save, Print, Send!

The 5th Wave   By Rich Tennant

"My God! I've gained 9 pixels!"

In this part . . .

*U*nless you're using Adobe PhotoDeluxe 4 solely to experience the inner joy that comes from clicking mouse buttons, the chapters in this part of the book are essential reading. (If you *are* clicking for clicking's sake, by the way, seek help.)

In Chapter 4, you find out how to save your images, a task that's a lot more complicated than you rightfully expect. You also get the lowdown on organizing your pictures in the new PhotoDeluxe photo organizer.

Chapter 5 shows you how to print your masterpieces and even gives some advice on buying a printer. Finally, Chapter 6 explores on-screen uses for your pictures and introduces you to Adobe's online photo-sharing program, which enables you to hang your work in the digital art gallery known as the World Wide Web.

Chapter 4

Saving Your Masterpiece

. . . .

In This Chapter

▶ Saving your images to disk

▶ Choosing the right file format

▶ Organizing your image files

▶ Tracking down images in the photo organizer

. . . .

*I*n the old days — you know, before Bill Gates owned the world — saving a piece of artwork was an easy proposition. Your kid came home from school toting a masterful rendition of a rainbow. You hung the picture on the refrigerator for a while and then stashed it in a memory box in the closet. No major effort required. At least, not until 20 years later, when you needed to remember where you put the memory box and which kid painted which rainbow.

Saving digital artwork is a bit more complex. You need to deal with technical issues, such as choosing a file format, and you also need to think about what storage medium is appropriate for your images. Incredibly geeky terms such as *JPEG, lossy compression,* and *GIF89A* rear their ugly heads.

This chapter helps you sort out all the mumbo-jumbo so that you can glide smoothly through the process of saving your images. In addition to explaining what file format to use for different projects, this chapter shows you how to organize and catalog your images using the new photo organizer.

Preserving Pictures

In PhotoDeluxe, as in most computer programs, you must save your image file before you close an image. Otherwise, PhotoDeluxe forgets about any changes you made to the photo. You should also save open pictures at regular intervals while you're working on them. Otherwise, you run the risk of losing hours of work if PhotoDeluxe freezes up or your computer shuts itself down in a fit of anger.

Saving images may seem like a thoroughly uninspiring topic — and, well, it is. Unfortunately, if you don't take the time to wade through the various issues related to saving files, your images may not live to see another day. So get some caffeine, crank up the stereo, or do whatever else you usually do to make sure that you don't nod off. Then plow through the next few sections, which explain the basics of saving files in PhotoDeluxe.

Understanding the PhotoDeluxe saving system

When you ask PhotoDeluxe to open an image, the program determines the image's file format. Discussed ad nauseam later in this chapter, *file format* simply refers to the method used to store image data. Different formats store data differently inside the image file. If you've hung around computer folk for a while, you've probably heard about the most popular formats for storing digital photos: TIFF, JPEG, and GIF.

Like many programs, PhotoDeluxe has its own unique method of saving images, known as the *native format,* or, in some circles, the *proprietary format.* The PhotoDeluxe native format goes by the initials PDD, except in the Business Edition of the program, where the format sometimes uses the alias PBD. To keep things simple, I stick with PDD in this book.

If you ask PhotoDeluxe to open a PDD file, the program opens the original image file, just as you would expect. If the image was stored in any other file format, PhotoDeluxe creates a working copy of the image, opens the copy, and converts the copy to the PDD format. Your edits are applied to the PDD copy, not to your original image.

Why would PhotoDeluxe go to the trouble of converting the image to PDD? Because PDD is designed to enable PhotoDeluxe to apply your edits more efficiently, thereby speeding up your editing work. In addition, the PDD format *supports* (can save) any image layers that you create. With the exception of the Adobe Photoshop format, PDD is the only format available for use in PhotoDeluxe that can save layers. (Chapter 11 explores the topic of layers.)

I bring up all this native format stuff because it comes into play when you save a file. Because of the PhotoDeluxe approach to file formats, you need to remember the following rules:

✔ **Always save in the PDD format until you're completely finished with your image.** Only then should you save the image in one of the other formats discussed in "Figuring Out Formats," later in this chapter.

✔ **The Save and Save As commands save images in the PDD format only.** To save in some other file format, select one of the commands on the File➪Export submenu. (Later sections in this chapter detail these saving options.)

✔ **Saving in any format but PDD merely saves a copy of the open image; the PDD version remains on-screen and active.** If you make further edits, PhotoDeluxe applies the changes to the PDD version, *not* to the version you saved in the other file format. If you want to update that other version, you need to choose the Export command again and resave the image.

✔ **If you're editing an image that has never been saved in the PDD format, the PDD version on-screen is temporary.** When you close the image, PhotoDeluxe asks whether you want to save the PDD version, even if you already saved the image in another format. If you say thanks but no thanks, PhotoDeluxe erases the PDD version.

✔ **Think long and hard before deleting the PDD version of an image.** After you save an image in another file format, you can delete the PDD version to free up some disk space. However, you may want to retain the PDD version if you saved the image in JPEG, GIF, or some other file format that throws away some image data in the saving process. (For more on that intriguing subject, see "Figuring Out Formats," later in this chapter.) You may also want to keep a PDD version of an image that contains layers so that you can manipulate the layers at a later date, if necessary.

Saving works in progress

As I mentioned a few paragraphs ago, you should save your pictures in the native PhotoDeluxe format, PDD, until you're completely finished working with them. If you need to create a copy of the image in some other format, wait until after you put the final editing touches on the picture.

To save an image in the PDD format for the first time, jog down the following path:

1. **Choose File➪Save or press Ctrl+S.**

   Either way, the dialog box shown in Figure 4-1 appears.

2. **Enter a filename into the File Name box.**

   The File Name box should be highlighted, which means that you can just start typing to replace the existing contents of the box. If the box isn't highlighted, double-click it and then type.

File list box   Up One Level

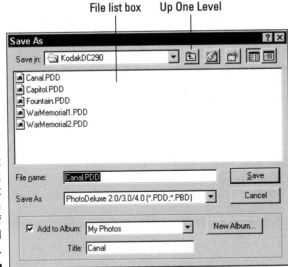

Figure 4-1:
Visit the
Save As
dialog box
to make
sure that
your work
doesn't
vanish in a
puff of
digital
smoke.

3. **Specify the drive and/or folder where you want to store the file.**

   From the Save In drop-down list, choose a folder or drive to display its contents in the file list box, labeled in Figure 4-1. Double-click a folder in the file list box to see what that folder contains. To move up a level in the folder/drive structure, click the Up One Level button, also labeled in the figure.

4. **Select PhotoDeluxe 2.0/3.0/4.0 (*.PDD, *.PBD) from the Save As drop-down list.**

   This option saves your image in the native format used by PhotoDeluxe Versions 2, 3, 4, and the Business Edition. The Save As drop-down list also provides an option for saving in the Version 1 format. Don't select that format unless you're completely done editing your picture and you need to open it in PhotoDeluxe 1. Be aware that when you open the saved picture in Version 1, the program makes two significant changes: First, if you have more than six image layers, PhotoDeluxe fuses them into one layer; and second, your text layer gets merged with the underlying image layer. (For more about layers and text, see Chapters 11 and 12.)

5. **Create a thumbnail for the photo organizer (optional).**

   If you select the Add to Album option at the bottom of the dialog box, PhotoDeluxe adds a thumbnail preview of your image to the photo organizer that comes with the program.

   First, select the album in which you want to store the thumbnail from the drop-down list next to the Add to Album check box. To create a new album, click New Album, which takes you to the Create Album dialog box. Type the album name, click Create Album, and click Done to return to the Save As dialog box. Next, double-click the Title option box and type a title for the image. The text you type appears with your thumbnail in the photo organizer window.

The title doesn't have to be the same as your actual image filename; for example, if your official filename is JK1014.PPD, you can give your thumbnail a title that's a little less obscure, such as *Lighthouse.* You don't need the three-letter file extension at the end of the title.

For more information about the photo organizer, read "Organizing Your Image Closet," later in this chapter.

6. **Click Save.**

PhotoDeluxe does your bidding and saves your image as instructed. Your image remains on-screen, tempting you to do more damage.

If you do any further editing, you must resave the image to retain the new changes. Unlike some programs, PhotoDeluxe doesn't offer an autosave feature that saves your image every so often without any input from you. That's good, because you can experiment freely with your image. If the program were saving your changes on its own, you might get stuck with some edits that you later decide you don't like. However, you have to assume the responsibility for remembering to save the image during your editing sessions. Only you can prevent image fires, as the saying goes.

To resave the image in a flash, just press Ctrl+S. If you like clicking, click File➪Save. PhotoDeluxe resaves the image without bothering you with the Save As dialog box.

When you close an image, PhotoDeluxe reminds you to save your latest round of changes if you haven't done so already.

Saving multiple copies of an image

At times, you may want to keep several versions of the same image. For example, say that you need to create a high-resolution image for a print piece but want a low-resolution version for a Web page. You can save the image once at the high resolution and then reduce the resolution for the Web page and save that low-resolution image under a different name.

Additionally, you may want to save a copy of your image to a different location on your hard drive or to a removable storage device, such as a floppy disk or a Zip disk.

To save an image with a different name or to another location, choose File➪ Save As. PhotoDeluxe displays the regular Save As dialog box, described earlier. Enter a new filename or choose a different storage location — or both — and click Save.

Like the Save command, the Save As command enables you to save in the native PhotoDeluxe format only. To save the image in some other format, use the process described in the next section.

Saving in Other Formats (Exporting)

If you're familiar with other image editors, you probably expected to be able to select from dozens of file formats when you chose the Save or Save As command. And when you encountered the PhotoDeluxe Save As dialog box, you no doubt said something like, "What the . . .?" or, if you're more wordy, "Hey, why can't I save this image in any format other than PDD? Has the world gone mad?" Or something like that.

Calm down. PhotoDeluxe can save your image in all the leading image file formats. The command you need just happens to be located in an out-of-the-way spot. My guess is that the folks at Adobe tucked the option away to ensure that users relied on the PDD format for everyday saving. Using the PDD format, after all, makes the program run more efficiently, which is why you should save to another format only if absolutely necessary and only after you're done applying all your edits to the image.

Really cool computer people use the term *export* when they mean saving a file in a format other than the program's native format.

Whatever term you prefer, you use the following process to save your file in any format but GIF. See "GIF: Another Web favorite," later in this chapter, for instructions on saving to GIF.

1. **Choose File⇨Export⇨File Format.**

   PhotoDeluxe displays the Export dialog box, which is a virtual twin of the Save As dialog box that you get when you choose the standard Save command (refer to Figure 4-1). But this time, formats other than PDD are available to you in the Save As drop-down list.

2. **Select your format from the Save As drop-down list.**

   Check out "Figuring Out Formats," later in this chapter, for a thorough review of the mainstream format options.

3. **Do all the other standard saving stuff.**

   In other words, follow Steps 2 through 6 in the preceding set of steps. Note that you can't create a photo organizer thumbnail when using some file formats. If the thumbnail options become unavailable after you select a file format, the program can't add a thumbnail to the organizer.

Depending on the file format you choose in Step 2, PhotoDeluxe may offer dialog boxes that contain additional saving options. The next portion of this chapter explains the options related to the major image file formats.

You may also see two controls in the Save As dialog box that don't show up when you choose the regular Save or Save As commands: Flatten Image and Don't Include Alpha Channels. If your image contains layers and you choose any format except the PhotoDeluxe format or the Adobe Photoshop format (PSD), PhotoDeluxe automatically selects the Flatten Image option, which merges all image layers into a single layer. When you select the PhotoDeluxe or Photoshop format, you can choose to flatten the layers or keep them separate. (Chapter 11 explains layers in depth.)

You can ignore the alpha channels thing altogether. This option is one of several that Adobe lifted from Photoshop when creating PhotoDeluxe, and it has no purpose whatsoever in PhotoDeluxe.

Whichever file format you choose, remember that saving an image in this fashion merely makes a copy of the PDD version that you see on-screen. If you make further edits, pressing Ctrl+S or choosing File⇨Save saves the PDD version of the image, *not* the one you saved in the new file format. To resave that image, you must choose the Export command and repeat the entire saving process. After you click Save, PhotoDeluxe tells you that the file already exists and asks whether you want to replace the file with the new image. Click Yes to do so. Click No if you think better of the whole idea.

Figuring Out Formats

In the computer world, everyone tries to outdo everyone else. Somebody comes up with a clever way to do something, and right away, other folks look for an even better way to do the exact same thing. This competition works out great for consumers because it gives us more options. But making sense of all those options takes some doing, especially if you're new to the language of the digital world, which consists mainly of acronyms and www-dot-coms.

Such is the case with image file *formats* (methods of storing image data). Computer wizards have developed dozens of formats, and dozens more are in the works, heaven help us all.

PhotoDeluxe can save your image in a variety of formats. Each format has its own unique advantages and disadvantages, and, unfortunately, no one format works well for all purposes. The good news is that many formats are either too obscure or too inefficient to be worth your attention, leaving just a few real contenders to consider. The following sections explain these first-tier formats, and Table 4-1 offers a quick-glance guide to which format you should use when.

Developers of file formats get extra points if they assign a format name that's highly technical, tells you absolutely nothing about the format's capabilities, and can be made even more mysterious by assigning an acronym that folks in the know can use to sound superior. As you read through the upcoming discussion, don't bother to memorize the proper name of each format — all you need to know are the acronyms. But you probably should pay attention to how the various acronyms are pronounced so that you aren't marked as easy prey by roving gangs of computer geeks.

Table 4-1	What Format Do I Use?
For This Purpose	*Use This Format*
Everyday editing in PhotoDeluxe	PDD
Saving an image for use on a Web page	JPEG or GIF
Creating a Web image with a transparent background	GIF
Sending an image as an e-mail attachment	JPEG
Publishing a picture in a printed document	TIFF
Placing a picture in an illustration or page-layout program	TIFF or EPS
Opening an image in Adobe Photoshop	PSD
Opening image files on a Macintosh computer	TIFF or JPEG
Creating a Windows resource file (screen saver, help file, and so on)	BMP

PDD: The everyday editing format

I believe that I droned on sufficiently about the native PhotoDeluxe format, PDD, also known as PBD in the Business Edition, earlier in this chapter (see "Understanding the PhotoDeluxe saving system"). Just to reinforce the fundamentals, here's a quick recap:

✔ **PDD enables PhotoDeluxe to carry out your commands as efficiently as possible.** For that reason, save in this format while you're in the process of editing an image. Convert images to another format only after you finish all your editing.

✔ **PDD is one of only two formats available to you in PhotoDeluxe that saves any individual layers that you create.** (Chapter 11 discusses layers.) The other format that supports layers is the Adobe Photoshop native format, PSD. Saving to other formats merges all layers into one.

✔ **The Save As dialog box enables you to save your image in either the Version 2/3/4 PDD format or the Version 1 PDD format.** Use the second option only if you need to open your image in Version 1. When you open the image in Version 1, you lose the ability to edit any existing text independently of the image. Version 1 also flattens any images that contain more than six layers.

PDD, by the way, is pronounced *puh-duh-duh*. Say it really fast, so that you sound like a sputtering lawn mower.

Oh, heck, I can't do that to you, no matter how entertaining it would be to hear a bunch of PhotoDeluxe users walking around making sputtering lawn mower sounds. The truth is that you should say *P-D-D*. Forgive me — sometimes spending long, lonely hours shackled to a computer brings out the worst in me.

TIFF: The file exchange format

TIFF (say it *tiff*, as in *petty little spat*) stands for Tagged Image File Format. Extra points to the format-naming committee on that one! You have my permission to forget what TIFF means. But do remember the following things about this format:

✔ **You can open TIFF files in most Macintosh and Windows-based programs.** If you need to share images across platforms or open the image in a program other than PhotoDeluxe, TIFF is a good option.

✔ **Rely on TIFF for print projects that demand the highest image quality.** Some formats, including JPEG and GIF, get rid of some image data in order to create smaller files, lowering image quality in the process. TIFF retains all vital image data.

✔ **Don't use TIFF for images you want to share online.** Because TIFF retains more image data, TIFF files are usually larger than JPEG or GIF files, which means TIFF files take longer to travel from place to place on the Internet or a corporate network. Most Web browsers and e-mail programs can't open TIFF images.

To save an image in the TIFF format, use the File⇨Export⇨File Format command. Follow the steps provided earlier in this chapter, in the section "Saving in Another Format (Exporting)." After you click the Save button, PhotoDeluxe displays the TIFF Options dialog box shown in Figure 4-2. If you're going to use the image on a Macintosh system, click the Macintosh option. For an image that you intend to use on a PC, click IBM PC instead.

Figure 4-2: You get these options when you save an image as a TIFF file.

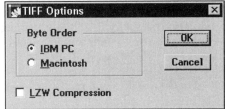

The TIFF Options dialog box offers one additional choice: LZW Compression. *Compression* is a method of eliminating some image data from a picture to make the file smaller. LZW compression is *lossless,* which means that only nonessential data gets tossed so that you don't lose image quality. (See the sidebar "Compression expressions: Lossy versus lossless" for details.)

Typically, you don't reduce your file size much by applying LZW compression, but feel free to select the option if you like. However, some programs can't open LZW-compressed images. If you have trouble opening a TIFF image in a program that's supposed to accept TIFF files, you may be able to fix the problem by resaving the image in PhotoDeluxe with LZW compression turned off.

Compression expressions: Lossy versus lossless

When you save an image in some file formats, you can *compress* the file. Compression sacrifices some image data in the name of smaller file sizes.

Several forms of compression exist. Some types of compression, such as LZW, remove only redundant image data and thus do no visible harm to your image. This type of compression is called *lossless compression.*

Other types of compression, including JPEG compression, are called *lossy* because they throw away more important image data, which can result in a loss of image quality.

The trade-off is file size. With lossless compression, you retain more image data, which usually results in better image quality, but creates a larger image file. With lossy compression, you get significantly smaller files but sometimes sacrifice more image quality than is acceptable. Ultimately, you have to decide which is more important, file size or image quality.

JPEG: The incredible shrinking format

JPEG (pronounced *jay-peg*) was developed by a committee called the Joint Photographic Experts Group — hence the name. The following list explains what you need to know about this format:

- **JPEG is widely supported on both the Macintosh and Windows platforms.** Translated into English, that means that you can open a JPEG image in just about any program that accepts images — Mac or Windows. This, as Martha Stewart would say, is a "good thing."

- **JPEG enables you to compress the image data so that the size of the file is significantly reduced.** For this reason, JPEG is one of the more popular formats on the World Wide Web. Smaller file sizes means that your Web site visitors spend less time downloading your images — also a "good thing."

- **JPEG compression is *lossy*, which means that it can lower image quality.** When you export a file to JPEG, you can specify how much compression you want to apply. The more compression, the more data you sacrifice, and the more you risk reducing image quality. (See the sidebar "Compression expressions: Lossy versus lossless" for more information about compression.)

  Just how much damage JPEG compression does depends on the image, however. Some images look okay even with a high degree of JPEG compression, whereas others turn incredibly ugly. You simply need to experiment to see how much compression is too much.

- **Each time you edit and resave a JPEG file, you do more damage to your image.** Merely opening and closing the image is fine, as is copying the image file. If you make changes and resave the image to JPEG, however, PhotoDeluxe recompresses the data during the saving process, which means more data loss.

To save an image as a JPEG file, take these steps:

1. **Make a backup copy of your original image.**

   Because saving to JPEG destroys some of your image data, *always* make a backup copy in a format that retains all the vital image information (PDD or TIFF).

2. **Choose File⇨Export⇨File Format to open the Export dialog box.**

3. **Specify the filename, storage location, and other options as usual.**

   If you need help, see the "Preserving Pictures" section earlier in this chapter.

4. Choose JPEG from the Save As drop-down list.

5. Click Save.

PhotoDeluxe displays the JPEG Options dialog box, as shown in Figure 4-3.

Figure 4-3:
Click the
Options
button to
choose a
compres-
sion level.

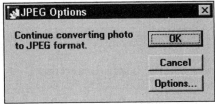

6. Click the Options button.

A second JPEG Options dialog box appears, as shown in Figure 4-4.

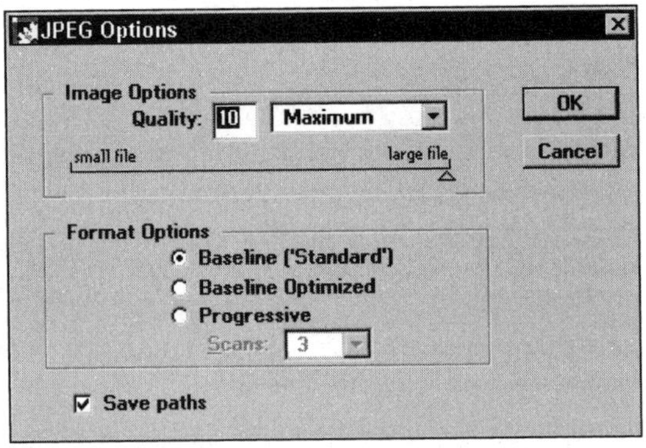

Figure 4-4:
Select
Maximum
from the
Quality
drop-down
list to apply
the least
amount of
JPEG com-
pression.

7. Choose a compression level.

The Quality setting, in the top half of the dialog box, controls how much JPEG compression PhotoDeluxe applies to your photo. The lower the Quality setting, the higher the compression amount and the smaller the file size. Of course, a lower Quality setting also means that more image data is dumped, increasing the chances that your image will suffer.

Not one to limit your options, PhotoDeluxe gives you three different ways to change the Quality setting. You can choose the value you want from the drop-down list, which offers four general settings: Maximum, High, Medium, and Low. If you want slightly more control, you can enter a value from 0 through 10 in the Quality option box.

Finally, you can drag the triangle on the slider bar. Drag to the left to apply lots of compression; drag to the right to apply minimum compression.

For Web images, a middle-of-the road setting is generally acceptable. For print images, apply a smaller amount of compression, keeping in mind that the damage done by compression tends to be more noticeable as you increase the print size of your image.

8. Choose a Format Options radio button.

You have three choices:

- Select Baseline ("Standard") for print images.

- Select Baseline Optimized if you're creating a Web image and you don't want any portion of your image to appear on-screen until all the image data is downloaded to the viewer's computer.

- Select Progressive if you want your image to appear gradually on the Web page as image data is downloaded. (See the sidebar "Creating progressive images.")

    The Scans value, which becomes available if you select Progressive, determines how many intermediate images the viewer sees before the total image is displayed. You can specify 3, 4, or 5 intermediate images; the default setting of 3 is fine.

9. Click OK.

You can ignore that Save Paths check box in the JPEG Options dialog box. The option enables you to take advantage of an editing feature available in Adobe Photoshop, but not in PhotoDeluxe. (Like other dialog boxes, Adobe took this one directly from Photoshop and didn't fully customize it for PhotoDeluxe.)

Determining exactly how much JPEG compression you can get away with is a matter of trial and error. After you save to JPEG, reopen the image to inspect it. (The picture that remains on-screen after you save is the PDD copy, not the JPEG file you just saved.) If you don't like what you see, open the backup copy that you created in Step 1 and export it to JPEG again, this time choosing a higher Quality setting.

Image-editing wonks use the term *jpegged* to refer to images that have been through the JPEG compression factory. Defects that appear in the image as a result of the compression process are called *JPEG artifacts*.

Creating progressive images

When you save an image in the two leading Web formats, JPEG and GIF, you can choose how you want the image to display when a viewer clicks onto your site.

If you save the image as a *progressive* image, the picture appears gradually as each bit of image data makes its way to the viewer's modem. Progressive images also go by the name *interlaced images*.

Images that you save without using the progressive option appear all at once, after every bit of image data makes its way to the viewer's modem.

I prefer progressive images because viewers have something to look at while they wait for the entire picture to arrive. Additionally, viewers can usually determine whether the picture is of interest to them before the download process finishes. That way they can click to something else without wasting time downloading the rest of the picture.

Progressive images do have drawbacks, however: First, they typically require more RAM to view. In addition, some older Web browsers gag on them. If your Web site visitors complain that they're having trouble viewing your images, resave the image without using the progressive feature.

GIF: Another Web favorite

The Graphics Interchange Format, better known as GIF, is another popular format for Web images. GIF was developed to enable CompuServe members to share images online, which is why the format is sometimes called CompuServe GIF. Regardless of whether you include the CompuServe part, you pronounce the GIF part *giff*, with a hard *g*, not *jiff*, like the peanut butter. Like other formats, GIF has features that make it suitable for some projects and not a good choice for others:

✔ **GIF images can contain a maximum of 256 colors.** To put it another way, GIF images are 8-bit images or less. (See Chapter 3 for details about bit depth.) When you save your picture, PhotoDeluxe strips your image down to 256 colors. Some people call this process *indexing* because the program consults a color index to determine what color to assign to pixels whose original colors aren't included in the 256-color palette.

If your image features large expanses of flat color, you may not notice a huge difference between your original image and the GIF version. Images that contain a broad spectrum of colors, on the other hand, usually turn blotchy, as illustrated in Color Plate 3-1. The top picture is a 24-bit, 16-million color image; the bottom picture is an 8-bit image, which means 256 colors. With only 256 colors, you just don't have enough shades to represent subtle color differences.

✔ **GIF files are small, making the format a popular choice for Web pictures.** Naturally, 256-color image files are smaller and require less time to download than full-color image files. For example, the 16-million-color image in Color Plate 3-1 consumes roughly three times as much space on disk as the 256-color version.

✔ **You can animate GIF images.** Most Web-page editing programs enable you to add effects that make your image shake, blink, or do other simple actions when viewed in a Web browser. (PhotoDeluxe doesn't offer a GIF animation tool, though.)

✔ **You can make portions of a GIF image transparent, so the Web page background is visible behind the image.** Figure 4-5 shows an example. I saved the telephone image on the left side of Figure 4-5 as a standard GIF, without the transparency feature. You see the telephone and the gray image background. To create the telephone image on the right side of the figure, I saved the image using the GIF transparency option. I made the gray background pixels transparent, so that the telephone appears to float over the Web page. All the background image pixels are still there — they're just invisible.

To save your image as a GIF file in PhotoDeluxe, you use the File⇨Export⇨ GIF 89a Export command. For details on what to do after you choose the command, flip to Chapter 6, which discusses all things Webbish.

Figure 4-5:
In the standard GIF image (left), the gray image background appears. In the transparent GIF image, the background pixels are invisible (right).

Special-use formats

In addition to the mainstream formats — TIFF, JPEG, and GIF — PhotoDeluxe can save and open files in several other formats. A few are so obscure or limited in their applications that I won't bore you by discussing them here. The following list discusses formats that may come in handy on occasion. If you need help saving to a format that the list doesn't include, check the PhotoDeluxe Help system (choose Help⇨Contents).

You can access all the following formats via the Export dialog box, which you open by choosing File⇨Export⇨File Format. If you need help navigating the dialog box, see "Preserving Pictures," earlier in this chapter.

- ✔ **PICT:** Pronounced *pict,* as in *picture,* PICT is the native graphics format for Macintosh computers. Use PICT only if you want to share your images with a Mac user who doesn't have any way to open TIFF or JPEG files. You can open PICT files inside SimpleText and other basic Mac programs. You can also use PICT to save images that are to be used as so-called *system resources* — images for an online help system, for example.

- ✔ **BMP:** The initials stand for *Windows Bitmap,* the native format for Windows graphics. Some people refer to BMP files as *bimp* files, but other folks use the less goofy-sounding *Windows bitmap.* BMP today is used mainly for images that will be used as Windows system resources, such as online Help systems and Windows *wallpaper* (the picture behind all the icons on your desktop). For instructions on how to create wallpaper, check out Chapter 6.

- ✔ **EPS:** EPS *(E-P-S)* stands for Encapsulated PostScript, which is a computer language used by most drawing and page-layout programs as well as by higher-end printers. EPS files are much larger than TIFF or JPEG files, so save to EPS only if your layout or drawing program can't work with anything else or if your commercial printer requests the file in EPS format. You can find out more about the various EPS options available to you by reading the PhotoDeluxe help system information.

- ✔ **PSD:** Say *P-S-D,* not *pssst.* PSD is the native format for Adobe Photoshop, big brother of Adobe PhotoDeluxe. Version 4 and higher of Photoshop can open PhotoDeluxe PDD files, but Version 3 can't. Save to PSD if you need to open your PhotoDeluxe file in Photoshop 3.

- ✔ **FlashPix:** A few years ago, an organization known as the Digital Imaging Group (DIG) developed the FlashPix format with the goal of enabling people to open and edit large image files on computers that had limited memory or slow processors. Once touted as the future star of digital imaging, FlashPix appears to be quietly fading away. Some software and hardware vendors have stopped supporting the format — and some never started. For that reason, I don't recommend saving files in the FlashPix format unless someone specifically asks you to provide a FlashPix file.

✔ **PDF:** This format, pronounced *P-D-F,* is the Adobe Acrobat native format. Acrobat is used to view electronic documents, such as online support manuals. The Acrobat document viewer is included on your PhotoDeluxe program CD and is also available for free at Adobe's Web site, www.adobe.com). Acrobat is available for Windows, Mac, UNIX, and DOS. So if you want to send your image to someone without any other means of viewing the picture, Acrobat is a convenient solution.

Unfortunately, PhotoDeluxe can't open PDF files — even those that you create in PhotoDeluxe. So be sure to save a backup copy of your image in another format before you export the picture to PDF. After you create your backup, choose File⇨Export⇨File Format or File⇨Export⇨Acrobat File. When you save your picture, you can choose from three quality options: Best, Good, and Draft. The better the image quality, the larger the image file.

As PhotoDeluxe saves the file, you see a message box indicating that the program is printing the file. Don't fret — you're not actually printing. The dialog box appears because somebody, somewhere, referred to the process of saving a PDF file as *printing to PDF,* and the terminology stuck.

Organizing Your Image Closet

Earlier versions of PhotoDeluxe included a photo cataloging program called EasyPhoto. In PhotoDeluxe 4, a new tool, to which Adobe assigned the unglamorous name "the photo organizer," replaces EasyPhoto.

PhotoDeluxe shares the photo organizer with Adobe ActiveShare, a stand-alone program included on the PhotoDeluxe program CD. (Chapter 6 covers the ActiveShare features that may be of interest to PhotoDeluxe users.) Any images and information that you put into the organizer in PhotoDeluxe appears when you view the organizer in ActiveShare, and vice versa.

However, I suggest that you do your organizing work in PhotoDeluxe, not ActiveShare. When you put a picture in the photo organizer in ActiveShare, the program makes a copy of the image file. That's fine in some cases — for example, if a colleague gives you an image disk, you can copy the pictures to your computer and add them to the organizer in one step. But if you're putting your own pictures into the organizer, you wind up with two copies of the same image, needlessly eating up precious file-storage space.

You don't have this double-image trouble when you add images to the organizer in PhotoDeluxe. In fact, you don't actually "add" images to the organizer — instead, you create thumbnail previews of the images. When you double-click a thumbnail in the organizer, PhotoDeluxe tracks down the actual image file and opens it for you. So if you want to organize the actual image files — for example, to put them inside one folder on your computer's hard drive — you need to use Windows Explorer or some other file-management utility.

Chapter 1 explains how to preview and open images stored in the photo organizer. The rest of this chapter explains how you put images into the organizer in a way that enables you to find them easily later.

Just so you know, people in the image-editing industry refer to the process of warehousing and organizing digital photos and other multimedia files as *digital asset management.* Some folks even shorten the phrase to DAM, as in "Stop playing with that DAM program and take out the trash!" But those of us who don't want to risk having our mouths washed out with soap avoid using the abbreviation.

Opening the photo organizer

To display the photo organizer window, shown in Figure 4-6, choose File⇨My Photos⇨Show My Photos. The window looks just like the window that you use to browse and open the sample images and clip art on the PhotoDeluxe CD-ROM. This organizer window, however, is reserved for your personal images — hence, the window name, My Photos. (To find out more about the sample images and clip art, check out Chapter 1.)

Figure 4-6:
The empty photo organizer awaits your pictures.

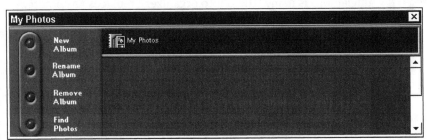

If you haven't yet opened and saved any pictures in PhotoDeluxe, your organizer window looks like the one in Figure 4-6 — which is to say, empty. Before you can preview and open images through the organizer, you have to create image thumbnails. Upcoming sections explain this process. Before you get to that step, you may want to create several *albums,* which enable you to group pictures together by category. The next section tells all.

Setting up albums

In a traditional filing cabinet, you typically find multiple hanging folders, each of which holds documents related to a different subject. In the PhotoDeluxe photo organizer, you can park similar images together in *albums*. For example, you can dedicate one album to all your family photographs and another album to your business images.

Subdividing your thumbnails into albums cuts down the time you spend hunting for pictures, especially if you're a prolific photographer. Instead of scrolling through hundreds of thumbnails to find that special picture of your cat wearing mouse ears, you head straight to your Cats album, where you have put all photos related to Fluffy.

When you first use the photo organizer, it contains just one album, appropriately named *My Photos*. To represent the album, PhotoDeluxe displays the My Photos icon, as shown in Figure 4-7. Unless you create additional albums, all photos that you put in the organizer go into this album.

Thumbnail

Figure 4-7: ┌Album management buttons   Album icon
Group
similar
images into
albums so
that you can
find your
pictures
easily
later on.

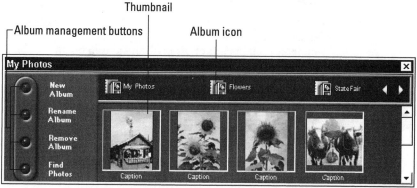

You create additional albums like so:

1. Click the New Album button in the photo organizer window.

After you click, you see the Create Album dialog box, shown in Figure 4-8.

If you get the urge to create an album when the photo organizer is closed, you can launch the organizer and open the Create Album dialog box in one quick step by choosing File⇨My Photos⇨Create New Album.

2. Type the album name in the New Album Name box.

Create Album

Albums:

Flowers
My Photos
StateFair

New Album Name:

Family

[**Create Album**] [**Done**]

Figure 4-8:
You can
create
several
albums with
one trip to
this dialog
box.

3. Click Create Album.

The new album name appears in the Albums list at the top of the dialog box. If you want to create additional albums, just keep typing in album names and clicking the Create Album button.

4. Click Done to close the dialog box.

Icons representing each of your new albums appear at the top of the organizer window, as illustrated in Figure 4-7. The original My Photos album icon remains intact, as does the album itself.

You also can create a new album as you're saving an image. See the instructions given earlier in this chapter, in the section "Saving works in progress," to find out where to locate the album controls when you're saving your image.

Adding thumbnails to an album

Before you can access your own images through the photo organizer, you must create thumbnails for them. You can create your thumbnails one at a time, as you work on each picture in PhotoDeluxe, or you can drag and drop pictures from Windows Explorer into the organizer.

As you read through the next two sections, which explain these options, remember that when you place a thumbnail in the photo organizer, you're not affecting the actual image file. If you want to change the storage location of an image file, you must do it by using Windows Explorer or by resaving the file in PhotoDeluxe to a different hard drive or folder.

Creating thumbnails for open images

You can create a thumbnail for an open picture in a few different ways. Which method you should use depends on whether you previously saved the image in the PhotoDeluxe format (PDD):

✔ **If you previously saved the image as a PDD file:** Open the album where you want to place the thumbnail by clicking the album's icon at the top of the photo organizer window. Then activate the Object Selection tool (choose Select⇨Selection Tools⇨Object Selection) and drag the picture from the picture window into the organizer window. A little plus sign appears next to your cursor as you drag.

PhotoDeluxe doesn't let you use this method if you made any changes to the picture since that last time you saved it. Nor can you go this route if you saved the picture in some other file format.

✔ **If you haven't saved the image as a PDD file, you can do either of the following:**

- **To save the image as a PDD file and add it to the organizer:** Choose either File⇨My Photos⇨Add Photo to Album. PhotoDeluxe displays the standard Save As dialog box. From there, follow the steps outlined earlier in this chapter, in the section "Saving works in progress."

- **To save the image in some other file format and add it to the organizer:** Use the same process but choose File⇨Export⇨File Format to get to the Save As dialog box. If the Add to Album button at the bottom of the dialog box appears greyed out — that is, unavailable — you selected a file format for which PhotoDeluxe can't create a thumbnail.

If you create a thumbnail for a picture and then save the picture in another format or with another name, be sure to give the second picture a different title than the first. Otherwise, you can't tell which image is which in the photo organizer.

Creating thumbnails without opening images

If you want to add more than a few images to the organizer at a time, don't bother with the methods explained in the preceding section. You can get the job done more quickly by dragging and dropping images from Windows Explorer into the organizer window. You can use this method for files saved in any format that PhotoDeluxe can open.

Follow these steps:

1. Open Windows Explorer.

If your keyboard includes a Microsoft Windows key (look between the Ctrl key and the Alt key), you can open Explorer in a flash by pressing that key along with the E key. No Windows key? Click the Windows Start button and choose Programs⇨Windows Explorer. You also can right-click the My Computer icon on your Windows desktop and choose Explore from the pop-up menu.

2. **Switch back to PhotoDeluxe and choose File⇨My Photos⇨Show My Photos to open the organizer.**

3. **Open the album where you want to store the pictures.**

   Just click the album icon at the top of the organizer window to open the album.

4. **Arrange the Explorer and PhotoDeluxe program windows so that you can see both windows on-screen.**

   In each program, click the middle window-control button, labeled in Figure 4-9. Then put your cursor along the edge of the window and drag inward to shrink the window. Drag the Explorer window and the photo organizer windows by their title bars if needed so that you can see both on-screen at the same time, as shown in the figure.

5. **In Explorer, locate and select the file(s) that you want to add to the organizer.**

   To select a range of files, as I did in the figure, click the first filename and then Shift+Click the last filename. If you want to select multiple files that aren't in the same range, click the first filename and Ctrl+Click each additional filename.

Click to change window sizes

Figure 4-9:
To create thumbnails for a batch of pictures, drag and drop the files from Explorer.

6. **Drag the selected block of files into the organizer window.**

   A little plus sign appears next to your cursor as you drag. When you release the mouse button, PhotoDeluxe spins and whirs a bit as it creates thumbnails for all the images.

   Even though the cursor you see on-screen looks the same as it does when you copy files from folder to folder in Explorer, you're not really copying files, just making thumbnails. If you want to move or copy your actual image files, work exclusively in Explorer.

PhotoDeluxe uses the filename as the image title in the photo organizer window. You can change the titles if you want; see the next section for details.

Adding thumbnail data

When you create an image thumbnail, PhotoDeluxe records the image filename and location along with the thumbnail. If you created a thumbnail through the Save As dialog box, PhotoDeluxe also records the title that you assigned to the picture.

You can add or change the title and also record some additional information about the image, such as the time and place you took the picture or the name of the subject. Including a title comes in especially handy down the road because you can use the organizer's Find Photo feature to display a list of all pictures that share a particular title.

To view the existing image data or add new data, take the following steps:

1. **Right-click the image thumbnail.**

   Be sure to click the thumbnail itself, not the title. PhotoDeluxe displays a tiny pop-up menu, as shown in Figure 4-10.

Figure 4-10: Right-click a thumbnail and click Properties to see image data.

2. Click Properties to display the Photo Information dialog box, shown in Figure 4-11.

You can also get PhotoDeluxe to reveal the dialog box by opening the image and then choosing File⇨My Photos⇨Show Photo Information. I prefer the right-click method, but I've got a lazy streak. You may get more satisfaction out of doing things the hard way.

Figure 4-11:
Add comments and other identifying information into the Photo Information dialog box.

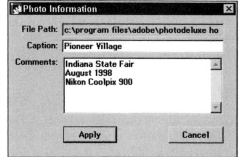

Photo Information

File Path: c:\program files\adobe\photodeluxe ho

Caption: Pioneer Village

Comments: Indiana State Fair
August 1998
Nikon Coolpix 900

Apply   Cancel

3. Type the new title into the Caption box.

PhotoDeluxe highlights the box for you when you open the dialog box, so you can just start typing. Whatever you put in the Caption box appears underneath the image in the photo organizer. If you previously gave the image a title by entering something into the Title box inside the Save As dialog box, PhotoDeluxe replaces the old title with the one you type in the Caption box.

4. Click Apply to save the information you added and to close the dialog box.

To view or change the photo information in the future, just right-click the thumbnail and choose Properties to redisplay the Photo Information dialog box.

If you want to change only the image title, you don't have to open the Photo Information dialog box. Instead, double-click the title in the photo organizer. A blinking cursor appears in the title, and the cursor changes to an I-beam, the universal cursor for adding or editing text. Press Delete to get rid of characters that follow the cursor; press Backspace to wipe out characters to the left of the cursor. Then type your new caption and press Enter.

Making changes to albums

Sooner or later, you'll want to update your albums, whether to delete a thumbnail for a photo that no longer exists or to reorganize thumbnails into a different set of albums.

PhotoDeluxe makes these maintenance chores pretty easy. You can accomplish everything without leaving the photo organizer window.

✔ **To delete a thumbnail:** Right-click it and choose Remove from the pop-up menu. Be sure to click the thumbnail itself, not the title, or the menu doesn't appear.

If for some reason you have trouble with this method, click the thumbnail to select it and then choose File⇨My Photos⇨Delete Photo from Album.

✔ **To move a thumbnail to a different album:** Drag the thumbnail to the album's icon.

✔ **To change the order of thumbnails in the same album:** Drag the thumbnails to where you want them to appear.

✔ **To delete an album and all the thumbnails in it:** Click the Remove Album button on the left side of the photo organizer window. If you like working harder than necessary, choose File⇨Show My Photos⇨Remove Album. PhotoDeluxe displays the Remove Album dialog box. Click the names of the albums you want to dump and click Delete. Click Done when you finish destroying albums.

✔ **To change the name of an album:** Open the album by clicking its icon; then click the Rename Album button, which opens the Rename Album dialog box. Type in the new name and click OK.

✔ **To get rid of orphan thumbnails:** If you move or delete an image file, you wind up with an *orphaned* thumbnail, which simply means that PhotoDeluxe no longer knows where to find the parent file that the thumbnail represents. You see a green warning icon at the bottom of an orphaned thumbnail. You may as well delete the thumbnail — you can't open the image using the thumbnail any more. If you moved the image file, you can create a new thumbnail to access the picture at its new location.

✔ **To refresh the organizer display:** After you make these changes to the organizer, PhotoDeluxe may not show them in the organizer right away. Right-click a thumbnail and choose Refresh from the pop-up menu to update the organizer.

Tracking down images in the organizer

Having trouble locating an image? Use the photo organizer's search feature to hunt the picture down. You can search for pictures by *keywords*. In the case of the photo organizer, a keyword is any word that appears in the image file-name or caption. However, you can search only one album at a time. To use the organizer, first open the album you want to search. Then take these steps:

1. **Click the Find Photos button to open the Find dialog box.**

2. **Type a keyword into the option box and click OK.**

   PhotoDeluxe displays thumbnails of any images in the current album whose filenames or captions include the keyword. All other thumbnails temporarily disappear. To bring back those other thumbnails, click the Restore Photos button, which temporarily replaces the Find button while you're conducting a search.

 If you plan on maintaining a very large image library, you may want to invest in a cataloging program that offers a more powerful and convenient search engine. ThumbsPlus, from Cerious Software (www.Cerious.com), is a good example. With that program and others like it, you can view your images in a format similar to that used by Windows Explorer, and you can manipulate your actual image files as well as create and browse thumbnails.

Moving and closing the organizer

You can keep the organizer window open as you work on your pictures. I recommend that you close the window, however, because the PhotoDeluxe window is cramped enough as it is. Click the close button in the upper-right corner of the organizer window to put the organizer away. To leave the organizer open but relocate it, drag it by its title bar.

Chapter 5

Getting into Print

● ●

In This Chapter

▶ Getting printed colors to match on-screen colors

▶ Sending an image to the printer

▶ Choosing the paper size and image orientation

▶ Improving the appearance of your prints

▶ Choosing the right printer for your home or office

▶ Getting an image professionally printed

● ●

*G*etting a digital image from your computer onto paper isn't a difficult proposition. You choose the Print command, and a minute or so later, your image comes creeping out of the printer.

Getting a *good* print of a digital image is another matter entirely. Any number of factors can hamper your efforts to reproduce your images on paper, from choosing the wrong image resolution to buying the wrong paper. For a process that seems, on the surface, like such a simple one, printing can often lead you into a complex maze of problems.

This chapter helps you understand the mechanics of putting pixels on paper so that you can get the best possible prints. In addition to covering the basics of sending an image to your printer, this chapter provides guidance on choosing a printer for your home or office, sending your images to a profes-sional for printing, and getting your printed colors to match your on-screen colors.

Calibrating Printer and Monitor

One pitfall of printing digital images is that the on-screen colors and the printed colors rarely match. Sometimes you get close, but many times printed and on-screen hues aren't even in the same ballpark. The "Why what you see isn't what you get" sidebar later in this chapter explains the reasons for this problem.

Version 4, like Version 3, includes a tool that may help resolve some of the differences. First, make sure that your monitor is set to display more than 256 colors. (Right-click an empty area of the Windows desktop and choose Properties to open the Display Properties dialog box and check your monitor settings.) Then take these steps to calibrate your printer and monitor:

1. **Choose File⇨Adjust Color Printing.**

   The Adjust Color Printing dialog box appears.

2. **Click the Adjust Color Printing radio button, if it's not already selected.**

3. **Select your printer type from the drop-down list.**

   If you don't see your printer type, choose Other or Generic Color Printer.

4. **Click the More button.**

   The More button transforms itself into the Less button, and the dialog box expands to reveal more options, as shown in Figure 5-1.

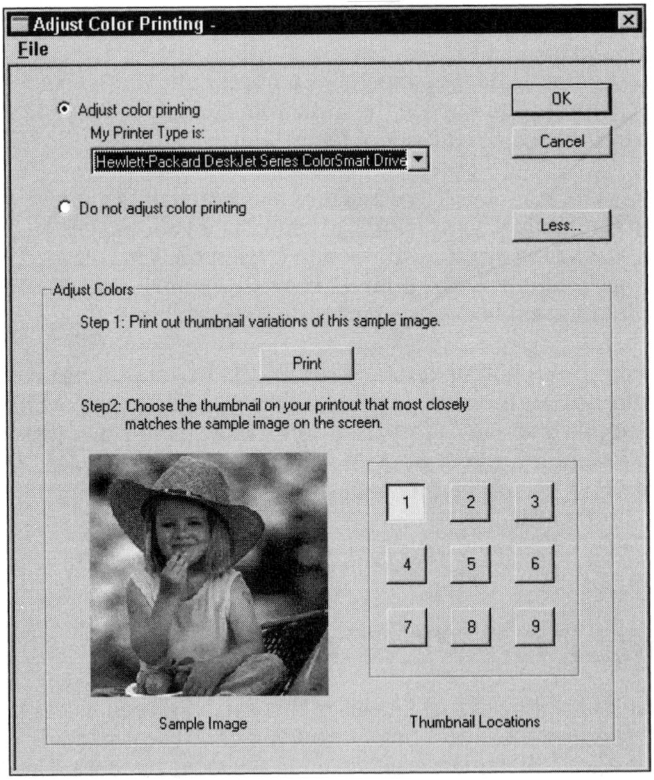

Figure 5-1:
PhotoDeluxe includes a tool that attempts to calibrate your monitor and printer.

Adjust Color Printing -

File

○ Adjust color printing
My Printer Type is:
Hewlett-Packard DeskJet Series ColorSmart Drive ▼

○ Do not adjust color printing

OK
Cancel
Less...

Adjust Colors

Step 1: Print out thumbnail variations of this sample image.

Print

Step2: Choose the thumbnail on your printout that most closely matches the sample image on the screen.

1	2	3
4	5	6
7	8	9

Sample Image   Thumbnail Locations

5. Click the Print button.

In order to start the calibration process, you need to print the sample image shown in the dialog box. After you click the Print button, the standard Print dialog box appears, just as when you print any other image. Choose your printer settings and send that image off to the printer.

6. Compare the printout with the on-screen image.

Nine different versions of the image appear on your printout. Find the one that most closely matches the image you see on-screen. Then click the corresponding thumbnail button in the Adjust Color Printing dialog box. For example, if the image in the middle of the page looks like the closest match, click the center thumbnail button (number 5).

7. Click OK to close the dialog box.

Now do a test print of your own image to compare the on-screen colors with printed colors. If you don't get decent color matching, try selecting a different thumbnail in the Adjust Color Printing dialog box and do another test print. If none of the thumbnail selections improve color matching, select the Do Not Adjust Color Printing option and give that setting a whirl. You can also check your printer manual to find out whether you can adjust color-related print options through the Print dialog box.

Even the most expensive color matching systems on the planet can't achieve perfect color synchronization between monitor and printer. Don't expect a total correction of color matching problems from the Adjust Color Printing command — consider yourself fortunate if your printer colors and monitor colors appear to be in the same ballpark.

Printing a Single Picture

Sending an image from PhotoDeluxe to the printer is a simple matter of choosing the File⇨Print command. But before you get to that command, you need to move through a few preparatory steps. The following steps outline the process of getting an open image into print. Don't panic when you see the length of these steps — after you go through them initially, you can probably skip several of them.

Before you print your image, be sure to visit the Photo Size dialog box to set the print size and image resolution of the picture. The settings you choose make a big impact on the quality of your printed image, so take the time to read all about sizing images in Chapter 3.

Why what you see isn't what you get

When you print your first color image, you may be dismayed at how much the colors on the printed page differ from those on your monitor. This color shift happens for a good reason: Monitors and printers create colors in two different ways.

Your monitor uses the *RGB color model* — which is a techie way of saying that it mixes red, green, and blue light to create all the colors that you see on-screen. Mixing full-intensity red, green, and blue light creates white, whereas a complete absence of red, green, and blue light makes black. If this concept seems foreign to you, imagine aiming red, green, and blue spotlights at the same spot. You get a white spotlight. Conversely, if you turn off all three lights, you get . . . a dark room.

Printers, on the other hand, create colors by mixing cyan, magenta, yellow, and black inks — otherwise known as the *CMYK color model.* If you mix full-strength cyan, magenta, yellow, and black ink, you get black, which is directly opposite of what you get if you mix full-intensity red, green, and blue light.

The mismatch between on-screen colors and printer colors arises not just because one device uses light and another uses ink, but because the CMYK and RGB *color spaces,* or

gamuts, are different. Put in plain English, that means that CMYK can't create as many different colors as RGB. Your printer just isn't capable of reproducing the most vivid colors that you see on-screen, so it substitutes the nearest matching color. Usually, this results in prints that appear duller than the on-screen version of the image. (Colors that can't be created by a particular color model are said to be *out of gamut,* by the way.)

PhotoDeluxe includes a tool designed to help calibrate monitor and printer. (See the section "Calibrating Printer and Monitor" in this chapter for details.) Most printer software enables you to tweak the printer's color settings as well. If you can't get acceptable results by using these two approaches, you may want to adjust the actual image colors, via the commands discussed in Chapter 7. Play with the Color Balance, Brightness/Contrast, and Saturation controls in PhotoDeluxe to compensate for the color shift that occurs with your printer.

Also remember that the type of paper you use, the brightness/contrast settings on your monitor, and the light in which you view your pictures all affect how your images look on paper versus how they appear on your monitor.

1. **Select the area to be printed.**

   You can print just a portion of the image by selecting that area before initiating the print process. See Chapter 9 for information on how to draw a selection outline. If you want to print the entire image, press Ctrl+D to get rid of any existing selection outlines.

   Alternatively, you can choose to print only certain layers in a multilayered image. Any visible layers print; hidden layers don't get to go to the dance. You hide and reveal layers by clicking the little eyeball icons in the Layers palette, a feature that Chapter 11 explains.

2. Choose File⇨Page Setup to display the Page Setup dialog box.

The dialog box varies depending on your printer and operating system; Figure 5-2 shows the dialog box for my color inkjet printer.

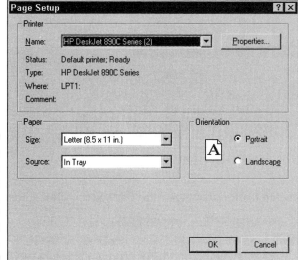

Figure 5-2: Select a printer, paper size, and page orientation here.

3. Choose a printer, paper size, and page orientation. Then click OK.

For any printer, you should be able to set these three basic printing options. The first two are easy enough, but if you're new to computing, you may not be aware of what the orientation options do.

Landscape orientation prints your image sideways on the page, with the top of your image running parallel to the long edge of the paper. The Portrait option prints your image normally, with the top of the image parallel to the short edge of the paper. The two settings were so named because landscape paintings usually have a horizontal orientation, and portrait paintings typically have a vertical orientation.

4. Preview the image.

Choose File⇨Print Preview or press Ctrl+/ (forward slash) to display a preview of your printed image. PhotoDeluxe presents a window showing how your image will appear on the page according to the choices you made in Steps 1 through 3. If the image doesn't fit on the page, you need to rethink either your paper size or your image size.

5. Press Ctrl+P or choose File⇨Print.

The Print dialog box, shown in Figure 5-3, bounds onto the playing field. The dialog box may look slightly different depending on your printer and operating system.

Figure 5-3:
The Print
dialog box
contains all
your printing
options.

Print

Printer: System Printer (HP DeskJet 890C Series (2))

Print Range
- ⦿ All
- ○ Selection
- ○ Pages
  - From: 1   To: 1

OK
Cancel
Setup...
ColorApp...

Print Quality: 300 dpi ▼   Copies: 1 ⬚
☐ Print to File   ☐ Collate Copies

PhotoDeluxe Output Quality:
- ⦿ Best
- ○ Better
- ○ Good
- ○ Draft

Click on Draft for fastest printing, click on Best for the highest quality printing.

6. **Click the Setup button to reopen the Page Setup dialog box.**

7. **Click the Properties button to select your print settings.**

   You're chauffeured to a dialog box that contains all the various settings available for your particular model of printer. I'm afraid that I can't help you determine which settings to use; printers simply vary too much from model to model. Consult your printer manual to see what settings are appropriate for your printing project.

8. **Click OK to return to the Page Setup dialog box.**

9. **Click OK to return to the Print dialog box.**

10. **Specify the number of copies, the print range, and the print quality.**

   If you selected a portion of your image in Step 1, you can print just the selection by choosing Selection as your Print Range option. (Note that the specific option names may vary slightly depending on your printer.) If you don't choose the Selection option, the entire image prints.

   The PhotoDeluxe Output Quality settings at the bottom of the dialog box don't override any printer-specific settings that you chose in Step 6. They do, however, control how much image data is sent to the printer.

   In order to keep your system from blowing its memory and storage-space stack, PhotoDeluxe limits the amount of data that you can send to the printer. The amount of data that PhotoDeluxe passes along to the printer depends on the capabilities of the printer you selected. The cap is proportionate to the printer's maximum *dpi* (the number of dots of ink the printer can apply to represent each inch of the image). For most printers, the image data is capped at 300 ppi (image pixels per inch); but for some printers, such as the Epson inkjets that can print at 1,440 dpi (printer ink dots per inch), the image resolution limit is just a tad higher.

If you choose the Best option in the Print dialog box, you send the maximum amount of data to the printer, within the allowable cap. In other words, if you set your image resolution to 300 ppi, all the image data goes to the printer. If you choose a lesser print quality, PhotoDeluxe sends a lower-resolution file to the printer to speed up printing time.

Bottom line: To achieve the best possible print quality, select the Best option. Use the other options for printing drafts of your image.

11. **Click OK to close the Print dialog box and send your image to the printer.**

Assuming that your printer and your computer are correctly connected and on speaking terms, the printer does its thing and then spits out your printed image.

As I said at the outset, you usually don't have to go through all this rigmarole every time you print. If you know that the image size and default settings in the Page Setup dialog box are okay, you can skip Steps 2 through 4, or at least wait until you open the Print dialog box to tweak the Page Setup options. Also, if the default settings for your specific printer are acceptable, you can skip Steps 6 through 9. Just press Ctrl+P, choose the number of copies, print range, and print quality, and then click OK.

Printing Multiple Copies on One Page

PhotoDeluxe 4, like Version 3 and the Business Edition, offers a special printing option, called the Print Multiple command, that simplifies the process of printing several copies of an image on the same page. You can use this feature to print your face on a sheet of business cards, for example, or to create reprints of a family photo for all your siblings.

To take advantage of the multiple-copy option, follow these steps:

1. **Choose File⇨Print Multiple.**

The Print Multiple dialog box, shown in Figure 5-4, appears.

2. **Select a paper type.**

The Paper Type option in the Print Multiple dialog box shows the selected paper. By default, PhotoDeluxe selects the paper size currently selected in the Page Setup dialog box. (See the preceding section for more information.) To select another paper type, click Change to display the Choose Paper Type dialog box, shown in Figure 5-5. Select a paper category from the top drop-down list and then choose a specific size from the scrolling list.

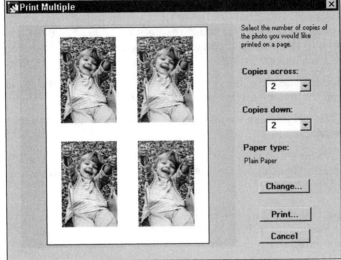

Figure 5-4:
Use the
Print
Multiple
command to
print several
copies of
the same
image on
one page.

Figure 5-5:
Select the
paper stock
you want to
use.

You can choose from three main categories:

- **Avery:** If you choose this option, you see a list of options that correspond with Avery labels, business cards, and other special stock. You can use these same options to print on products from other manufacturers, as long as the stock sizes match those listed for the Avery products.

- **Standard Photo Print Size**: If you want to print your image in, er, standard photo sizes — 5 x 7 inches, 8 x 10 inches, and so on, select this option.

- **Plain Paper**: This one returns you to the default paper option, which uses the page size you defined in the Page Setup dialog box.

3. **If you changed the paper size, click OK to return to the Print Multiple dialog box.**

4. **Specify the number of copies that you want to print on each page.**

   Use the Copies Across and Copies Down drop-down lists to specify how many rows and columns of images you want to print. The choices that are available in the drop-down list are based on the paper size you selected and the size of your image. (PhotoDeluxe looks at the paper size and figures out the maximum number of copies that can fit on the page.)

5. **Click Print.**

If you choose the Get & Fix Photo or Cards & More Guided Activities button and then click the Print icon, you see an option called Print Standard Sizes. This Guided Activity provides templates that help you print multiple pictures at an assortment of standard photo sizes on one page. I don't like this Guided Activity because PhotoDeluxe automatically resizes your pictures to fit the template and sets the image resolution for you. In addition, the Guided Activity doesn't really make the project any easier than if you did it on your own.

If you want to print several different images on a page, create a blank image that's sized to match your paper dimensions. Set the resolution to the value recommended by your printer. Then open each picture you want to print, size it, and copy it into the new image. Keep in mind that PhotoDeluxe changes the resolution of a copied picture to match that of its new home, so for good results, your pictures need a resolution close to the resolution of the new image. (See Chapter 3 for more information about resolution and how it affects print quality.)

Getting the Most from Your Printer

How good printed pictures look depends a great deal on the quality of the printer. No matter what printer you use, however, you can improve your prints by keeping these tips in mind:

✔ **Use the right printer cable:** I know, it sounds like a silly thing to worry about, but newer printers require a special cable known as a *bi-directional IEEE 1284 compliant cable* in order to operate correctly. For whatever reason, these cables aren't included with most printers; you have to buy them separately. Because the special cables are more expensive than the garden-variety printer cable, many people opt for the cheaper type. Unfortunately, those cheaper cables can interfere with the communication between your printer and computer and affect your printer's performance.

✔ **Send the printer enough pixels:** Face the facts, you're not going to get a decent print from a low-resolution image, no matter how good your printer. By the same token, setting the image resolution too high can also lead to decreased print quality. Most consumer-model printers do their best work with an image resolution of 250 to 300 ppi. Check your printer manual for specific recommendations about image resolution, because each model is geared to accept a certain optimum resolution.

When you prepare your pictures for printing, don't mix up printer resolution — measured in *dpi* — and image resolution — measured in *ppi.* For more on sorting out the two terms, read Chapter 3.

✔ **Buy good paper:** For everyday drafts of images, plain paper is fine. When you really want the best printouts, upgrade to premium photo stock. You will be amazed at the difference in the look of your printed images. (This tip doesn't apply if you use a dye-sub or thermal-autochrome printer, which can print on only one kind of stock. See "Shopping for a Printer," later in this chapter, for more information about different types of printers.)

✔ **Don't neglect routine printer maintenance:** Follow your printer manual's suggestions for maintaining the machine. If you work with an inkjet printer, for example, you probably need to align the print heads every now and then. Also, use the ink, dye, or toner that the manufacturer recommends for best performance.

✔ **Get creative:** Most printers sold for the home and small-office consumer offer accessories that enable you to reproduce your images on a variety of media, from T-shirts to coffee mugs to greeting cards. Explore these special printing options when you want to preserve a special image. A picture on paper is nice, but the same scene on a coffee mug or T-shirt is a true keepsake.

Shopping for a New Printer

I know that when you read that headline, you hoped that I was going to share privileged information about the best buys in printers. Sorry, but I have to disappoint you. Printer manufacturers are turning out new models at breakneck speed, and any printer I recommended today would surely be surpassed by a newer, better model before this book made it to the bookstore. Then you'd just end up hating me for steering you toward an outdated product. I can, however, offer you some general buying advice, which I do in the next two sections.

What type of printer is right for me?

The printers available to the average home or small-business user fall into a few distinct categories. These different types of printers each cater to a special market niche, so you need to carefully consider your printing needs before you go shopping. The following sections offer a quick look at the advantages and disadvantages of each of the main categories of machines.

Inkjet printers

The most popular choice among home and small-office users, inkjet printers reproduce your images by spraying tiny drops of ink onto the page. Inkjets deliver a reasonable facsimile of a photograph at an economical price — you can get a good inkjet for less than $300. If you opt for an inkjet, the following tips can help you make a good choice:

- ✔ **Choose a model that uses multiple ink cartridges over models that use a single cartridge.** Some inkjets have four ink cartridges, one each for the cyan, yellow, magenta, and black ink. Others have just two cartridges — one for the black and one for the cyan, magenta, and yellow — or just one cartridge that holds all four inks. Your printer uses up the different colors of ink at different rates, however, because no picture requires the exact same amount of each color. If all your inks share one or two cartridges, you usually end up throwing away some unused ink when one color is gone. For long-term cost savings, a printer with multiple ink cartridges wins over a printer with a single cartridge.

- ✔ **Don't settle for faux black.** Lower-priced printers sometimes omit the black ink, blending the other ink colors to simulate black. Unfortunately, black areas usually wind up looking muddy brown, not black.

- ✔ **Find out what the printer is designed to do best.** Certain inkjets are geared toward people whose primary concern is output that comes as close to a traditional photograph as possible. These printers, sometimes called *photocentric printers,* print your image on glossy photo stock and may or may not be able to print on regular paper. They typically consume a lot of ink per print, and the glossy photo stock is expensive, too — about $1 per 8½ x 11 sheet. Also, photocentric printers usually don't do a good job on text because they're not engineered for that purpose.

  Other inkjet printers are designed for people who want their printers to do dual duty as a text printer and a graphics printer. These models can handle plain paper as well as glossy paper, but they may not match the glossy-print quality of the models designed expressly for photo printing.

Dye-sub printers

Dye-sub is short for *dye-sublimation*. Dye-sub printers transfer colored dye to the paper using a heat process, which is why they are sometimes known as *thermal dye* printers.

Dye-sub printers do the best job at creating prints that look and feel like traditional photographs. However, they can print only on special coated stock; you can't print plain-paper drafts of your images. And that special coated stock is, of course, more expensive than the plain paper that an inkjet can use. Most dye-subs for the consumer market can't print anything larger than snapshot size images, either.

A dye-sub printer is ideal if you want a second printer just for printing top-quality images. The printer cost is about the same as for a good-quality inkjet. But if you need to print text documents or drafts on plain paper, a dye-sub printer isn't for you.

Thermo-Autochrome printers

Thermo-Autochrome machines print on light-sensitive paper instead of applying ink, toner, or dye to the page. The process is similar to the one used in older-model fax machines (the ones that print on thermal paper rather than plain paper). You can take home a Thermo-Autochrome printer for about $300.

Like dye-sub printers, these printers aren't suitable in situations where you need one printer for images and text documents. Thermo-Autochrome printers can't print on plain paper, and most models create snapshot-size printouts only. More importantly, these printers don't do such a hot job on images. However, some models offer a feature that enables you to print stickers — for kid's scrapbooks, employee badges, and the like — which make them attractive to some users with special needs.

Micro Dry printers

A few printers made by Alps Electric use ribbon cartridges that are coated with dry, resin-based ink called Micro Dry ink. (These cartridges look like the ones you used to put in a typewriter — remember those?) The printer heats the ink and transfers it to the paper during the printing process.

Costing about the same as a good inkjet printer, Micro Dry printers can print on plain and glossy stock, and because the ink is dry, you don't get the smearing and page-warping that sometimes happens with inkjet printing. In addition, Micro Dry prints don't fade with exposure to light, a problem with prints from inkjets, dye-subs, and lasers. However, some users of these printers complain of problems with slight *color banding.* On light areas of the image, you can sometimes see tiny strokes of individual ink colors rather than a nice, smooth blend of color.

Some Alps models offer dual printing modes: You can print with the standard Micro Dry inks or put in special ink cartridges for dye-sub printing on glossy stock. This dual-mode option can work out well for users who need to print on plain paper for text and everyday image work but also want to generate dye-sub quality prints of really special images.

Laser printers

Laser printers transfer toner to paper using a heat process that's more complex than I care to explain and probably doesn't matter to you, anyway. Color lasers cost far more than inkjets — expect to pay $1,000 and up. Lasers can produce good output on plain paper, although a high-quality laser paper usually delivers better results.

Some laser printers do a better job than inkjets at printing photos, while others do not. But where laser printers really shine is in quantity printing situations. If you need to print large numbers of images on a daily basis, consider a laser printer, inkjet printers just aren't geared for that type of demanding performance. In other words, laser printers are suitable for office settings, but typically not for casual users. On top of their high cost, laser printers eat up a big chunk of desk space. These babies are *big*.

More shopping tips

After you determine what category of printer serves your needs best, the following tips can help you narrow down your choices even further.

- ✔ **Don't focus solely on dpi.** Printer vendors make a big deal about their printers' *dpi* — the number of dots of color that the printer can create per linear inch. The truth is that dpi is not as critical as the manufacturers would have you believe. The real story is in the technology the printer uses. For example, a dye-sub printer that has a resolution of 300 dpi creates far superior prints to an inkjet that has double the resolution.

  Even among similar types of printers, dpi can be misleading. For example, different brands of inkjet printers spray ink onto the page differently, which can affect print quality more than dpi. Again, the highest dpi doesn't always deliver the best results. When comparing output, trust your eyes, not the dpi marketing hype.

- ✔ **Do your research.** Check out the current issues of computer magazines for reviews on the specific model you're considering. If you're on the Internet, point your newsgroup reader toward `comp.periphs.printers` to see what other users have to say about various printers. I've found that the people who are using the printers every day often have better information about what's good and what's not than the experts. After all, reviewers evaluate a printer only for a limited time period — real users work with the thing on an ongoing basis.

> ✔ **Consider consumables.** Factor in the cost of paper and ink into your pricing decision, not just the initial cost of the printer. If you're thinking of buying a particular model because it can print on plain paper, be sure that you can get acceptable quality with that plain paper. On some models, the plain-paper output is so dismal that you soon find yourself printing only on upgraded paper stock.

Giving the Job to a Pro

On those occasions when you have special printing needs, you may want to consider getting your picture professionally printed.

If you need high-end output for a four-color brochure or magazine, plan to take your image to a professional service bureau or a commercial printer. The price varies according to the size and scope of the job, naturally. Be sure to consult with the customer service representative to find out the appropriate image resolution, what file format to use when saving the image, and what type of removable storage media the printer can accept (Zip disk, floppy, and so on). Also, because this kind of printing typically requires that images be converted to the CMYK color model, be sure to tell the service rep that you're submitting an RGB file and need to have it converted. Unfortunately, PhotoDeluxe can't do the conversion for you.

What if you want just one really good print of an image? You may want to locate a printer or digital-imaging lab that can print your picture on a professional photographic printer. Alternatively, many retail photo-processing labs now can print digital images on regular photographic paper. The price is quite reasonable — around $1 for a 4-x-6-inch snapshot and $10 for an 8-x-10 print.

If you can't find an outlet in your area that can do the job, many online companies provide this service. You just e-mail your picture files, order your prints, and wait for the prints to arrive in the mail. The Adobe ActiveShare Web site, which Chapter 6 covers, is just one of dozens of sites that can print your pictures.

Chapter 6

Showing Off Online
(and On-Screen)

● ●

In This Chapter

▶ Preparing pictures for the Web and other on-screen uses

▶ Taking advantage of GIF transparency

▶ Attaching pictures to e-mail messages

▶ Using images as wallpaper and screen savers

▶ Posting pictures on the Adobe ActiveShare Web site

▶ Creating an eCircle

▶ Sending photo postcards

▶ Turning pictures into digital jigsaw puzzles

● ●

*I*f you want to share your pictures with several people, you have two choices. You can print as many copies as you need, stuff the prints into envelopes, and head for the mailbox — an expensive proposition, considering the cost of decent photo paper and postage. You may also pay in terms of your mental health when standing in line for an eternity at the post office to find out how much postage you need to slap on each envelope.

This chapter introduces you to a picture-sharing method that's easier not only on your wallet, but on your schedule and mood: *electronic distribution*. That's a fancy phrase that means sharing your pictures via the Internet, either by posting them on a Web site or by attaching them to e-mail. Yes, you have to take a few steps to get your pictures ready for online sharing, but the prep work takes no more time than you need to prepare images for printing. And with online sharing, you don't even have to leave the comfort of your home or office.

In addition to explaining online picture-sharing, this chapter covers other on-screen uses for your images, such as creating screen savers and desktop wallpaper. You even find out how to turn a favorite picture into a digital jigsaw puzzle that you can put together during the time you would otherwise be glaring at the post office clerk.

Preparing Pictures for the Screen

You need to take two important steps to make your images fit for on-screen use. Take these steps *only* after you do all editing other than setting the image size. Until then, save your picture periodically in the PhotoDeluxe native format, PDD. (Chapter 4 explains that process and all the horrible, ugly things that can happen if you don't take the time to choose that Save command.)

When you're satisfied with your picture, do this screen-prep two-step:

1. **Size your picture using pixels as the unit of measurement.**

   Chapter 3 covers this issue in detail, but here's a quick recap: Choose Size⇨Photo Size and select Pixels as the unit of measurement for the Width and Height values. Specify how many pixels wide and how many pixels tall you want your picture to be, keeping in mind the one-to-one relationship between image size and screen-display size. For example, if you want your picture to fill half the screen on a monitor that's running at the 640 x 480-pixel display setting, make the image 320 pixels wide and 240 pixels tall.

   Don't forget to save a backup copy of your picture before changing the number of pixels in your picture! *Resampling* — adding or deleting pixels — can lower your image quality, and you may want a top-quality version of the picture some day. Chapter 3 explains how resampling affects your picture; see Chapter 4 to find out how to save your backup copy.

2. **Save the file in the JPEG or GIF file format.**

   The de facto standards for screen images, JPEG and GIF, each offer advantages and disadvantages that you need to understand before saving in one format or the other. Chapter 4 tells you everything you need to know to make an informed decision. Here are the basics in a nutshell:

   • JPEG can handle full-color images, making it the best choice when image quality is vital. JPEG also is more reliable for pictures that you want to attach to e-mail messages; some e-mail programs shun GIF images. You can apply JPEG compression to make the image file smaller — and to therefore faster transmit and download over the Internet. If you apply a very high degree of JPEG compression, however, you wreck your pictures.

   • GIF can save a maximum of 256 colors. Limiting your pictures to that small color spectrum often creates blotchy, unsatisfactory pictures (refer to Color Plate 3-1). On the plus side, fewer colors means smaller file sizes. GIF also offers two features that make it popular for Web pages. First, you can make some pixels in your picture transparent, so that the underlying page background shows through. If you're really feeling creative, you also can *animate* GIF images — make them spin, blink, and otherwise distract the eye.

To find out how to save your picture as a JPEG file, head back to Chapter 4. The following two sections in this chapter explain how to create a GIF image that incorporates transparent areas and one that doesn't. Unfortunately, PhotoDeluxe can't add animation effects to your pictures; you need a Web-page editing program such as Adobe PageMill for that task.

That's it: from PhotoDeluxe to the big — or small — screen in two steps. After you take these steps, you can use your picture in any of the ways suggested in this chapter or in any other on-screen project you can dream up.

Depending on how you want to share your picture, you may not even have to take these two steps. PhotoDeluxe provides a few Guided Activities that automate the process of sizing and saving an image for online sharing, for example. Check the instructions given in upcoming sections in this chapter to find out whether you need to do the sizing/saving chores yourself or can turn them over to PhotoDeluxe.

Creating GIF Images

You can make selected areas of your image transparent if you save your picture as a GIF file. When you put the picture on a Web page, you can see the page background through the transparent image areas. You don't actually delete any pixels in the image — you just make some of them invisible. Figure 6-1 illustrates the difference between a GIF that incorporates transparency and one that doesn't.

Figure 6-1:
Parts of a standard GIF image (left) become invisible when I save the picture using the GIF transparency option (right).

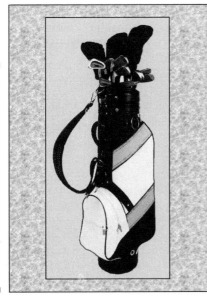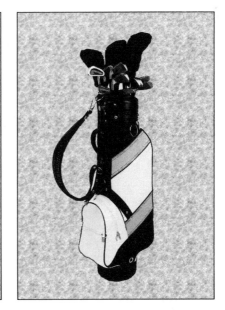

The next two sections provide specifics on creating both a see-through GIF image and a fully opaque one. Before you jump in, pay a brief visit to Chapter 4 to get the full details about GIF, because the format does have a few downsides.

Creating a GIF with transparent pixels

GIF transparency works on a pixel-color basis. You specify what colors you want to make transparent, and *any* pixels of that color become invisible.

For example, if you have a multicolor vase set against a blue background and you tell PhotoDeluxe to make blue pixels transparent, the background disappears — and so do any blue areas of the vase. To prevent portions of your vase from disappearing, you need to change the image background to some color that doesn't show up on the vase, too. (When you look at the images in Figure 6-1, you're looking at grayscale versions of the color originals. In the original golf-bag picture, the background fades from medium blue to dark blue; the golf bag is red, white, and grey. So when I specified that I wanted to make the blue pixels transparent, none of the golf bag pixels disappeared.)

The steps for creating a transparent GIF seem complicated at first glance, but they're actually pretty simple:

1. **Choose File⇨Export⇨GIF89a Export.**

   If you're intrigued by that *89a* stuff, here's the deal: The inventors of this format decided to use *89a* to let people know that they were using a version of the format laid out in 1989. The first version of GIF was born in 1987, so it got the equally user-friendly tag *87a*. With the older GIF, you can't animate your image or make areas of the picture transparent.

   At any rate, when you choose this command, PhotoDeluxe summons the GIF89a Export Options dialog box, whose name is nearly larger than the dialog box itself. Figure 6-2 shows the dialog box.

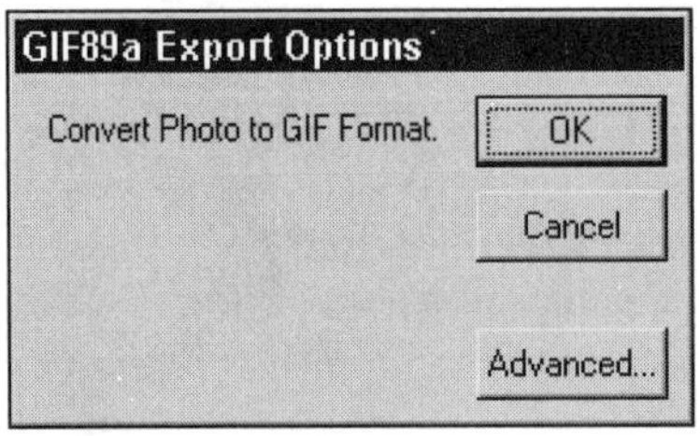

Figure 6-2:
Click the
Advanced
button to
reveal con-
trols that
make pixels
invisible.

GIF89a Export Options
Convert Photo to GIF Format.   [OK]
[Cancel]
[Advanced...]

2. Click the Advanced button.

Now you see the dialog box shown in Figure 6-3. Staying true to the highly technical format name, this dialog box contains a batch of controls with highly technical labels. Don't freak out — the options aren't as complex as they appear.

Figure 6-3:
Click the
color
swatch to
specify how
transparent
pixels
should
appear
when you
view the
image in
PhotoDeluxe.

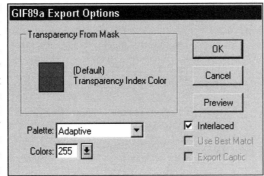

3. Set the transparency preview color.

Okay, once more, in English: When you view your image in PhotoDeluxe, the program uses a particular color, called the *preview color,* to represent transparent pixels. This coloring of transparent pixels happens only in PhotoDeluxe; the pixels are invisible when you view the image on a Web page.

By default, the preview color is the same gray once commonly used as a background color for Web pages. If your image contains many *non*transparent pixels that are a similar shade of gray, change the preview color to some other shade so that you can more easily distinguish transparent pixels from opaque pixels when you view the image in PhotoDeluxe. To change the color, click the Transparency Index Color swatch and select a color from the Color Picker. If you need help using the Color Picker, see Chapter 10.

4. Decide whether you want an interlaced image.

GIF, like JPEG, enables you to decide how you want your image to appear on the viewer's screen.

- If you turn on the Interlaced option, the image appears bit by bit as the image data makes its way to the viewer's modem.

• If you turn off the Interlaced option, the viewer sees nothing until all the image data is received.

There is no right or wrong choice here; just pick the one that makes you happy. For more information, see the sidebar related to progressive images in Chapter 4.

5. Ignore the Palette and Colors options.

Unless you're an advanced Web designer and know what you're doing in terms of defining a color palette — or unless someone who *is* experienced tells you what to do — leave the Palette option set to Adaptive and the Colors option to 255.

6. Click Preview.

The Select Transparent Colors dialog box shown in Figure 6-4 appears. Here's where you tell PhotoDeluxe which colors to make invisible.

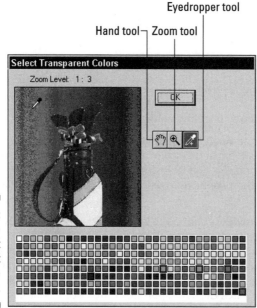

Eyedropper tool

Hand tool ⌐ Zoom tool

Figure 6-4:
Click the colors that you want to make transparent.

7. Click the Eyedropper button and then click the colors that you want to make transparent.

You can either click the color in the image preview at the top of the dialog box or click a color swatch at the bottom of the dialog box. After you click a color, its swatch becomes surrounded by a heavy black outline. All pixels of that color turn the color that you selected as your preview color in Step 3. In Figure 6-4, I set the transparency preview color to dark gray.

If you change your mind about making a color transparent, either Ctrl+Click the swatch to make the color opaque again or Ctrl+Click the color in the image preview. You can tell that the color is deselected because the heavy black outline disappears from around the color swatch.

Click the Zoom button and then click in the image preview to zoom in for a closer look at your image. Alt+Click to zoom out. Click the Hand button and drag in the image preview to display hidden portions of the image.

After you select your colors with the Eyedropper, zoom way in and scroll around the entire image. Make sure that you didn't leave any stray pixels behind. When you're zoomed out, those stray pixels can be difficult to see. Also inspect the portions of the image that you *don't* want to make transparent to make sure that you haven't selected any colors that are in those areas.

8. **Click OK to close the Select Transparent Colors dialog box.**

9. **Click OK again.**

PhotoDeluxe takes you to the Export GIF89 dialog box, which looks suspiciously like the standard Export dialog box. Indeed, the two dialog boxes work exactly the same. Choose a filename and a file location and click Save. (If you need help navigating the dialog box, see Chapter 4.)

PhotoDeluxe saves a *copy* of your image in the GIF format. The original PDD version of the image remains on-screen. To see how well you did at making the right pixels transparent, you must open the GIF version of your image. The PDD version on-screen looks the same as it did before you saved to GIF. If you did leave some pixels behind and want to make them transparent — or you went too far and want to restore some pixels to their original opacity — just repeat the preceding steps.

If you don't already have a copy of your original image, save the PDD version before you close it. Remember that in the process of creating your GIF file, you not only made some of your pixels transparent, but also reduced your image to 256 colors. If you ever need all those colors back and you don't save the original image, you're sunk.

Creating a GIF image without transparency

If you want to save your image as a GIF file but don't care to make any pixels transparent, follow these steps:

1. **Choose File⇨Export⇨GIF89a Export command.**

PhotoDeluxe opens the GIF89a Export Options dialog box, shown in Figure 6-2, in the preceding section.

2. **Click OK.**

PhotoDeluxe displays the Export GIF89a dialog box, which is a clone of the standard Export dialog box, which is itself an offshoot of the Save As dialog box.

3. **Assign your image a name and location on disk.**

   If you need help, see Chapter 4.

4. **Click Save.**

   PhotoDeluxe saves a copy of your image in the GIF format as instructed.

Because GIF can save only 256 colors, PhotoDeluxe strips your image down to that bare minimum when you click the Save button. Open the GIF file to see what effect the color reduction had on the image; as explained earlier, the on-screen image is the original PDD version and doesn't reflect the new color palette. If you haven't already saved a backup copy of the original image, be sure to do so before you close the PDD version.

If you don't like what you see when you open the GIF version of your image, delete the file. Reopen the *original* image — the one you started with before you saved to GIF for the first time. Now you're back to square one.

When you follow the steps for creating a GIF image without transparency, you create an interlaced GIF image. If you want to create a *non*interlaced image, take a side trip between Step 1 and Step 2. Click the Advanced button in the GIF89A Export Options dialog box, deselect the Interlaced check box in the next dialog box, and click OK twice; then go ahead with the rest of the steps.

E-Mailing Photos

Want to send a picture to someone via e-mail? PhotoDeluxe provides a Guided Activities wizard for that task, but I can't recommend it. For one thing, the wizard saves your picture in the JPEG format and applies JPEG compression by default. Although you can turn off the compression option, you don't get the opportunity to send your picture in any other format, which you may occasionally need to do. More importantly, you actually can get the job done more easily and more quickly by preparing your picture yourself and sending it directly from your e-mail program.

If your only goal is to enable others to see your pictures, follow the instructions given earlier in this chapter ("Preparing Pictures for the Screen") to size and save your images. Choose JPEG as your file format; some e-mail viewers can't handle GIF.

If you want recipients to be able to output a high-quality print of your picture, size the picture as you would if you were going to print it yourself. (See Chapter 3 for how-to's.) Save the file in the TIFF format to retain the best image quality. Remember, though, that TIFF files are much bigger than compressed JPEG files, which means that a TIFF image takes longer to send and receive. Give the recipients a heads-up so that they know that their computers will be tied up for a while during the downloading process.

If you're sending pictures to computer novices, also explain that they will need to save the pictures to disk and then open them in a program that can work with TIFF images — e-mail programs and Web browsers can't.

When you're ready to send your image, open your e-mail program, create your message, and attach the image file as you would any other file. If you're new to the whole e-mail business, take the following steps to tackle the project in Netscape Communicator, Version 4.7. The steps are similar for other versions of the program as well as for most other e-mail programs. Check your e-mail program's Help system if you run into trouble.

1. **Connect to the Internet and launch Communicator.**

2. **Open Netscape Messenger by choosing Communicator⇨Messenger or pressing Ctrl+2.**

3. **Click the New icon or choose File⇨New⇨Message to open the Composition window.**

   Figure 6-5 gives you a look at the window.

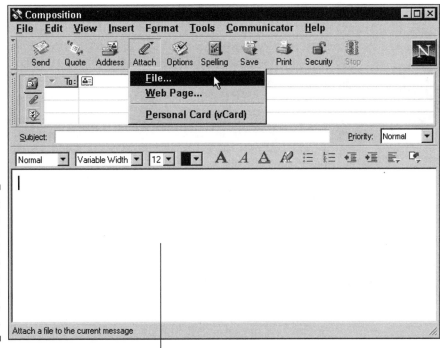

Figure 6-5:
Click the Attach button and select File to choose the picture file you want to send.

Message area

4. **Enter the recipient's e-mail address in the To box.**

   If you want to mail the picture to a second person, click the line below the To box and enter the second e-mail address. You can keep adding as many addresses as you want by using the same process. You also can click the To button, to the left of the box, and select another addressing option from the menu. For example, if you want to copy a colleague on the message, choose CC from the menu.

5. **Type a message subject header in the Subject box.**

   "Wow, what a picture!" is always effective.

6. **In the Message area, type any thoughts you want to send with the picture (see Figure 6-5).**

7. **Click the Attach button and select File from the pop-up menu, as shown in the figure.**

   Alternatively, choose File⇨Attach⇨File. Up pops the Files to Attach dialog box. Whaddya know, it looks and works just like the Open dialog box that you use to open files in just about every Windows program on earth.

8. **Locate the file that you want to send, click it, and click the Open button.**

   Don't worry — you're not really going to open the file. Somebody just got lazy about changing the button name in the dialog box.

   In this e-mail program and some others, you can select more than one image file by clicking the first file and then Ctrl+Clicking the others.

   After you close the dialog box, a list of the attached files appears in the area of the Composition window where you earlier entered your recipient's e-mail address. To redisplay the list of recipients, click the little card file icon to the left of the box. To check the list of attachments again, click the paper-clip icon just below the card-file icon.

9. **Click the Send button, or press Ctrl+Enter, or choose File⇨Send Now.**

   Your image shoots through your modem and out into cyberspace.

Hanging New Computer Wallpaper

Tired of looking at the same old background on your computer desktop? You can create a custom background featuring your favorite digital image, as shown in Figure 6-6.

In computerese, the background is known as *wallpaper*.

Figure 6-6:
Replace
your boring
desktop
wallpaper
with a
favorite
image.

To hang new wallpaper, follow these redecorating steps:

1. **Open your image.**

2. **Choose Size⇨Photo Size and check the image pixel dimensions.**

   Set the unit of measurement to pixels for both the Width and Height values. Assuming that you want your wallpaper to fill the entire screen, you need to match the pixel dimensions of the image to your monitor display setting. In the figure, for example, I had my monitor set to display 800 pixels horizontally by 600 pixels vertically, so that's how big I made the image. If you want to *tile* your image — that is, repeat the same picture many times across the screen — you of course want to make the image size smaller than the monitor display setting.

3. **Choose File⇨Export⇨Windows Wallpaper.**

   PhotoDeluxe makes a copy of your image and saves the copy in the BMP file format, which is the right format to use for wallpaper in Windows. The file, named *PhotoDeluxe*, is stored in the main Windows folder with the regular Windows wallpaper files.

   PhotoDeluxe automatically selects the new file as your system wallpaper. To see your new environment, minimize the PhotoDeluxe program window and any other open windows. (If your keyboard has a Microsoft Windows key, you can press that key and the M key to minimize all open windows simultaneously.)

4. Close your open image without saving it.

Changing the pixel count, which you may have done in Step 2, can harm image quality, and you may need the original quality some day. As long as you don't save the open image, your original remains untouched.

Also, PhotoDeluxe saves a copy of the resized image in Step 2, so you don't need to save another copy unless you need the resized version in format other than BMP.

To control whether Windows uses a single copy of your picture as wallpaper or tiles the image across the screen, you need to select an option in the Windows Display Properties dialog box. Here's how:

1. Right-click an empty area on the Windows desktop.

2. Choose Properties from the pop-menu to open the Display Properties dialog box.

3. Click the Background tab.

4. Choose a Display option.

In Windows 95, you can choose from Tile, which repeats your image as many times as necessary in order to fill the screen, or Center, which displays a single image in the center of the screen.

If you use Windows 98, you get one additional option: Stretch. As its name implies, this option stretches your picture to fill the screen. Because this option can make your picture appear distorted or jagged, I recommend that you avoid it unless your picture is only slightly smaller than the screen size.

5. Click OK.

PhotoDeluxe can store only one image as wallpaper at a time. If you want to change the wallpaper image, open the new image and choose the Windows Wallpaper command again. PhotoDeluxe asks whether you want to replace the existing wallpaper image. Click OK to go ahead.

Even though PhotoDeluxe can't deal with more than one wallpaper image at a time, you can keep several images on hand to use as wallpaper by saving your image manually as a BMP file. (See Chapter 4 for information on how to save in the BMP format.) Then, to select an image for use as your wallpaper, head for the Background tab of the Display Properties dialog box, as covered in the preceding steps. Click the Browse button, track down the BMP image file you want to use, and click Open.

To switch back to the wallpaper you created by using the Windows Wallpaper command, choose PhotoDeluxe from the list of wallpaper files in the Display Properties dialog box.

Staring at Your Face in the Monitor

In the early days of computing, you could damage your monitor by leaving the same data displayed for a long time. The data *burned* into the screen, leaving a faint image that never went away.

This phenomenon led to the *screen saver,* a program that displays a changing pattern of images or text during times when the computer is inactive — or, more accurately, when the computer operator is inactive. By continually altering the monitor display, the screen saver prevents burn-in.

You don't need to worry about burn-in with today's monitors, but so many entertaining screen savers have been designed that people like to use them anyway. After all, when you're daydreaming instead of working, wouldn't you rather watch a really cool screen saver than stare at your half-completed project on-screen?

With PhotoDeluxe, you can do the computer geeks in your office one better by designing a custom screen saver that features your own images. The best way to do this is to use a Guided Activities wizard.

 The wizard requires you to select images that currently appear in the My Photos organizer. If you want any text to appear with an image in the screen saver, open the Photo Information dialog box for the image and type the text into the Comments box. Chapter 4 explains how to do all this stuff, if you need help.

After you put all the images you want to use into the My Photos organizer, create your screen saver as follows:

1. **Click the Get & Fix Photo button (the top Guided Activities button).**

2. **Click the Save & Send icon and choose Screen Saver from the drop-down menu.**

3. **Click the Select tab and then click the My Photos icon.**

   PhotoDeluxe displays the My Photos window, if the window isn't already open, and then creates a new album named Screen Saver.

4. **Click the album that contains the pictures you want to put in the screen saver.**

5. **Drag the image thumbnails to the Screen Saver album icon.**

   You can select images from more than one album if you want.

6. **Click the Create tab and click the Create icon.**

   PhotoDeluxe makes a copy of each image in the Screen Saver album, saves the copy in the BMP format, and then generates the screen saver.

7. **Click the Done tab to close the wizard.**

If you want to change the pictures in your screen saver, you must work through the entire wizard again. You can't add a picture to the screen saver by dragging a thumbnail to the Screen Saver album or by specifying that PhotoDeluxe create a thumbnail in the Screen Saver album when you save a new file. By the same token, deleting a thumbnail from the Screen Saver album doesn't remove the image from the actual screen saver.

You can, however, use the File⇨Export⇨Screen Saver command to add an open image to the screen saver. First, save the file in the PDD format and give it a unique name. Otherwise, PhotoDeluxe names the screen saver copy of the image *Untitled1.bmp.* If you open another file and apply the Screen Saver command — again, without saving the file with a unique name — that file gets the name *Untitled1.bmp,* too. PhotoDeluxe doesn't let you keep more than one picture with the same name in the screen saver; you have to overwrite the old *Untitled1.bmp* with the new one.

After you create your screen saver, you need to tell Windows that you want to use the thing. Here's the drill:

1. **Right-click an empty area in the Windows desktop and choose Properties from the pop-up menu.**

2. **Click the Screen Saver tab.**

3. **Choose PhotoDeluxe from the Screen Saver drop-down list.**

4. **Click the Settings button.**

   A tiny dialog box opens; it contains one option. If you want the screen saver to display the image comments along with the image, select the Show Captions check box if you use Windows 95; select Show Comments in Windows 98. (You can find out how to add comments in Chapter 4, in the section that covers the photo organizer.)

5. **Click OK to return to the Display Properties dialog box.**

6. **Click the Preview button.**

   Windows shows you how the screen saver will look. Click to exit the preview and return to the Display Properties dialog box.

7. **Set the delay time.**

   Tell Windows how many minutes you want the computer to be idle before the screen saver appears by entering a value in the Wait option box.

8. **Click OK to put the Display Properties dialog box away.**

   The next time you nod off and ignore your computer for the length of time you specified in Step 7, the screen saver does its thing.

Sharing Pictures the Adobe Way

A few years ago, a number of traditional photography companies — Kodak, Fujifilm, and the like — began to offer free Internet services that enabled people to create online photo albums, send e-mail picture postcards, and do other photo-related projects. As the popularity of online picture-sharing grew, so too did the number of Web sites providing similar services.

Adobe recently got into the act by launching its ActiveShare service with partner eCircles (`www.ecircles.com`), a leading online community. Using the service, you can create *eCircles,* which are like online private clubs. You start an eCircle and then send e-mail invitations to other people you want to be part of the group. Group members can post messages, share online photo albums, send picture postcards, trade music files, participate in live text and voice chats, and even post a wish list of all the goodies they want to receive for their next birthday, anniversary, or other occasion that demands gifts.

For folks who want to enjoy these activities but don't want to get involved with digital imaging beyond the basics, Adobe provides free ActiveShare software. This program offers limited photo-editing capabilities and is mainly designed to simplify the process of sharing pictures via the ActiveShare Web site.

You probably noticed that Adobe includes a copy of the ActiveShare software on your PhotoDeluxe program CD, and you may be wondering whether you need to install it. In a word, nope. In two words, please don't. You can access all the photo-related ActiveShare features from inside PhotoDeluxe or your Web browser. More importantly, ActiveShare and PhotoDeluxe take very different approaches to some critical file-management tasks. Trust me, things get confusing if you try to work with both ActiveShare and PhotoDeluxe.

Because online products and services change so rapidly, I hesitate to explore the ActiveShare service too deeply in this book. Any instructions that I give you today may well change tomorrow, or even this evening. I figure, however, that Adobe will at least continue to offer the features that you can access via PhotoDeluxe — if only because discontinuing them would create a nightmare for the Adobe technical support staff.

With that approach in mind, the next sections explain how to create an eCircle, put together an online photo album, and send digital picture postcards and picture puzzles. For other issues — and to get any updates regarding the features I do discuss here — be sure to explore the ActiveShare Web site (`www.AdobeActiveShare.com`). I encourage you to spend some time exploring the site. It offers a fun and very well done array of features, most of which are absolutely free.

Creating an eCircle

Before you can take advantage of the online services, you must register as a member. As part of the registration, you also create your first eCircle. Here's how to do this from inside PhotoDeluxe:

1. **Click the Share button.**

   The Share button is the bottom Guided Activities button. When you click the button, the Guided Activities project area displays icons related to photo-sharing.

2. **Click the Web Sharing icon.**

   Now you can access other icons related to Web activities. Click the green arrows at either end of those icons to scroll through the available activities.

3. **Click the Tell Me More icon.**

   At this point, PhotoDeluxe attempts to launch your Internet connection and Web browser. If PhotoDeluxe isn't successful, connect to the Internet and start your browser as you normally do; then switch back to PhotoDeluxe and click the Tell Me More icon.

   When you make the link with the Web, you see a Web page looking something like the one in Figure 6-7. This page explains more about eCircles and includes links for finding additional details and also for signing up with the program.

4. **Click the Sign Up link, as shown in the figure.**

   You're shown a Web page containing a form for entering your name, address, and other pertinent information. Be sure to complete all boxes marked as Required information. You can provide the rest of the information if you like or leave those fields blank.

5. **Click the Next button at the bottom of the form to continue the registration process.**

   Adobe asks you to enter a login (user) name and password. After you do so, click the link for reviewing the terms of agreement for the eCircles service. The terms appear in a new window. When you've read the terms, close the window.

6. **Click the Sign Up button.**

   You see a message confirming that you're registered and inviting you to visit your first eCircle.

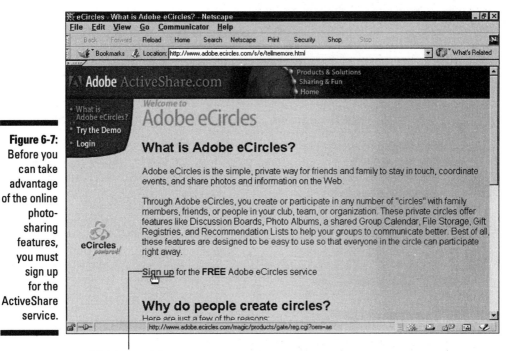

Figure 6-7:
Before you
can take
advantage
of the online
photo-
sharing
features,
you must
sign up
for the
ActiveShare
service.

Click here to join

7. **Click the Go to My Circles button.**

On the Web page that appears, you can customize your eCircle pages
and invite other people to join the circle. To do so, click your First Circle
link and follow the prompts on the pages that appear. Shortly after you
register, you should receive an e-mail confirming your membership. The
e-mail contains your user name and password. I suggest that you print
the message and file it somewhere you can find it easily if you forget the
name and password you selected.

You can travel directly to the page where you log in by clicking the Share
Guided Activities button, then the Web Sharing icon (if the icon isn't already
selected), and then the Web Community icon. If you don't have PhotoDeluxe
open, point your Web browser to www.adobe.ecircles.com to log in. After
you log in, your eCircle home page appears automatically.

Creating and posting photo albums

Everyone who joins your eCircle can create and post digital photo albums.
This feature provides a convenient way to share pictures with a bunch of

people — you no longer have to e-mail the photo to each person individually. After you post pictures on the site, members of your circle can save the photo so that they have their own copy of the picture file.

When you create and post your photo albums via PhotoDeluxe, the program automatically compresses them to reduce the files to a size acceptable for the Web. If you put pictures in your album that haven't been saved in the JPEG format, the program also creates a JPEG version. That JPEG version is the one that appears on the Web.

PhotoDeluxe does not, however, *resize* your photos. You must do that yourself. Follow the guidelines found in Chapter 3, in the section on sizing pictures for on-screen use.

Because your image files are compressed and limited in pixel count, you typically can't produce a good print from images in an online album. If someone wants to print one of your pictures, you should send your original image file as an e-mail attachment, as explained earlier in this chapter.

To create and post a photo album, take these steps:

1. **Click the Share button (the bottom Guided Activities button).**

2. **Click the Web Sharing icon, if it's not already selected.**

3. **Click the Share on the Web icon.**

   The Guided Activities area changes to show tabs related to creating and posting Web photo albums.

4. **Click the Open Web Album tab and then click the Web Album icon.**

   PhotoDeluxe opens a special photo organizer window, named Post to Web. You use this window to specify what pictures you want to include in your album.

5. **Click the Get Photos tab and add your pictures to the photo organizer window.**

   The easiest way to get the job done is to click the My Photos icon, which opens the My Photos organizer. You then can drag thumbnails from the My Photos window into the Post to Web organizer window, as I'm doing in Figure 6-8. You also can drag open pictures into the Post to Web album, as long as you first save those pictures in the PDD format (see Chapter 4).

6. **Click the Post tab (in the Guided Activities tabs) and then click the Post to Web icon.**

   PhotoDeluxe responds with the dialog box shown in Figure 6-9.

Figure 6-8:
Drag the
pictures you
want to
share into
the Web
Album
organizer
window.

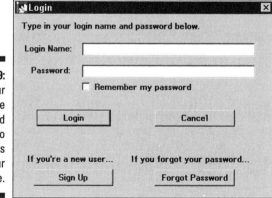

Figure 6-9:
Enter your
login name
and
password to
gain access
to your
eCircle.

7. **Enter your login name and your password and then click the Login button.**

   If you don't want to enter your password every time, select the Remember My Password option.

PhotoDeluxe attempts to start your Internet connection software and your Web browser. If the program isn't successful, leave the PhotoDeluxe program window and do the job manually, as you normally do to surf the Web. After you connect, you see the dialog box shown in Figure 6-10.

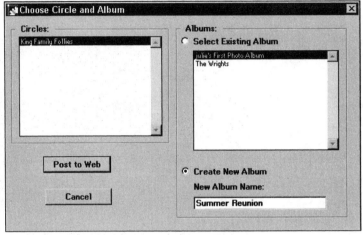

Figure 6-10: Choose the album where you want to put your pictures.

8. **Select the eCircle and album where you want PhotoDeluxe to put your pictures.**

   If you belong to more than one eCircle, you see all the circle names in the Circles list. Click the name of the circle where you want to share the album.

   Next, select an album. When you first register to create an eCircle, Adobe creates one default album for you. In my case, Adobe assigned the album name Julie's First Photo Album. If you want to put your pictures in that album or in any other existing album, click the Select Existing Album button and then click the album name. To create a brand new album, click the Create New Album button and type in an album name, as I did in Figure 6-10.

9. **Click the Post to Web button in the dialog box.**

   PhotoDeluxe displays a dialog box that tells you how long you have to goof off while the pictures are uploaded to your eCircle album, as shown in Figure 6-11. Note that PhotoDeluxe estimates how long the album transmission will take on a 28.8K modem. If you have a faster modem and Internet connection, your upload time should be shorter.

10. **If you want to proceed, click Add Photo(s) Now.**

    PhotoDeluxe posts your photo album to the Web.

You can click the Cancel button to bail and post the album later. From there, click the Done tab in the Guided Activities project tabs. When you're ready to post your album, just start the wizard again. PhotoDeluxe saves your Post to Web album and retains all the thumbnails you already added to the album.

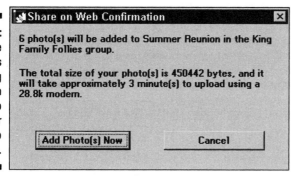

Figure 6-11:
PhotoDeluxe
estimates
how long
your album
will take to
go from your
computer to
your eCircle.

When PhotoDeluxe finishes sending your album, it asks whether you want to view it. If you select Yes, your album page appears in your Web browser window. Figure 6-12 shows how an album that I created looks on-screen.

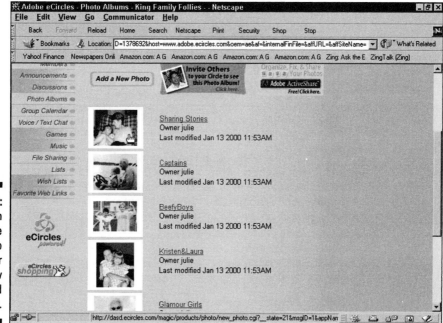

Figure 6-12:
Click an
image
thumbnail to
see a larger
view
and add
comments.

After you create an album, you can add a photo to it directly from your eCircle Web page if you prefer. Open the album and then click the Add a New Photos button. You're asked to locate and select the image file you want to add to the album. Don't forget — you need a picture that's sized appropriately for on-screen viewing and then saved in the JPEG format.

Viewing and managing albums

When people want to log in to your eCircle and open an album, they'll no doubt call you for help, what with you being the resident digital photo expert and all. So that you don't look foolish, get familiar with the process:

✔ From the initial eCircles page that appears when you first log in, click the link for the eCircle you want to enter. You then see a page showing links and graphical icons for everyone in your circle. If you click those links, you can see address and e-mail information for each member.

To get to the photo albums, click the Photo Albums button on the far left side of the Web page. You then see a list of links for any albums that have been posted by members of your eCircle. Click the link for the album that you want to see.

✔ Initially, the album appears as shown in Figure 6-12, in the preceding section. To view the image at full size, as shown in Figure 6-13, click the image thumbnail.

✔ If you scroll down the page, you see buttons for deleting and renaming the picture. However, only the person who posted the picture can make these changes. Click the buttons and follow the instructions to delete or rename the picture.

✔ Anyone can post comments, which appear beneath the image, as shown in Figure 6-13. To put in your two cents' worth, scroll down past the comment display area, type your text into the Add Your Comments box, and click Add Comment.

✔ To scroll through the album and see each image at the larger size, click the left- and right-pointing arrow buttons labeled in Figure 6-13. To close the image and return to the thumbnails that appear on the album's opening page, click the Back to Photo List button.

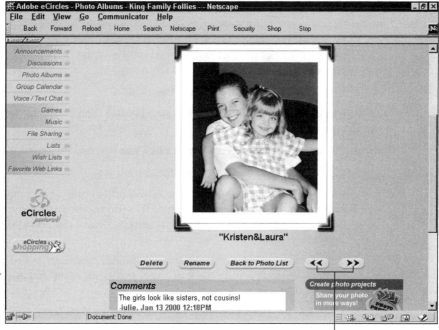

Figure 6-13:
After you
click an
image
thumbnail,
you can see
the image at
full size.

Click to scroll through photos

Sending a picture postcard or puzzle

If you want to share a picture with just one or two folks in an eCircle or with
someone who isn't part of your eCircle, you can either attach the picture to
an e-mail message (see the section "E-Mailing photos," earlier in this chapter)
or send a private picture postcard. PhotoDeluxe places the card in a special
area of the Adobe ActiveShare Web site and sends an e-mail message to each
recipient to announce the postcard's arrival. People who get the e-mail can
then click a link in the message to see the postcard. You also receive e-mail
confirmation that the picture arrived safely.

This project, like the others involving the ActiveShare features, works only
via the Guided Activities wizards. Here's what you need to do:

1. **Open the picture that you want to send.**

   In this case, you do *not* need to resize your picture or save it as a JPEG. PhotoDeluxe takes care of all that nasty business for you. Note that the program works with a copy of your image — the on-screen PDD version remains untouched.

2. **Click the Share Guided Activities button.**

3. **Click the Web Projects icon to display the Web Projects Guided Activities tabs.**

4. **Click the Choose tab and then click the Picture Postcard icon.**

5. **Click the E-mail tab and click the E-mail icon.**

   PhotoDeluxe displays a box where you must enter your e-mail address and the recipient's e-mail address. To send the postcard to more than one person, just type all the addresses, adding a comma and a space between each.

   You also can enter a caption and a personal message, just as you would write a message on the back of a real postcard. After you add all this information, click OK.

6. **Click the Post tab and then click the Post to Web icon.**

   You get the same login dialog box you get when posting an album to your eCircle (refer back to Figure 6-9).

7. **Enter your login name and password — if they're not already entered — and click the Login button.**

   In a few moments, PhotoDeluxe displays a message box to tell you that your postcard made its way to the ActiveShare Web site and that the recipient was sent an e-mail announcing that fact. For some reason, the Login dialog box remains on-screen; click the Close button (the little X) at the right end of the dialog box title bar to remove the box if it bothers you. Otherwise, you can just click the Done tab to close both the dialog box and the wizard.

For even more fun, send your picture as a jigsaw puzzle. The process is the same as for sending an e-mail message, except that you click the Picture Puzzle icon in Step 5 instead of the Picture Postcard icon.

As with picture postcards, you supply the e-mail addresses of the people who can play the puzzle. Those people get an e-mail message with a link to the puzzle. Of course, you, too, get to join in the fun. Figure 6-14 shows a puzzle that I created from a family photo.

Adobe keeps your postcards and puzzles on its site for 30 days. After that, they're deleted.

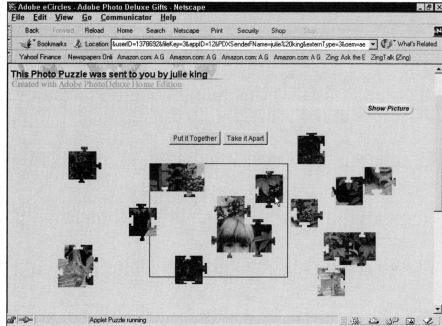

Figure 6-14:
You can create online jigsaw puzzles out of your favorite pictures.

Part III
Editing Boot Camp

In this part . . .

*I*n the early days of computing, people often used the phrase, "Garbage in, garbage out." The saying referred to the fact that the output you generated from a computer depended on the quality of the data that you fed *into* the computer.

With image editing, the "garbage in, garbage out" motto gets turned on its ear, spun around the room, and flung against the wall. Using Adobe PhotoDeluxe 4, you can turn a stinky, rotten image into a compelling digital master-piece — or, at least, a much improved version of its former self.

This part presents the basic techniques for enhancing your images. You find out how to apply color corrections, fix soft focus, move or copy a portion of your image from one spot to another, and perform all manner of other essential editing tasks. I even show you how to cover up unsightly image blemishes using some top-secret patching techniques.

Capable as PhotoDeluxe is at making something out of nothing, though, you still need to be wary of PEBKAC* errors. These image-killing mistakes occur when users apply edits willy-nilly, using no restraint at all and *certainly* without taking the time to read the insightful and always entertaining instructions found in this book. So consider yourself reminded — unless you want to ruin perfectly good images and make awful images worse, you have to actually *read* the sentences, paragraphs, and pages in this part.

*PEBKAC (pronounced *pebb-kaaaaaack!*): Problem Exists Between Keyboard and Chair

Chapter 7

Everyday Edits

- -

In This Chapter

▶ Approaching your edits from the right perspective

▶ Undoing mistakes

▶ Cropping out unwanted image elements

▶ Adjusting image brightness and contrast

▶ Making your colors more vivid

▶ Correcting out-of-whack colors

▶ Modifying the image canvas area

▶ Adding borders and drop shadows

- -

*I*n the 1950s, my grandmother bought a state-of-the-art sewing machine capable of producing about a zillion different stitches. That machine is still alive and kicking, having been used to sew everything from a dress for my first high school dance to curtains for my first house. But in all those years, we used but a handful of the machine's many features. The truth is, you can accomplish 99 percent of all sewing projects with a few basic stitches.

In case you're wondering where this "Sewing with Julie" introduction is going, let me jump right to the analogy: The tools discussed in this chapter are like the basic features on my vintage sewing machine. They're not the fanciest tools in the PhotoDeluxe collection, but they're the ones you rely on day in and day out to give your images a more professional, finished look.

Among other things, this chapter explains how to crop an image; adjust color balance, contrast, and brightness; and apply a simple image border. You also get a primer on image-editing safety — that is, how to approach your editing so that you don't ruin your picture in the process of trying to improve it. With the information gleaned from this chapter, you can stitch up any frayed image edges in no time.

Touching Up Like a Pro

PhotoDeluxe gives you several powerful tools for cleaning up images, but if you don't use the tools carefully, you can do more harm than good. To keep your pictures safe, keep the following rules in mind:

- ✔ **Don't rely exclusively on the "quick fix" tools.** PhotoDeluxe offers several tools that promise to correct common image problems automatically, with little effort on your part. These tools include filters for removing the dreaded "red eye" problem that crops up in many snapshots, getting rid of dust and scratches that tend to make their way into scanned images, and correcting image exposure.

  On some images, the automatic correction tools do an acceptable job. But just as often, they either do no good or cause a new problem while fixing another. In this chapter and Chapter 8, I introduce you to these tool, explain the best way to use them, and suggest alternative solutions when a quick fix doesn't fix.

- ✔ **Use selections to limit the effects of your edits.** As Chapter 8 explains, you can use the PhotoDeluxe selection tools to rope off a portion of the image so that your edits affect only that area. In most cases, selective correction is the way to go. For example, suppose that the foreground of your image is too dark, and the background is too light. If you raise the brightness of the whole image, the foreground may look better, but the background looks even more overexposed. For better results, select the foreground before you lighten the image.

- ✔ **Edit on a separate layer.** To give yourself an editing safety net, copy the layer that you want to edit to a new layer and edit there. That way, you can simply delete the new layer and start over if you muck things up. Your original layer remains untouched.

  Chapter 11 explores layers fully. In case you don't want to trek to that chapter right now, here's a quick how-to: To duplicate a layer, display the Layers palette, shown in Figure 7-1, by choosing View⇨Show Layers. In the palette, drag the layer to the New Layer icon, as illustrated in the figure. Your cursor changes into a little hand to show that you've grabbed the layer (also shown in the figure). When you release the mouse button, PhotoDeluxe creates your duplicate layer and makes it active. Any edits you make while the duplicate layer is active don't affect the rest of the image. If you mess up and want to delete the duplicate layer, drag it to the Trash icon in the Layers palette.

  When you're done editing, mush the new layer and the original layer together by choosing Merge Layers from the palette menu, unfurled in Figure 7-1. (Click the little triangle to make the menu appear.) As long as you keep the opacity of the new layer at 100 percent, your edited layer blots out everything in the underlying layer.

Click to display menu — Layers palette menu

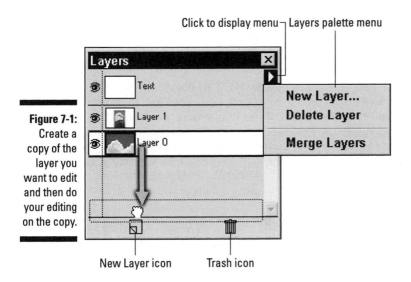

Figure 7-1:
Create a
copy of the
layer you
want to edit
and then do
your editing
on the copy.

New Layer icon   Trash icon

✔ **Save a backup copy of your original image in the PhotoDeluxe format (PDD) before you begin editing.** If you happen to totally destroy an image, you can choose the File⇨Revert to Last Saved command (discussed later in this chapter) to go back to square one.

✔ **Use a light hand when applying image correction commands.** Otherwise, your edits become obvious and your images look amateurish.

Speaking of looking amateurish, if you want to avoid sounding like a beginner, refer to image correction commands (those that adjust brightness, sharpness, and so on) as *filters,* not commands. Please don't ask me why — this is just one of those lingo things that the digital imaging crowd started, and you have to go along if you want to fit in.

Undoing Editing Goofs

If you make an edit that you regret, PhotoDeluxe gives you several ways to fix things:

✔ **Choose Edit⇨Undo:** This command undoes your most recent editing action. Choose Undo immediately after you mess up, or your opportunity to correct your mistake vanishes.

Don't go to all the trouble of choosing the Undo command from the Edit menu, however. Instead, press Ctrl+Z or click the Undo button in the image-editing window.

PhotoDeluxe even gives you a way to correct a mistaken Undo. If you choose Undo and then think better of it, simply choose the command again. You must do so before you make any other editing move, or you can't undo your undo.

✔ **Choose File⇨Revert to Last Saved:** This command restores your image to the way it appeared the last time you saved it. Use this option when you want to undo a whole series of blunders. But remember, you don't have access to the Revert to Last Saved command unless you saved your image before you started editing. Also, Revert to Last Saved works only for images saved in the PDD file format. So save early, save often, and save in the PDD format until you're completely finished editing your image. See Chapter 4 for complete details about saving files in PhotoDeluxe.

✔ **Delete your editing layer:** As I explained in the preceding section, doing your editing work on a duplicate image layer affords you an extra, er, layer of protection. If you're not happy with your edits, you simply trash the editing layer, create a new editing layer, and start over. To delete a layer, choose drag the layer name to the Trash icon in the palette. You can find out more about all this intriguing layers stuff in Chapter 11.

Snipping Away Parts of Your Image

To trim away unwanted portions of your image — otherwise known as *cropping* your image — snip your way through these steps:

1. **Press Ctrl+7 or choose Size⇨Trim to pick up the Crop tool.**

2. **Drag to create a crop outline.**

   Starting at one corner of the area you want to *retain,* drag to the opposite corner. As you drag, PhotoDeluxe displays a dotted outline to represent the crop boundary, as shown in the left side of Figure 7-2. When you release the mouse button at the end of your drag, the dotted outline changes into a solid outline with a little square at each corner.

   Call those little squares *handles* if you want to sound like an image-editing pro.

3. **Adjust the crop outline if necessary.**

   Place your cursor over one of the crop handles until the cursor becomes a double-headed arrow. You can then adjust the outline as follows:

   • Drag any handle to enlarge or shrink the outline.

   • Drag inside the outline to move it. If you're a former Version 2.0 or Business Edition user, note that you no longer have to press Ctrl as you drag to move the outline.

Crop outline

Figure 7-2:
After
dragging to
enclose the
area you
want to
retain (left),
click to crop
away every-
thing else
(right).

Crop cursor

4. Click outside the crop outline or press Enter.

Here's another important cropping change from Version 2.0 and the Business Edition: In Version 4, you can't just click anywhere as you could in those earlier versions of the program.

After you click, PhotoDeluxe snips off the unwanted portions of the image, leaving just the area inside the outline, as shown in the right side of Figure 7-2.

If you decide midstream that you don't want to crop your image, you can press the Esc key (sometimes labeled Escape) any time before taking Step 4. After you press Esc, the crop outline vanishes, as does the Crop tool.

You can rotate and crop your image at the same time by applying the Crop tool in a special way. Take a look at the image on the left in Figure 7-3. Some people say that shot, taken from a sailboat in St. Maarten, was the result of too many island cocktails. I say that our sailboat was rocked by waves just as I pressed the shutter button. Either way, I used the Crop tool to trim the image and right the ship.

If you want to perform the same trick on your picture, Alt+Drag a crop handle clockwise or counterclockwise, as shown in the left image of Figure 7-3. When you click outside the crop outline, PhotoDeluxe rotates and crops your picture.

To make sure that you rotate the image to the right degree, line up one side of the crop outline with an image element that should be perfectly vertical or horizontal. For example, I aligned the bottom edge of my crop outline in Figure 7-3 with the horizon line. Then I enlarged the outline to the size that you see in the figure.

Crop handle   Double-arrow cursor

Figure 7-3:
You can
rotate and
crop in one
step.

Don't apply the rotating crop too many times to the same image. Each time you rotate the image, PhotoDeluxe reorganizes the pixels to come up with the rotated version, and the process can degrade your picture.

Fixing Brightness and Contrast

PhotoDeluxe provides a variety of ways to adjust both the brightness and contrast of your images. Just to be sure that we're on the same page terminology-wise, I want to define exactly what I mean by these terms, as well as some others related to brightness and contrast:

- ✔ *Brightness* refers to the overall lightness or darkness of an image. Photographers use the term *exposure* to mean the same thing, but most image-editing programs, including PhotoDeluxe, use brightness.

  You adjust brightness to correct *overexposed* (too bright) or *underexposed* (too dark) pictures. If you raise the Brightness value in PhotoDeluxe, you make all pixels in the image lighter; lowering the value makes all pixels darker.

- ✔ *Contrast* refers to how much difference exists between the brightness of one pixel and its neighbors. In areas of high contrast, the brightness difference is large; in low-contrast areas, all the pixels have similar brightness values. The best images have a good balance of bright, dark, and medium pixels — or, in photography terms, *highlights, shadows,* and *midtones.*

Practically speaking, you usually adjust the Contrast control to increase contrast rather than to decrease it. Raising the contrast can bring out details in an image because the eye can more easily see where one element begins and another ends. However, if you raise the contrast too much, you actually destroy detail because you lose midtones — all your pixels become either very bright or very dark.

To get a better idea of all this contrast stuff, see Figure 7-4. The upper-left image shows the original, too-dark scan of an old family photo. I increased the brightness of the picture to create the upper-right image. As you can see, PhotoDeluxe lighted all pixels to the same degree. Next, I raised the contrast to create the lower-left image. PhotoDeluxe made the dark pixels darker and the light pixels lighter, improving the image significantly. To create the final image, I applied the Instant Fix filter to the original image. This filter offers a variation on the standard PhotoDeluxe brightness and contrast controls. In the image in the figure, Instant Fix did a fine job, but it's not always the answer, for reasons you can read about later in this chapter.

Now that you understand the basic lingo, the next three sections explain different ways to adjust brightness and contrast in your image.

Applying automatic brightness/contrast filters

You can find three automatic filters for adjusting brightness and contrast on the Effects➪Extensis Instant Fix Tools submenu. These filters come from Extensis, a company that makes many *plug-ins* (add-on tools) for image-editing programs.

When you apply one of these filters, the program analyzes your image and then makes the adjustment it deems appropriate. The image characteristics that get altered depend on the filter you select:

- ✔ **Intellifix Instant Fix** adjusts both brightness and contrast. At the same time, the filter plays with color balance, a topic that you can explore later in this chapter. Don't get this filter confused with the Instant Fix filter on the Quality menu; the two filters do very different things.

- ✔ **Auto Brightness** alters the image brightness only.

- ✔ **Auto Contrast** plays with contrast only.

These filters work okay on some images. On other images, however, they either don't result in any noticeable improvement or, worse, alter the colors in your image in unwanted ways.

Original

Increased Brightness

Increased Contrast

Instant Fix filter

Figure 7-4:
To correct
my original
scan, I first
raised the
brightness
and then
increased
the contrast.
In the
lower-right
image, I
applied just
the Instant
Fix filter to
the original.

Don't ignore these instant correction tools altogether — by all means, give them a whirl. You may find that one of these filters is just the ticket for correcting a recurring problem with images from your digital camera or scanner, for example.

But my guess is that you aren't going to be satisfied with these filters very often. For better results, use the options described in the next two sections.

Leveling the brightness field

The Quality menu contains a filter named Instant Fix. Although its name is similar to the Intellifix Instant Fix filter (which you find on the Effects➪ Extensis Instant Fix Tools submenu), the two filters work very differently.

When you choose Quality➪Instant Fix, PhotoDeluxe ponders your image and then adjusts it so that you have an even distribution of lights, darks, and midtones. The brightest pixels in the image become pure white; the darkest pixels become black; the rest are distributed evenly along the brightness scale from black to white.

If your image already has a good balance of highlights, midtones, and shadows, this filter doesn't change your picture very much. For pictures like the original image in Figure 7-4, on the other hand, Instant Fix can work quite well. Note that the filter created a slightly different — and better — result than I got by adjusting the image brightness and contrast independently. Why? Because the Instant Fix spreads the pixels out over the greatest possible range of brightness values, something that you can't always achieve by raising the brightness and contrast values.

Notice that the brightest pixels are about the same in both lower examples. In the Instant Fix example, however, the darkest areas are blacker than in the other image. You could raise the contrast in the left image to make the dark pixels blacker, but in doing so, you would also make the light pixels lighter. Areas that are light gray would become white, eliminating the subtle shadows in the christening gown.

After my glowing recommendation of this filter, I should warn you that, on some pictures, it may shift your colors in unwanted ways. For an example, take a look at Color Plate 7-1. The left image is my original daisy, which I scanned from a print photograph. The print darkened and faded in the ten years or so since I shot the picture, giving the flower a dim, gloomy face. Nobody likes a depressed daisy, so I put the image through the Instant Fix filter. The result, shown in the middle image of Color Plate 7-1, is a much brighter daisy. But the filter shifted the image colors dramatically, and although the new flower is lovely, it doesn't reflect the original scene accurately. To create the more satisfactory version on the right, I adjusted the brightness, contrast, and color balance independently.

Here's how I would approach the Instant Fix filter if I were you: Apply it before doing any other color corrections. If the result comes close to what you're after, great. You can tweak the brightness and contrast as necessary by using the Brightness/Contrast command and correct any color balance problems using the Color Balance command.

If, however, you don't like what you see, press Ctrl+Z or click the Undo button. Then adjust the brightness and contrast by using the controls outlined in the next section. See "Balancing Out-of-Kilter Colors," later in this chapter, for information on refining the color balance in your pictures.

Tweaking brightness and contrast manually

To adjust brightness or contrast — or both — by a specific degree, choose Quality⇨Brightness/Contrast or press Ctrl+B to display the dialog box shown in Figure 7-5.

Figure 7-5:
You can
make
manual
adjustments
to bright-
ness and
contrast
here.

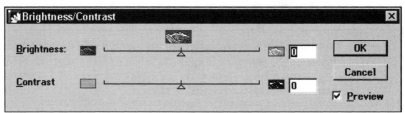

I'm guessing that you can figure out what's what in this dialog box all by your lonesome, but a few hints may help:

✔ Adjust the Brightness and Contrast values by dragging the slider triangles under the slider bars or typing new values in the Brightness or Contrast option boxes. If you want to lower the value, enter a minus sign before the value. Otherwise, PhotoDeluxe assumes that you want to enter a positive value.

✔ You also can raise or lower the value in the active option box (the one that's highlighted) by using the arrow keys on your keyboard. Press the up-arrow to raise the value by 1, press the down-arrow to lower the value by 1. Press Shift+↑ to raise the value by 10; press Shift+↓ to lower the value by 10. (To make an option box active, double-click it.)

✔ Select the Preview check box to preview the results of your changes in the image window.

When preparing images for print, keep in mind that pictures tend to darken when printed. If you're creating images for on-screen display, be aware that images on Macintosh monitors usually appear brighter than images on PC screens. You may want to reduce the brightness beyond what looks good on your PC screen if most of your expected audience will view the image on a Mac.

Making Your Colors More Vivid

If you watch much TV, you're probably aware of a current trend among commercials: the digital manipulation of colors. One popular trick is boosting the *saturation,* or intensity, of some or all colors in a scene. Skies are eye-popping blue, not just the ordinary blue that you see when you wander outside and look up. Grass is astoundingly green, unlike anything you could grow even if you dumped a boatload of chemicals on your lawn.

You can create the same kind of vivid colors in PhotoDeluxe, although I encourage you to keep the saturation in the realm of the believable. Pump up the saturation too much, and your image looks unnatural.

With that caution in mind, if you find yourself with an image that looks a little washed out, like the one in the left half of Color Plate 7-2, the Saturation filter can work wonders. By boosting the saturation, you can bring dull colors back to life, as I did in the right image in the color plate.

To crank up your colors, walk this way:

1. **Choose Quality⇨Hue/Saturation or press Ctrl+U.**

   PhotoDeluxe drags out the Hue/Saturation dialog box, shown in Figure 7-6.

Figure 7-6:
Strengthen colors with the Saturation filter.

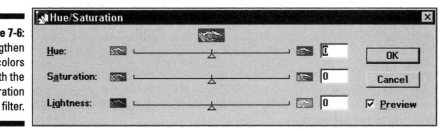

2. **Drag the Saturation slider to the right to increase saturation.**

   Alternatively, double-click the corresponding option box and enter a value from the keyboard. Higher numbers increase the color intensity; lower values fade colors. Keep the Preview check box selected so that you can preview the results of your changes in the image window.

   To reduce the saturation, drag the slider to the left. To lower the saturation from its original level, drag the slider past the midpoint of the slider bar or enter a negative number in the option box. (You must type the minus sign before your value.)

   At any time, you can reset the saturation and start over without closing the dialog box. Press Alt to convert the Cancel button to the Reset button and then click that Reset button. PhotoDeluxe returns your image to the way it was when you opened the dialog box.

3. **Click OK or press Enter to finish the job.**

Don't confuse the Lightness control in the Hue/Saturation dialog box with the Brightness control in the Brightness/Contrast dialog box. Increasing the Lightness value has a negative effect on image contrast, so don't use this control to make your images lighter unless you want to create a faded-out look. Instead, use the Brightness and Contrast filters, discussed in the preceding section.

The Hue control in the Hue/Saturation dialog box shifts your image pixels around the color wheel, an effect discussed in Chapter 10.

Balancing Out-of-Kilter Colors

Old photographs, images from digital cameras, and scanned pictures often have problems with *color balance.* The image in Color Plate 7-3 offers a perfect example. I shot this picture in Lake Tahoe after I made the mistake of buying some outdated film from a souvenir shop. Unfortunately, I didn't notice the expiration date until after I shot the entire roll of film. As a result, my snowman is bending over backward to figure out why pink snow is blanketing the California/Nevada border.

Well, live and learn — and in the meantime, fix problems like this in PhotoDeluxe. You have three color-correction tools at your disposal. Read about your options in the next few sections and then choose the approach that you find easiest.

The Color Balance filter

Using the Color Balance filter, you can adjust the colors in your image while previewing your changes in the image window. You also can make more subtle adjustments than you can with the other two color-correction filters.

To open the Color Balance dialog box, shown in Figure 7-7, choose Quality⇨ Color Balance or press Ctrl+Y. You know, *Y,* as in "Y are my colors so out of whack?"

Figure 7-7:
Correct
color
balance
problems
here.

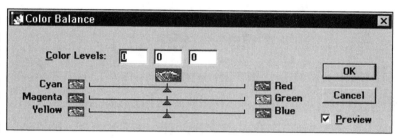

The dialog box controls work as follows:

✔ Drag the slider triangles to shift the color balance away from the color at one end of the slider bar and toward the color at the other end. If you want to remove a red cast from an image, for example, drag the slider toward the Cyan end of the top slider bar. PhotoDeluxe decreases the amount of red in your image and increases the amount of cyan, which lives opposite red on the color wheel. In Color Plate 7-3, I reduced the red, increased the green, and added just a bit more blue to get rid of the pink snowfall effect.

✔ As you drag the sliders, the values in the Color Levels option boxes change to reflect your decisions. The first option box corresponds to the Cyan/Red slider bar, the middle box to the Magenta/Green slider bar, and the third box to the Yellow/Blue slider bar.

✔ If you have a batch of images that all suffer from the same color balance problem, you may want to note the values that you enter in the Color Levels option boxes. That way, you can enter the same values for all the images to achieve a consistent color balance.

✔ Values in the Color Levels boxes can range from +100 to –100. (If you're entering a negative value, you must type in the minus sign before the value, but if you're entering a positive number, you don't need to type a plus sign.) Values higher or lower than +30 or –30 tend to create blotchy, unnatural results, so use moderation.

✔ To reset the color balance to the values that were in place when you opened the dialog box, press the Alt key and click the Reset button, which appears in place of the Cancel button when you press Alt.

The Variations filter

To try another approach to color correction, choose Quality⇨Variations or Effects⇨Adjust⇨Variations. Both commands display the Variations dialog box, shown in Figure 7-8.

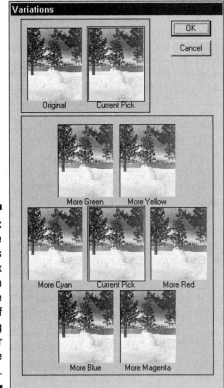

Figure 7-8:
The Variations dialog box offers an alternative method of correcting color balance problems.

The dialog box contains thumbnail views of your image. To raise the amount of one color, click the corresponding thumbnail. For example, to add green to the image, click the More Green thumbnail. To reduce the amount of a color, click the *opposite* thumbnail. If you want your image to contain less green, for example, click the More Magenta thumbnail.

As you click the More thumbnails, the Current Pick thumbnails show you the effect of your changes. The Original thumbnail shows how your image looked when you opened the dialog box. If you decide that you want to return to the original colors and try again, press Alt and then click the Reset button. (The Cancel button becomes the Reset button when you press Alt.) Want to abandon the idea of playing with colors altogether? Click Cancel to close the dialog box without applying your changes.

Unfortunately, you can't preview your changes in the image window as you can when using the Color Balance command; you have to rely on the thumbnails. Also, you're limited to adding and subtracting colors in preset increments. You can't make small adjustments as you can in the Color Balance dialog box. For this reason, I prefer working with Color Balance to using Variations.

Removing a fluorescent glow

Pictures shot in fluorescent lighting, the de facto standard for office lights in large corporations, often exhibit a greenish cast. PhotoDeluxe provides a filter that's geared solely to removing that green glow. Like the other automatic filters, the Fix Fluorescent Light filter works okay on some pictures; on others, it doesn't.

If you want to try the filter, choose Effects⇨Extensis Instant Fix Tools⇨ Fix Fluorescent Light. Did your picture lose its ugly green cast? Great. If not, click Undo and use the Color Balance or Variations command (both explained in the preceding sections) to get the job done.

To be honest, I think that you'll likely try this filter once and then ignore it in favor of the other two color correction tools from that point on. If you shoot lots of pictures in fluorescent lighting, and the filter offers just the right fix, more power to you. You're one click and maybe ten seconds ahead of the rest of us. If you want to save yourself even more time, consider getting a camera filter that's designed to prevent the cast from occurring in the first place.

Changing the Canvas Size

As Chapter 2 explains, every PhotoDeluxe image rests on a transparent *canvas*. On occasion, you may want to change the canvas size. The most common reason for enlarging the canvas is to join two images together.

Suppose that you have two 640-x-480-pixel images. One image shows your kitchen, as it appeared 30 years ago, when you thought you couldn't live without an avocado green stove and dishwasher. Another image shows your kitchen after you came to your senses and replaced those green monstrosities with sleek, almond-colored appliances. Now, for whatever reason, you decide that you want to place the two kitchen images side-by-side in the same image — a before-and-after illustration of your decorating project, perhaps. You open the first image, double the width of the canvas, and copy and paste the second image onto the new canvas area.

To change the Canvas Size, follow these steps:

1. **Choose Size⇨Canvas Size to display the Canvas Size dialog box, shown in Figure 7-9.**

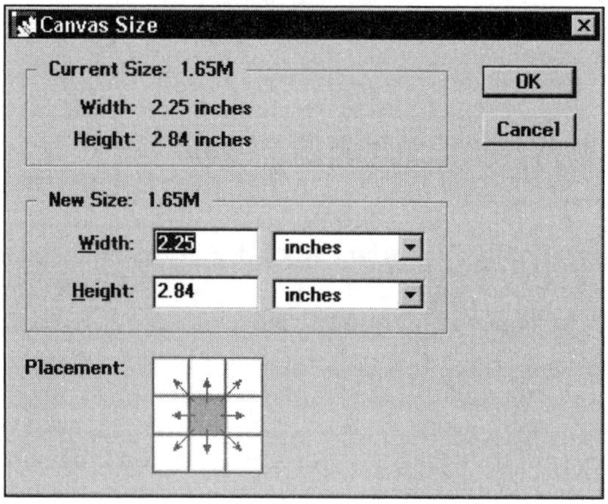

Figure 7-9:
Reduce or enlarge the image canvas by entering new Width and Height values.

2. **Select the unit of measure that you want to use from the drop-down lists next to the Width and Height option boxes.**

   If you choose Percent as your unit of measurement, you can enlarge or reduce the canvas a percentage of the original size as opposed to entering specific dimensions. I don't believe that I've ever used the Percent option, mind you, but I wanted you to know that it was there.

   The Columns option, available for the Width value only, can come in handy when you want to match your canvas size to the width of the columns in a newsletter or some other document. Before you can use this option, you need to travel to the Units dialog box (File⇨Preferences⇨ Units) and enter the column size and *gutter* size (the distance between columns).

3. **Enter the new canvas size in the Width and Height option boxes.**

   If you selected Percent as your unit of measurement, enter the percent by which you want to enlarge or decrease the canvas. A value of 100 percent leaves your canvas unchanged. Anything less than 100 percent reduces the canvas; any value over 100 enlarges the canvas.

If you selected Columns for the Width unit of measurement, change the Width value to however many columns you want the image to consume. For example, if you want an image to stretch across two columns, enter 2 as the Width value. You can read more about working with Columns as your unit of measurement in Chapter 2.

4. **Click a square in the Placement grid to specify where you want your image positioned on the new canvas.**

   If you click the center square, PhotoDeluxe positions your image smack dab in the middle of the new canvas.

5. **Click OK or press Enter to close the dialog box and create your new canvas.**

   If you enter a canvas size that's smaller than your original canvas, PhotoDeluxe warns you that some of your existing image is destined for the cutting room floor. Click Proceed if you want to go ahead.

The Canvas Size command can come in handy when you want to trim just a few pixels off your image — a precision maneuver that can be difficult using the Crop tool. Just choose Pixels as your unit of measurement, enter the new image dimensions, and click OK to trim away the unwanted pixels.

Always trim away any excess canvas when you complete your image. Those extra canvas pixels do nothing but make your file size larger, so get rid of them by using the Crop tool or the Canvas Size command.

Adding a Border

If you have a lot of time on your hands, you may have noticed that all the images in this book are surrounded by a black border. The following steps explain how you can surround your images with a similar border — or one of a different color.

Don't apply your border until after you finish any color corrections, resizing, or sharpening. All these commands can result in a blurry or off-color border because they affect the border pixels just like the other pixels in the image.

1. **Select the area that you want to outline.**

   Press Ctrl+A to select the entire image; use the selection tools to select just a portion of the picture. (See Chapter 9 for help.)

2. **Choose Effects⇨Outline.**

   PhotoDeluxe rushes to the closet and drags out the Outline dialog box, shown in Figure 7-10.

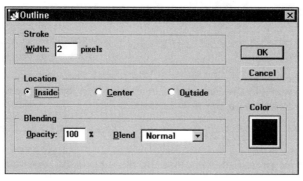

Figure 7-10:
Add a
border to
your image
by using the
Outline
command.

3. **Enter a Width value to set the border thickness.**

   Remember, PhotoDeluxe uses pixels as the unit of measurement here. Because of that, the effective size of the border on your printed images changes if you increase or decrease the image resolution. To find out more about all this pixel and resolution stuff, see Chapter 3.

   By the way, professional image editors refer to borders as *strokes*. That's because what you really do when you apply a border is lay down a stroke of color along the selection outline — or so they say. Anyway, now you know why you see the word Stroke above the Width option in the Outline dialog box.

4. **Choose a Location radio button to set the border placement.**

   To put the border inside the selection outline, choose Inside. If you choose Center, the border rides the selection outline like a cowboy straddling a fence. Outside, surprisingly enough, places the border just outside the selection outline.

   If you selected the whole image before you chose the Outline command, Inside is your only option. The Outside option calls for the stroke to be placed outside the selection outline, and PhotoDeluxe has no empty canvas area on which to paint the stroke — your image covers the entire thing. You can choose the command, but your image is completely unaffected by it. If you want to apply the Outline command with the Outside option, enlarge the canvas size first.

   Similarly, Center asks PhotoDeluxe to place one-half of the stroke outside the selection outline. Unless you first enlarge the canvas, the program doesn't have anywhere to put the half that goes outside the outline, so you wind up with a border that's one-half the size you specified in the Width option box.

5. **Choose an Opacity value and a Blend mode.**

   These options enable you to vary the opacity of the border and alter the way that the border pixels blend with the original image pixels. These options work the same as they do for the painting tools, Selection Fill command, and image layers. For more details, check out Chapter 10. For a solid border, leave the Opacity value at 100 and the Blend mode at Normal.

6. **Click the Color square to change the border color, if necessary.**

   When you click the square, PhotoDeluxe displays the Color Picker dialog box. Chapter 10 explains how to select a color from the dialog box, if you need help.

7. **Click OK or press Enter.**

Adding a Drop Shadow

To wrap up this chapter, I want to fill you in on one more common image-editing task: adding a drop shadow behind an object. Figure 7-11 shows examples of two drop shadows created via the Drop Shadow command.

Figure 7-11: A hard-edged drop shadow (left) and a softer version (right).

Here's the process for creating shadows:

1. **Select the portion of the image to which you want to apply the shadow.**

   Chapter 9 explores selection techniques. To select the entire image, press Ctrl+A.

If you want to apply the shadow to the entire image, be sure to increase the canvas size first by using the Canvas Size command discussed earlier in this chapter. Otherwise, your drop shadow is hidden from view by the image.

2. Choose Effects⇨Drop Shadow.

The Drop Shadow dialog box shown in Figure 7-12 appears.

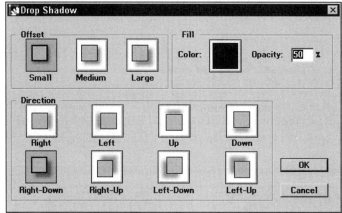

Figure 7-12:
Choose the size and direction of your drop shadow here.

3. Choose your shadow size and direction.

Click an icon in the Offset area to specify the size of your shadow — Small, Medium, or Large. Click a Direction icon to tell PhotoDeluxe how to orient the shadow with respect to the image.

4. Change the shadow color (optional).

The Color icon shows the current shadow color. To change the color, click the icon and select the color from the Color Picker dialog box. (Chapter 10 explains the Color Picker in detail.)

5. Set the shadow opacity.

For a solid shadow like the one in the left half of Figure 7-12, set the opacity value to 100 percent. You can always adjust the opacity later, so don't sweat this decision too much now.

6. Click OK or press Enter.

PhotoDeluxe creates a copy of the original selection and places the copy on a new layer. The program also adds a new layer to hold the shadow.

Chapter 11 explains layers fully, but the important thing to know for this project is that because PhotoDeluxe puts the shadow on its own layer, you can alter the shadow if necessary. You can move the shadow and adjust its opacity and softness, as follows:

- ✔ **Move the shadow:** Grab the Object Selection tool (Select⇨Selection Tools⇨Object), click the shadow, and then drag the shadow into place. You also can press Ctrl+G to select the Move tool and then press the arrow keys on your keyboard to nudge the shadow into place. One press of an arrow key moves the shadow one pixel; press Shift along with an arrow key to move the shadow ten pixels.

- ✔ **Change the shadow opacity:** First, display the Layers palette (choose View⇨Show Layers). Next, double-click the shadow layer in the palette to open the Layer Options dialog box. Enter a new Opacity value and click OK.

- ✔ **Soften the shadow edges:** To create a soft, fuzzy shadow like the one in the right half of Figure 7-11, apply the Soften blur filter to the shadow layer. Click the Shadow layer in the Layers palette and then choose Effects⇨Blur⇨Soften. Raise the Radius value in the Soften dialog box until you achieve an effect you like. Be sure to select the Preview check box so that you can preview the results of your Radius setting in the image window.

After you get the shadow just right, you may want to merge the shadow layer and the other image layers together by choosing the Merge Layers command from the Layers palette menu. If you want to retain the right to shift the shadow layer around in the future, however, leave the layers as they are. To delete the shadow altogether, just drag the shadow layer to the Trash icon in the Layers palette.

Chapter 8
Turning Garbage into Gold

. . . .

In This Chapter

▶ Getting rid of red eyes

▶ Fooling the eye with hocus focus

▶ Mastering the Unsharp Mask filter

▶ Eliminating dust, scratches, speckles, and jaggies

▶ Creating a patch to cover up unwanted image elements and flaws

▶ Hiding moiré patterns and decreasing image noise

. . . .

Most weekend mornings, you can find me plopped in front of the TV, watching gardening shows. I don't do much actual gardening myself, mind you, because it requires a zillion times more energy and time than I have to spare. Still, I enjoy watching TV gardeners spin the fantasy that anybody can turn a scraggly plot of land into a blooming oasis in 30 minutes, give or take a few commercial breaks.

This chapter is the digital imaging equivalent of a do-it-yourself gardening show, with one exception: With the techniques I show you in the next few pages, you really *can* turn a rotten image into an acceptable, if not altogether terrific, picture. You can remove scratches and dust from scanned images, get rid of those glowing red eyes that occur in many snapshots, and even use some digital sleight-of-hand to bring blurry images into sharper focus.

Within the same amount of time that those TV gardeners spend rescuing another homeowner from the depths of landscape despair, you can raise a whole crop of prize-winning pictures. And the best part is, no smelly fertilizer is required.

Removing Red Eye

May as well start with a biggie: how to fix the red-eye phenomenon that occurs when you take pictures with most point-and-shoot cameras. Red eye is caused by the camera's flash reflecting in your subjects' eyes, creating a demonic-looking effect. The top image in Color Plate 8-1 shows an example.

PhotoDeluxe offers a special filter that's supposed to replace the unwanted red pixels in the eye with a more natural color. To give this filter a try, do the following:

1. **Select the red portion of the eye.**

   You can draw around the red-eye zone with the Oval tool or click the red pixels with the Color Wand. Both selection tools are explained in Chapter 9. Zoom in on your image so that you limit your selection to the red-eye portion as much as possible.

2. **Choose Effects⇨PhotoDeluxe⇨Remove Red Eye.**

   PhotoDeluxe replaces the red pixels with darkish, blue-black pixels.

Well, that's the way it's supposed to happen, anyway. If the red-eye area is very large, only a small area of red is replaced, as illustrated by the second image in Color Plate 7-1. You have to keep reapplying the filter over and over and over to replace all the red-eye pixels. Alternatively, if the red-eye area is very small, PhotoDeluxe may recolor more pixels than you want. The result can be an unnatural dark blob rather than a proper pupil.

If your red-eye area happens to be just the right size, the filter may work okay. Go ahead and give the filter a try; if the results are less than satisfactory, press Ctrl+Z or click the Undo button in the image window. Then use the more professional — and more successful — approach described in the following steps:

1. **Open the Layers palette (View⇨Show Layers) and click the layer that contains your eye pixels.**

   You can find more information about layers in Chapter 11.

2. **Select the red-eye areas.**

   Zoom way in on each eye and use the selection tools discussed in Chapter 9 to select the red pixels. The Color Wand works well for this job.

   Be careful not to select the white pixels usually found in the eye area. The white areas give the eye its natural highlights, and you want to preserve them.

3. **Click the New Layer icon in the Layers palette.**

   The icon lives to the left of the Trash icon at the bottom of the Layers palette. When you click the icon, the New Layer dialog box appears.

4. **Accept the default layer settings, and click OK.**

   PhotoDeluxe creates a new layer immediately above the red-eye layer and transfers your selection outline to the new layer.

5. **Choose Effects⇨Selection Fill or press Ctrl+9 to display the Selection Fill dialog box.**

   Chapter 10 explores this dialog box in detail.

6. **Click the Color icon, select the color you want to use as the new eye color from the Color Picker, and click OK.**

   Chapter 10 offers information about the Color Picker, too.

   To get a natural-looking eye, select your color by moving your cursor into the image window while the Color Picker is open and clicking the darkest portion of the eyeball. For example, I clicked the dark ring around the outside of the iris in Color Plate 8-1. Absolute black tends to give the eyes a stark, unnatural look.

7. **Click the Selection icon in the Selection Fill dialog box.**

8. **Set the Opacity value to 100 and the Blend mode to Normal.**

9. **Click OK or press Enter.**

   PhotoDeluxe creates your new eye pixels on the layer you added in Step 3. If you're unhappy with the results, double-click the layer name in the Layers palette to display the Layer Options dialog box. Fool around with the Opacity value and Blend mode until you get a natural-looking eye.

   If you want to try filling the eye with another color, drag the layer to the Trash icon in the Layers palette. Create another new layer and try again. Your eyeball selection remains intact, so you can easily experiment with different colors.

   After you fill the red-eye area, zoom out to view the results of your handiwork; when you're zoomed way in, the eye is likely to look odd no matter how well you've done the job.

10. **Choose Merge Layers from the Layers palette menu to flatten your image.**

    Click the right-pointing arrowhead in the top-right corner of the palette to display the menu. For more info about the Merge Layers command, see Chapter 11.

For a variation on this technique, choose Effects⇨Feather instead of Selection Fill in Step 5. The Feather command, described in Chapter 9, softens the harsh edges of a selection outline so that the color you use to fill the red-eye area fades in gradually from the edge of the selection. In the Feather dialog box, click the Color icon to choose your new eye color, set the Feather value to 1 to 3 pixels, and click the Fill Selection icon. Click OK to wrap things up.

Creating the Illusion of Sharper Focus

Digital images have an annoying tendency to appear a little soft, as if the photographer didn't get the focus quite right when shooting the picture. Aging celebrities appreciate the soft-focus effect because it makes wrinkles and other evidence of long life less noticeable. But unless you're specifically going for that petroleum-jelly-on-the-lens look, you'll want to run most images through one of the PhotoDeluxe sharpening filters. You have several sharpening options, all explained in the upcoming sections.

How sharpening fools the eye

Technically, no image-editing program can restore focus to a soft image. What PhotoDeluxe and other programs with sharpening filters do is create the *illusion* of sharper focus with some clever pixel manipulation.

Sharpening fools the eye by adding small halos along the borders between dark and light areas of the image. (Image-editing gurus refer to those borders as *edges.*) The dark side of the border gets a dark halo; the light side gets a light halo. The effect is increased contrast between the two regions, which makes the eye think that focus has improved. Artists have been using this technique for centuries, as have photographers with advanced darkroom experience.

For a look at this concept in action, see the left column in Figure 8-1 and Color Plate 8-2. The top-left image is the original — four simple bands of color. The lower-left image was sharpened using the Sharpen More filter. Along the border between each band of color, the filter created a dark halo on one side and a light halo on the other.

Managed with a steady hand — or in this case, mouse — sharpening can dramatically improve an image. But too much sharpening can give your image the *jaggies,* making the individual pixels more noticeable. Sharpening also emphasizes any pixelization that may be present in your image. Done to an extreme, sharpening can even create unwanted color shifts.

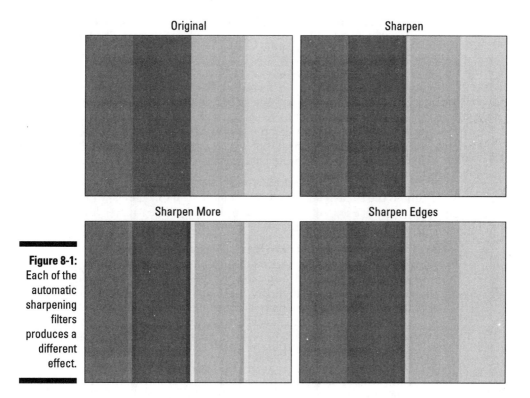

Figure 8-1: Each of the automatic sharpening filters produces a different effect.

Your sharpening options

PhotoDeluxe offers several sharpening filters, all found on the Effects menu. All are one-shot filters, with the exception of the curiously named Unsharp Mask filter. *One-shot* means that PhotoDeluxe applies the sharpening automatically when you choose the filter; you don't have the option of adjusting the amount of sharpening. Unsharp Mask, the best sharpening tool of the bunch, enables you to control different aspects of the sharpening effect.

Each of the sharpening filters works differently, producing a specific effect. The following list explains how each filter approaches sharpening.

✔ **Effects⇨Sharpen⇨Sharpen:** This filter applies subtle light and dark halos along the edges of the image (areas where contrasting pixels meet). For an example of the Sharpen filter in action, look at the top-right image in Figure 8-1 and Color Plate 8-2. This filter, by the way, is also found on the Quality menu. The results are the same no matter which menu you use to access the filter.

✔ **Effects➪Sharpen➪Sharpen More:** As its name implies, this filter adds halos that are stronger than those applied by Sharpen. The lower-left example in Figure 8-1 and Color Plate 8-2 provide an illustration.

✔ **Effects➪Sharpen➪Sharpen Edges:** If you select this filter, PhotoDeluxe applies the same level of sharpening as when you use Sharpen, but only along borders where there is a significant change in contrast. For example, see the lower-right image in Figure 8-1 and Color Plate 8-2. You see the sharpening halos along the border between the two middle bands, where the contrast is high, but not along the border between the outside bands and their interior neighbors, where contrast is low.

✔ **Effects➪Extensis Instant Fix Tools➪Auto Sharpen:** This filter produces about the same results as Sharpen More. In fact, I dare say that you won't notice any difference — but please feel free to try. I don't think you've had enough to do lately, anyway.

✔ **Effects➪Sharpen➪Unsharp Mask:** The most sophisticated of the sharpening filters, Unsharp Mask enables you to control how and where you want your halos added. You can specify how intense you want PhotoDeluxe to make the halos, how big to make them, and how different two pixels must be before sharpening is applied. This filter is discussed in detail in the next section, but for now take a peek at Color Plate 8-3, where you can see some of the sharpening variations that are possible with Unsharp Mask.

As with most things in life, the option that requires the most work, Unsharp Mask, typically delivers the best results. Sharpen usually doesn't go far enough, Sharpen More and Auto Sharpen tend to go too far, and Sharpen Edges often creates unnatural shifts between sharpened areas and unsharpened areas.

To see how each of the sharpening filters works on a real-life image, set your sights on Figure 8-2 and Color Plate 8-4. The original feather image, shown in the center of the figure, was perfectly focused in its original print state but came out of my scanner decidedly soft.

Passing the image through the Sharpen filter helped a little, but not enough (top-left image). Sharpen More (top right) made things a little too crisp — the feather looks almost brittle in some areas. Sharpen Edges (lower left) did a good job in high-contrast areas, but the interior of the feather looks too soft because the filter didn't find any significant edges to sharpen.

Using the Unsharp Mask filter, I was able to adjust the sharpening so that both background and feather appear in good focus while retaining the, uh, featheriness of the feather. The inset areas in the upper-left corner of each example give you a closer look at the differences in each sharpening filter's effect. Head for the next section to find out how to successfully sharpen your own images by playing with the Unsharp Mask controls.

Figure 8-2:
I applied four sharpening filters to my original image (center). Sharpen (top left), Sharpen More (top right), and Sharpen Edges (lower left) either sharpened too little or too much. With Unsharp Mask, I created a custom effect to achieve just the right amount of sharpening (lower right).

Unsharp Mask: The best solution

In case you're wondering where this filter got its odd name, *unsharp masking* is a technique used in traditional photography to create the illusion of sharper focus. At any rate, choosing Effects⇨Sharpen⇨Unsharp Mask brings to life the Unsharp Mask dialog box, shown in Figure 8-3.

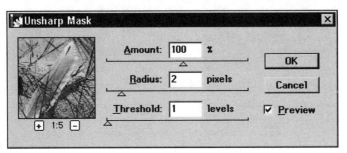

Figure 8-3: For expert sharpening, open the Unsharp Mask dialog box.

The Amount, Radius, and Threshold settings enable you to tell PhotoDeluxe exactly how you want your image to be sharpened. The controls work as follows:

✔ **Amount determines the intensity of the sharpening halos**. (Read "How sharpening fools the eye," earlier in this section, if you don't know what I'm talking about.) A higher value creates stronger halos, as illustrated by Color Plate 8-2 and Figure 8-4. The left column shows the results of using an Amount value of 100 percent, and the right column shows the effect of doubling the Amount value to 200 percent.

For best results, apply the filter with a lower value — say, in the 50 to 100 percent range. If the sharpening effect is too minimal, apply the filter a second time. You usually get more natural-looking results by applying the filter several times at low Amount values than you do applying it once with a large Amount value.

✔ **Radius determines the range of pixels affected by the sharpening.** If you use a low Radius value, the haloing is concentrated in a narrow region, as in the top row of Color Plate 8-3 and Figure 8-4, where I set the Radius value to 1. If you use a high Radius value, the haloing is distributed over a broader area and fades out gradually, as illustrated in the bottom row of Color Plate 8-3 and Figure 8-4. For these two examples, I set the Radius value to 2.

Usually, a setting of 0.5 to 1 is appropriate for on-screen images. Print images do better with slightly higher Radius values — say, 1 to 2. Anything above 2 tends to create artificial-looking results and can even have the effect of softening your edges, which is the exact opposite of what you're trying to accomplish.

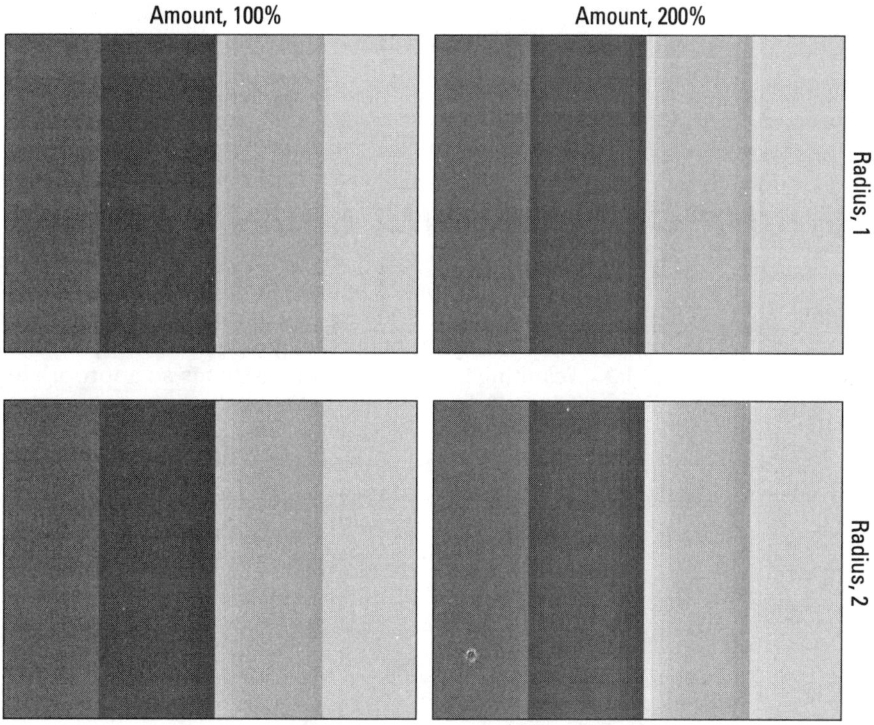

Amount, 100% Amount, 200%

Radius, 1

Radius, 2

Figure 8-4:
The top row shows the result of sharpening with a Radius value of 1, Threshold value of 0, and two different Amount values. In the bottom row, the Radius value is 2.

Keep in mind, too, that you may need to adjust the Radius value as well as other sharpening values to accommodate different printers. An image output on a home inkjet printer, for example, usually requires a bit more sharpening than those output on a high-resolution, commercial printer.

✔ **Threshold controls the level of contrast that must occur before sharpening is applied.** If you leave the Threshold value set at 0, the slightest difference in contrast results in sharpening. If you raise the value, PhotoDeluxe is more selective; it sharpens the edges only in areas of high contrast, similar to what happens when you use the Sharpen Edges command.

Usually, you can leave the Threshold value at 0. If your image contains areas that are soft looking in real life — such as a baby's skin — you may get better results using a slightly higher Threshold value.

Also bear in mind that sharpening tends to exaggerate the jagged edges or speckles that sometimes show up in images that have been overly compressed or were captured in insufficient lighting. Raising the Threshold value to 1 or 2 can sometimes enable you to sharpen the image without making those defects more noticeable.

Every image requires different Unsharp Mask settings, so experiment to find the right Amount, Radius, and Threshold values for your image. For the record, I used an Amount value of 100, a Radius value of 2, and a Threshold value of 1 to create the bottom-right example in Figure 8-2 and Color Plate 8-4.

Wiping Off Dust and Other Crud

If you work with scanned images much, you're probably familiar with the kind of problems illustrated in Figure 8-5. During the scanning process, a bit of dust or some other tiny bit of flotsam got between the photograph and the scanner glass, resulting in the dark smudge that is so appropriately labeled *crud* in Figure 8-5. As if that weren't bad enough, the original print (and negative) came back from the processing lab with a big scratch running all the way from one side of the picture to the other — a defect that the scanner faithfully reproduced. Poor Beastie — such a noble creature deserves better.

Faithful family friend   Scratch   Crud

Figure 8-5: This poor doggie suffers from embarrassing image defects.

PhotoDeluxe offers a Dust & Scratches filter that is designed to remove scratches, dust bunnies, and other impurities from your image. But the filter can sometimes do more harm than good, and you often get better results by cleaning up your images manually, using the Clone tool. The next two sections describe both options.

Applying the Dust & Scratches filter

The Dust & Scratches filter works by searching for areas of high contrast and then blurring the pixels in the immediate vicinity. For example, if you have a white scratch across black fur, as in Figure 8-5, PhotoDeluxe "sees" those white pixels as a defect and blurs the area.

All well and good — except that PhotoDeluxe isn't really capable of determining which contrasting pixels represent image defects and which represent image detail. As you can see in Figure 8-6, the filter did a good job of making the scratch and scanner crud less noticeable. But in the process, it destroyed the focus of the image. Everywhere a light pixel met up with a dark pixel — which happens a lot in this picture — PhotoDeluxe applied the blurring effect, resulting in an unacceptably soft image.

Figure 8-6: Applying the Dust & Scratches filter to the entire image blurs my furry friend too much.

Applying Dust & Scratches to your entire image, as I did in Figure 8-6, rarely yields good results. By applying the filter to small, selected areas, however, you sometimes can remove defects without compromising your image. Follow these steps:

1. **Select the defect.**

   Using the tools discussed in Chapter 9, select the defect and a few surrounding pixels. The smaller the selection, the better.

2. Choose Quality⇨Remove Dust/Scratches.

Alternatively, choose Effects⇨Noise⇨Dust/Scratches; this filter appears both on the Effects menu and Quality menu. However you select the filter, the dialog box shown in Figure 8-7 appears.

Figure 8-7:
Adjust the blurring applied by the Dust & Scratches filter here.

3. Set the Threshold value to 0.

The Threshold value determines how different two pixels must be before PhotoDeluxe blurs them. If you drag the Threshold slider all the way to the left or enter 0 in the option box, all pixels inside the selection are fair game. You refine the Threshold value later; for now, set it at 0.

4. Set the Radius value.

The Radius value tells PhotoDeluxe how big an area to scan when it searches for differing pixels. The smaller the Radius value, the less damage to your image. Use the smallest possible Radius value that hides the defects.

Be sure to select the Preview check box so that you can preview the results of the filter in the image window as well as in the preview area inside the dialog box. Remember, you can drag inside the preview area to see a hidden portion of the image. Click the plus and minus buttons beneath the preview area to zoom in and out on your image.

5. Raise the Threshold level.

Now you can play with that Threshold level that you initially set to 0. Raise the value as much as you can without bringing the defect back into view.

6. Click OK.

Keep repeating these steps until you've cleared your image of all unwanted dirt, dust, and other specks. Using the filter this way takes a bit more time but delivers much better results than trying to clean up your entire image with one pass of the filter.

Each time you select and blur a defect, examine the image closely. If you wind up with an area that's noticeably blurry compared with the rest of the image, press Ctrl+Z to undo your work. Set aside the Dust & Scratches filter and try eradicating the flaw by using the technique discussed in the next section.

Cloning good pixels over bad

One of the more useful weapons in the PhotoDeluxe bag of tricks is the Clone tool, which enables you to copy "good" pixels and paint them over image defects. To create Figure 8-8 from the original, scratch-and-dent version in Figure 8-5, I cloned pixels from just below the scratch and used the clones to cover the scratch, removing the defect without the blurring that accompanies the Dust & Scratches filter. I used the same method to cover up the speck of scanner crud in the upper-right corner of the picture. (Any other specks you may see in the picture occurred during the printing process, when bits of flotsam and jetsam sometimes settle on the paper.)

Figure 8-8: Cloning good pixels over defective pixels eliminates defects without ruining focus.

I rely on the Clone tool almost every day to cover up blemishes in images, whether I'm trying to rid a picture of tiny dust flecks or some larger defect, like an ex-boyfriend. Unfortunately, the Clone tool is also one of the more difficult tools for new users to grasp, in part because no real-life equivalent exists. The Brush tool is easy — you drag with it to paint a stroke of color, just like you do with a real paintbrush. But the Clone tool? Only those wacky scientists in that sheep-growing lab seem to have one, and I doubt that their Clone tool works much like the one in PhotoDeluxe.

The best way to figure out the Clone tool is to try it out for yourself. Cloning is one of those things that doesn't make much sense until you actually see it on-screen. So open an image, find a flaw, and take the following steps:

1. **Zoom in on the defect.**

   You need a close-up view for successful cloning. Figure 8-9 shows a magnified view of the scratch area from Figure 8-5. You're looking at the forehead area between Beastie's eyes. The row of light gray pixels is the scratch.

Clone tool cursor   Clone tool cursor

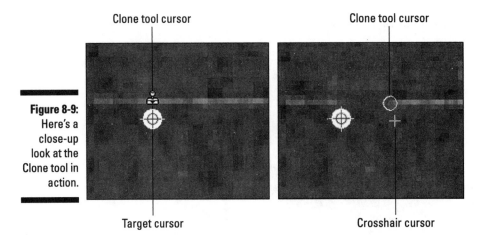

Figure 8-9: Here's a close-up look at the Clone tool in action.

Target cursor   Crosshair cursor

2. **Open the Layers palette (View⇨Show Layers) and click the layer that contains the pixels you want to clone.**

   See Chapter 11 for the lowdown on layers.

3. **Choose Tools⇨Clone.**

   PhotoDeluxe opens the Clone palette and displays two cursors in the image window, as shown in Figure 8-9. One cursor is the mouse cursor; you have to move your mouse pointer into the image window to see that cursor.

4. **Position the target cursor over the good pixels that you want to clone.**

   Drag the target cursor (labeled in Figure 8-9) so that it's directly over the pixels that you want to use to cover up the flaw. In Figure 8-9, I positioned the target cursor just below the scratch.

5. **In the Layers palette, click the name of the layer that contains the pixels that you want to cover up.**

   You can skip this step if you have only one image layer plus the Text layer.

   For safety's sake, you may want to duplicate the layer so that you can clone on a copy of the layer instead of the original. To copy the layer, just drag it to the New Layer icon in the bottom-left corner of the Layers palette. If you mess up, you can just delete the duplicate layer and start over.

6. **Position the Clone tool cursor over the first bad pixel(s) that you want to cover up.**

   I positioned the Clone tool cursor (also labeled in the figure) on the scratch, just above the target cursor in Figure 8-9.

   By default, the Clone tool cursor looks like a rubber stamp, as in the left image in Figure 8-9. This cursor is a carryover from Photoshop, where the Clone tool is called the Rubber Stamp tool. Whether the rubber stamp icon was a conscious decision or an oversight by the folks at Adobe, I don't know — but I do know that the rubber stamp cursor gets in the way when you're trying to make precise edits.

   To get a clearer view of what you're doing, press Ctrl+K or choose File➪Preferences➪Cursors to open the Cursors dialog box. Select Brush Size in the Painting Options portion of the dialog box and then click OK. Now the Clone tool cursor is a circle that reflects the size of the brush tip you choose, as shown in the right half of Figure 8-9. (You choose the brush tip in the next step.)

7. **Choose a brush size and softness in the Clone palette, shown in Figure 8-10.**

   The Clone palette, like the Brushes palette described in Chapter 10, contains icons representing different brush tips for the Clone tool. You can choose a soft, fuzzy brush or a hard-edged one, and you can vary the size of your brush as well. If you choose a big, soft brush, you clone in big, fuzzy strokes, as if you were painting with a large paintbrush. If you choose a small, hard-edged brush, you clone in small, sharp strokes, as if you were drawing with a hard pencil.

Figure 8-10:
Click a
brush icon
to set the
size and
softness of
the Clone
tool.

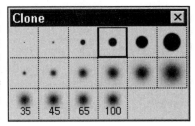

Click the icon for the size and shape of brush that you want to use. The top six brushes are hard-edged; the rest are fuzzy. The bottom four icons give you a 35-, 45-, 65-, or 100-pixel brush size. (The icons would be too big for the palette if they represented the actual brush size.)

In Figure 8-9, I chose a hard brush that was the size of the scratch I wanted to cover up. If you're trying to cover up a larger defect, however, you get better results if you keep the brush size small and clone in small increments instead of trying to clone over the entire problem area with one or two strokes of the Clone tool.

8. **Click or drag to clone.**

If you click, the pixels underneath the target cursor are cloned onto the pixels underneath the Clone tool cursor. You can click at several different spots on the defect to clone the same target pixels over and over again.

Alternatively, you can drag the Clone tool cursor to clone pixels along the length and direction of your drag. (Stay with me here.) As soon as you begin dragging, a crosshair cursor emerges from the target cursor, as shown in the right side of Figure 8-9. That crosshair cursor shows you what pixels are being cloned onto the pixels underneath the Clone tool cursor. For example, in the right half of Figure 8-9, I dragged the Clone tool cursor from its original position, just above the target cursor, to the right along the scratch pixels. As I dragged, the Clone tool picked up the pixels underneath the crosshair cursor and painted them onto the scratch.

When you release the mouse button, the crosshair cursor scurries back to the target cursor. If you click or drag, you begin cloning from the original target area again. You can reposition the target cursor before you do more cloning if you like.

Successful cloning takes some practice, but I promise that after you become familiar with this tool, you'll never want to be without it. The following tips provide some additional hints for getting the most from your cloning experiments:

✔ You can vary the opacity of the pixels you paint with the Clone tool by pressing number keys. Before you begin cloning, press 0 to make your cloned pixels fully opaque, so that they cover up the underlying pixels completely. Press any number between 1 and 9 to make the pixels translucent, so that some of the underlying pixels show through the cloned pixels. Lower numbers make the cloned pixels more transparent. Using a medium transparency sometimes helps cloned pixels blend with original pixels more naturally.

PhotoDeluxe doesn't have a palette or menu item that tells you what opacity value is in force, and the opacity value stays in effect until you change it. If the Clone tool doesn't seem to work, you may have lowered the opacity in a previous editing job. Press 0 to return the tool to full opacity.

✔ Try to avoid cloning repeatedly from the same source *(target)* pixels. You wind up with too many similar pixels, creating an unnatural, obvious edit. Instead, clone several times from different target areas. If the scratch in Figure 8-9 were a little larger, for example, I would have cloned once from the bottom of the scratch and once from the top.

✔ You can clone pixels from one image to another. Open both image windows side by side, as discussed in Chapter 1, and click the window of the image that contains the pixels that you want to clone. Choose the Clone tool and position the target cursor. Finally, move your cursor into the other window and click or drag to begin cloning.

Creating a Digital Patch

The Clone tool, discussed in the preceding section, works well for hiding small image elements or defects. For larger problems, you may want to create a patch to cover up the offending pixels. For example, consider Figure 8-11. I like the way this statue is set in silhouette against a fair sky. I'd like it a lot more without that ugly construction tower — or whatever it is — and stray tree branches in the bottom-right corner of the image.

You could clone pixels from the surrounding sky over the offending elements, but that technique would require quite a bit of clicking and dragging with the Clone tool. A more efficient fix is to select a large area of sky, copy the selection, and use the copy as a patch to hide the crane and branches.

There's one fly in the ointment: All the selection tools in Version 4, as in Versions 2 and 3, draw hard-edged selections, which usually results in an obvious patch, like the one in the left image in Figure 8-12. The SmartSelect tool in the Business Edition offers an option that enables you to create soft-edged (feathered) selections, which create less noticeable patches. For some reason, the Version 4 SmartSelect tool lacks the option.

Figure 8-11:
That ugly
metal
construction
thing has to
go.

Figure 8-12:
A standard
patch is
noticeable
(left), but a
feathered
patch
blends in
seamlessly
with the
surrounding
area (right).

You still can create a seamless patch, but you have to do a little fancy foot-work. To make your patch blend in with the surrounding area like the right example in Figure 8-12, take these steps:

1. **Choose View⇨Show Layers and View⇨Show Selections.**

   PhotoDeluxe displays the Layers and Selections palettes, which are essential to this job.

   You can find out all about the Layers palette in Chapter 11. Chapter 9 covers the Selections palette and all the selection tools.

2. **In the Layers palette, click the layer that contains the pixels that you want to use as your patch.**

3. **Duplicate the layer by dragging it to the New Layer icon.**

   The New Layer icon is that double-box thingy in the bottom-left corner of the palette. PhotoDeluxe adds your duplicate layer directly above the original. The duplicate layer is active, which means that your edits affect that layer only.

4. **Select the pixels that you want to use as a patch.**

   Use the selection tools discussed in Chapter 9 to enclose the patch pixels in a selection outline. Try to grab pixels that are as close as possible in color and brightness to those that now surround the area you want to cover. To create the patch for Figure 8-11, for example, I used the Oval tool to select a patch of sky just to the left of the tower. Select an area that's a little larger than the object you want to hide; the next step reduces the size of the patch slightly.

   Creating a patch that matches the shape of an irregular object can be difficult. To simplify things, draw the selection outline around the object and then move the outline onto the area that you plan to use as your patch. You move the outline by putting your cursor inside the outline and Ctrl+Alt+Dragging it into place. Again, you need to draw your initial selection outline a little beyond the boundaries of the object.

   When patching an area like that in Figure 8-11, you get more natural results if you create several small patches, taken from different areas surrounding the unwanted pixels, rather than creating one large patch. In my case, I covered the tower and tree branches with four or five patches created from different areas of sky.

5. **Choose Effects⇨Feather to display the Feather dialog box.**

   You see the dialog box in Figure 8-13. By using this command, you can manipulates the pixels so that the selected area fades gradually from full opacity to full transparency around the edges. The effect, known as *feathering,* causes the selection to blend in naturally with the surrounding pixels.

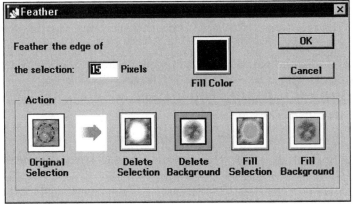

Figure 8-13:
The Feather
command is
key to
creating a
natural-
looking
patch.

6. **Enter a feather value in the option box in the top-left corner of the dialog box.**

   Higher values make your selection edges fuzzier. I used a value of 15 to create my patch. If your patch is very small, you may need a smaller feather value. (You can find out more about other Feather command uses in Chapter 9, by the way.)

7. **Click the Delete Background icon and click OK.**

   Your duplicate layer now contains a nicely feathered patch. To see the patch without the underlying background, Alt+Click the Eyeball icon to the left of the layer name in the Layers palette. Alt+Click again to make all your image layers visible again.

8. **Click the None icon in the Selections palette or press Ctrl+D to get rid of the selection outline.**

   This step is critical to the patching process. If you don't lose the selection outline, you wind up with a hard-edged patch after you take the next steps.

9. **Select the Move tool.**

   Click the Move icon in the Selections palette or press Ctrl+G.

10. **Drag or nudge the patch into place.**

    To nudge the patch in small increments, press the arrow keys on your keyboard. One press of an arrow key moves the patch one pixel; Shift+Arrow moves the patch ten pixels.

    If your patch isn't quite large enough to cover the image blemish, drag the patch layer to the New Layer icon to create a second patch on another layer. Use the second patch to hide more of the unwanted element.

11. To merge all layers together, choose Merge Layers from the Layers palette menu.

Click the right-pointing triangle in the top-right corner of the palette to display the menu.

Choosing this command glues all image layers together, which means that you can no longer adjust the patch. You may want to print your image to get a good look at your patching job before merging layers. If you don't like results, drag the patch layer or layers to the Trash icon in the Layers palette and start over.

The steps for creating a patch seem long and involved, but after you work through them a few times, you'll see how easy it is to erase reality from your images.

Fading Away Noise, Jaggies, and Moiré Patterns

When digital imaging gurus turn up their noses at an image, they often diss the photo because it suffers from one of three problems: noise, jaggies, or moiré patterns. For those of you who don't have your official digital-imaging decoder rings handy, the three terms mean the following:

- ✔ *Noise* refers to speckles that give the image a grainy look. Noise often occurs in images that were shot in low light.

- ✔ *Jaggies* refers to a blocky, pixelated effect caused by oversharpening, applying too much JPEG compression, or overenlarging an image.

- ✔ *Moiré* patterns occur when you scan pictures in magazines, books, and newspapers. These pictures are printed using a pattern of small dots of ink known as *halftone cells.* Although you can't see the halftone cells in the original, scanners pick up the dots in the pattern unevenly, resulting in visible rows of dots running through your picture. (You pronounce the problem *mor-ay,* like the eel, in case you were wondering.)

The following sections offer some tips for fixing all three unsightly blemishes.

Quieting noise

If your image suffers from *noise* — speckles that give the image a grainy look — you can sometimes correct the problem by applying one of the following filters:

✔ **Despeckle:** This filter searches for *edges* (areas of high contrast) in the image. It then applies a slight blur to everything *but* the edge areas to make the noise less pronounced.

Unfortunately, Despeckle is a *one-shot filter* — you don't have any control over how much blurring is applied. Sometimes the filter works great, but other times it blurs the image too much. To give Despeckle a try, choose Effects⇨Noise⇨Despeckle.

✔ **Reduce Graininess:** With this filter, you can control the amount of blurring. Choose Effects⇨Noise⇨Reduce Graininess to display the Reduce Graininess dialog box. Drag the Smoothness slider triangle to raise or lower the intensity of the blur. Use the lowest possible Smoothness value that rids your image of noise. Unfortunately, you can't preview the effects of this filter in the image window; you have to rely on the preview inside the dialog box. (Tip: Click the Example button if you're not quite sure what noise looks like.)

For best results with either of these filters, select the noisy areas of the image and apply the filter only to the selection. If you have to apply the filter to the whole image — that is, if the entire image is noisy — you can sometimes firm up the focus after you blur by applying the Unsharp Mask filter. Raise the Threshold level as necessary to prevent the noise from reappearing.

Softening jaggies

PhotoDeluxe also provides a filter designed to correct *pixelization,* more commonly known as *jaggies.* Choose Effects⇨Noise⇨JPEG Clean Up to open the JPEG Clean Up dialog box and experiment with the filter. The filter got its name because pixelization often results from applying too much JPEG compression to an image. See Chapter 4 to find out more about JPEG and compression; click the Example button in the dialog box to get a good look at pixelization.

Like the Despeckle and Reduce Graininess filters, this filter works by applying a subtle blur to the image. In the dialog box, raise the Smoothness value to intensify the blurring effect. You can preview the effects of the filter in the dialog box, but not in the image window.

Muting moiré

When you scan pictures from newspapers, magazines, and other commercially printed publications, you can wind up with *moiré patterns* — rows of tiny dots running through your picture. The problem occurs because of the way the scanner sees and reproduces the halftone dots in the original image. You can see what I mean by looking at Figure 8-14.

Figure 8-14:
Moiré
patterns
can appear
when you
scan
magazine or
newspaper
pictures.

To make moiré patterns disappear — or, to try, anyway — choose
Effects⇨Noise⇨Remove Moire Pattern. You see the dialog box shown in
Figure 8-15.

Figure 8-15:
Align the
blinking line
with the
lines in the
moiré
pattern.

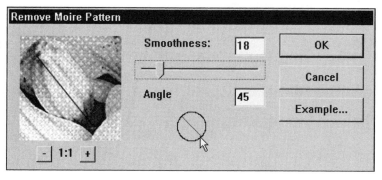

Try to align the blinking line in the image preview portion of the dialog box as
closely as possible with the lines in the moiré pattern. Drag around the
perimeter of the Angle circle, as shown in the figure, or enter a value in the
Angle option box to change the angle of the blinking line. Because adjusting
the Angle value precisely is difficult using the drag method, you may want to
drag to get close to the value you want and then use the type-in-the-number
approach to fine-tune the value.

As with the other filters discussed in this section, this filter does its magic by
blurring the image. The Smoothness value determines how much blurring
PhotoDeluxe applies. Use the lowest possible value that makes the moiré pattern disappear. You can preview the filter effects in the dialog box only.

Some scanners provide a moiré-removal filter inside their scanning software. If yours does, try using that feature to reduce or eliminate the moiré pattern in the scanning stage, rather than trying to do after-the-fact correction in PhotoDeluxe.

Chapter 9

Getting Selective

● ●

In This Chapter

▶ Telling PhotoDeluxe what part of the picture you want to edit

▶ Uncovering the Selections palette

▶ Drawing round, oval, and irregular selections

▶ Selecting by color

▶ Tracing the edges of an object with the SmartSelect tool

▶ Refining a selection outline

▶ Moving, copying, and rotating selected pixels

▶ Feathering selections before filling or deleting

● ●

*B*efore you paint a room, you stick masking tape over baseboards, window frames, and other areas that you don't want to paint. If you're smart, you also put down a drop cloth so that if you dribble paint from your brush — or kick an entire paint can over — your floor doesn't suffer the consequences.

In PhotoDeluxe, *selection tools* serve as the digital equivalent of masking tape and drop cloths. Using the selection tools, you can protect portions of your image from being altered when you apply filters, special effects, and other edits. For example, if you want to sharpen your picture's main subject but leave the background blurry, select the subject before applying a sharpening filter. Any pixels not selected are unaffected by your edit.

Selecting is one of the more important aspects of image editing, which is why I devote an entire chapter to the subject. You find out how to maneuver the PhotoDeluxe selection tools, select intricate image elements easily, and refine a selection outline after you initially create it. In addition, this chapter explains how to move, copy, and rotate selected elements. As if all that weren't tantalizing enough, you also find out how to create a special type of selection that enables you to fade your image into the background.

You say "marquee," I say "selection outline"

When you select a portion of your picture, PhotoDeluxe surrounds the selected pixels with either a blinking, dashed line or a solid line, depending on what selection tool you use. Common folk refer to these selection boundary-markers as *selection outlines.* If you linger where image-editing enthusiasts gather, though, you may hear the following terms when the discussion turns to selections. Just so you can decode the conversation, here's a guide to the alternative lingo:

✔ People with a graphic design or printing background often refer to the act of selecting pixels as *masking.* Deselected areas are said to be *masked.*

✔ People who like to use fancy words for common things call the selection outline a *marquee.* To this audience, those blinking, dashed lines look like the lights in a theatre marquee; hence the name. Some folks are so enamored with the word *marquee* that they use it both as a noun, referring to the selection outline, and as a verb, referring to the act of creating a selection outline. For

example, whereas you and I might say, "Select the purple cow," they would say, "Marquee the violet bovine creature." I don't use *marquee* as a verb because I fear that if I do, my grade-school teachers will hunt me down and make me write "I shall not abuse the English language" 100 times on the blackboard.

✔ Another image-editing camp prefers to use the term *marching ants* because they think that the selection outline looks more like ants on parade than marquee lights. Even if I squint real hard, I don't see this association, but you may have a more active imagination than I do.

For the record, I stick with *selection outline* in this book, even though doing so puts my membership in the Society for Highfalutin' Computer Language at risk. I call the blinking outline a *standard selection outline* and the solid outline a — uh, *solid outline.* Sorry to be so dull. Hopefully, the clarity afforded by this simplistic terminology makes up for the lack of creative nomenclature.

Knowing When to Select

Pick up the selection tools if you want to do any of the following:

✔ **Limit the effects of your edits to certain areas of the image.** Any paint tools, special effects, or image-correction commands affect only selected pixels. You can brighten one portion of your image while leaving the rest alone, for example. You can even print just the selected area if you want.

✔ **Apply selection-oriented commands.** PhotoDeluxe requires that you select a portion of your picture before you use certain commands, such as the Drop Shadow command. You also must create a selection to move, copy, paste, or delete a portion of your picture.

If a command appears *grayed out* — unavailable — in a menu, you probably need to create a selection outline before you go any further. The File⇨Revert to Last Saved command is an exception; this command remains unavailable until you save your picture in the PhotoDeluxe file format.

✔ **Give yourself some extra editing protection.** Selections are your best defense against a slip of the mouse when you use the Brush, Line, Smudge, Clone, and Eraser tools. Suppose that you want to use the Brush tool to paint a man's tie. If you have a steady hand, you may be able to apply paint precisely to the tie pixels without touching any of the surrounding shirt pixels. Most people, however, don't have that kind of hand-to-eye coordination, especially when a mouse is involved. By selecting the tie, you make sure that any errant swipes of the Brush tool don't paint pixels that you didn't intend to change.

In other words, selections are an everyday part of editing life. Thankfully, most selection jobs are fairly easy, and PhotoDeluxe gives you some sophisticated tools for tackling the more complex selection challenges you may face.

Exploring the Selections Palette

You can access the PhotoDeluxe selection tools by choosing them from the Select menu. But the Selections palette, shown in Figure 9-1, offers quicker access to the selection tools and also provides some selection features not available on the Select menu.

Figure 9-1:
Keep the
Selections
palette
handy.

To display this tiny but power-packed palette, choose View⇨Show Selections. If necessary, you can relocate the palette by dragging its *title bar* (the area that contains the name of the palette). To put the Selections palette away, click the Close button (the X on the title bar) or choose View⇨Hide Selections.

Upcoming sections provide details about all the palette options, but here's a quick guide:

- ✔ Select the tool that you want to use from the drop-down list at the top of the palette.

- ✔ The icons beneath the drop-down list enable you to start a new selection outline or refine an existing outline. The icons disappear when you work with the Object Selection tool because they're not relevant to that tool.

- ✔ By clicking the buttons at the bottom of the palette, you can select all pixels on the current image layer, wipe out any existing selection outlines, or reverse the selection outline so that you select the opposite part of the picture.

Reviewing Your Tool Choices

You can choose from nine selection tools, each of which approaches the pixel-picking process from a different angle:

- ✔ **Rectangle, Oval, Circle, and Square:** These tools draw — drum roll, please — rectangular, oval, circular, or perfectly square selection outlines. Forgive me for insulting your intelligence.

- ✔ **Color Wand:** Use the Color Wand to select an area that's dissimilar in color from its surroundings — for example, a red rose set against a blue background.

- ✔ **Polygon and Trace:** With these tools, you can draw freehand selection outlines. I don't find these tools terribly easy to use for drawing precise selection outlines, but you may have better control of your mouse than I do.

- ✔ **SmartSelect:** A blend of the freehand selection tools and the Color Wand, the SmartSelect automatically places a selection outline along the border between contrasting pixels as you drag your mouse.

- ✔ **Object Selection:** This tool selects all pixels on the current image layer and then displays handles that you can use to rotate and resize the selected area. You also use this tool to select individual text blocks on the Text layer.

You can read more about the Object Selection tool in the next section; see the section that follows ("Selecting Parts of a Layer") to find out how to use the other selection tools.

Selecting an Entire Layer

As you know if you've flipped through Chapter 11, PhotoDeluxe offers a feature called *layers*. If you came to this chapter first, here's a bare-bones explanation: Imagine a stack of clear sheets of acetate, and you get the basic idea behind layers. You put different picture elements on different layers so that you can edit each element independently from the rest of the picture.

All PhotoDeluxe images start life with two layers. One layer, the Text layer, holds text that you create with the Text tool; the other layer, named Layer 0, contains everything else. To keep things simple, I use the term *image layer* to mean any layer but the Text layer. You can create as many additional image layers as you want, but you can't create additional Text layers.

On the Text layer, you can select only one text item at a time. On an image layer, you can select the whole kit and caboodle.

Use any of these techniques to select all pixels on a layer:

- ✔ Click the All button in the Selections palette.
- ✔ Press Ctrl+A.
- ✔ Choose Select⇨All.
- ✔ Select the Object Selection tool and click any element on the layer.
- ✔ Click the layer name in the Layers palette. As long as you don't have an existing selection outline, PhotoDeluxe automatically selects all pixels on the layer.

PhotoDeluxe requires that you select your layer in a particular way before you can apply certain types of edits. If you can't access a command after using one of the first three selection methods, try selecting the layer using either of the other two methods, or vice versa.

After you select an image layer, one of three things happens:

- ✔ If you selected the layer by using one of the first three methods, PhotoDeluxe surrounds the layer with a standard selection outline — the blinking dashed line. You can see an example a few sections away, in Figure 9-2.
- ✔ If you clicked a layer element with the Object Selection tool, a solid outline appears around the layer. The outline has Resize and Rotate handles at its corners. Peek ahead to Figure 9-8 in the section "Rotating and flipping selections" for a look.
- ✔ If you simply clicked the layer name in the Layers palette, PhotoDeluxe appears to ignore you. It doesn't display a selection outline at all. Don't fret — your layer really is selected.

"Manipulating Selections," later in this chapter, contains more information on using the Resize and Rotate handles as well as other ways to resize and rotate your selection. For the full scoop on creating and editing text, take two giant steps to Chapter 12.

Selecting Parts of a Layer

If you want to select a single bit of text on the Text layer, you simply click it with the Object Selection tool. (Chapter 12 offers more details.) When you want to select a portion of an image layer, put the Object Selection tool aside and focus on the remaining eight selection tools.

You can find out how to use each tool in the following sections. Before you dive in, though, I want to point out a few important aspects of using these tools:

- ✔ **You can grab pixels on the active layer only.** Suppose that you have a blue sky on Layer 1 and a red airplane on Layer 2. If Layer 1 is active and you want to select the airplane pixels, you need to make Layer 2 active. (Click its name in the Layers palette.) In other words, although *you* can see all layers at once, the selection tools can't.

- ✔ **You can transfer a selection outline between image layers.** After you create a selection outline, you can move the outline — not the enclosed pixels, just the outline — to another layer by clicking that layer's name in the Layers palette.

- ✔ **Clicking can eradicate your outline, so be careful.** You lose your selection outline if you click with any selection tool but the Object Selection tool when either the Add or Reduce button isn't selected in the Selections palette. In some cases, you can get the selection outline back by choosing the Undo command immediately. (Press Ctrl+Z or click the Undo button at the top of the image window.)

  If you click with the Object Selection tool, PhotoDeluxe locates the layer that contains the pixel you clicked and then selects all pixels on that layer.

Again, if you're confused about all this layer stuff, head for Chapter 11, which sorts things out for you.

The basic shape tools

The Rectangle, Oval, Square, and Circle tools create rectangular, oval, square, and circular selections. Gosh, you'd think that with all this computer experience under my belt, I could come up with a more complicated-sounding description than that, wouldn't you? Hope they don't take away my geek card or anything.

Anyway, to select an area with any of these tools, just drag from one side of the area to another. Alt+Drag to draw the selection outline from the center of the area outward. As you drag, a standard selection outline appears, as shown in Figure 9-2.

Figure 9-2: Drag from one corner to another with the Rectangle tool.

Selection outline ⌐   Rectangle cursor

Here's a secret: You don't really need the Square or Circle tools. To draw a square selection outline, you can just press Shift while you drag with the Rectangle tool. To create a perfect circle, Shift+Drag with the Oval tool.

And here's another tip: You can press Ctrl+M to grab the Rectangle tool quickly.

Some people who are new to image editing expect these basic selection tools to perform like similarly named tools in drawing programs such as CorelDraw or Adobe Illustrator, in which the tools create filled shapes. In PhotoDeluxe, if you want to create a filled shape — a blue square, for example — you must first draw the selection outline and then fill the selection with blue by applying the Selection Fill command. The next chapter covers this command.

The Color Wand

The Color Wand, as its name implies — sorta — bases the selection outline on pixel color. When you click with this tool, PhotoDeluxe analyzes the color of the pixel you click and then selects a contiguous area of similarly colored pixels.

Suppose that you have a skyline image like the top-left picture in Color Plate 9-1. Clicking to the right of the main tower selects an expanse of blue sky pixels, as indicated by the selection outline. The similarly colored pixels on the left of the tower aren't selected because the tower pixels come between those sky pixels and the pixel I originally clicked. That's what I mean by a *contiguous* area of color — the selection outline stops at the point where PhotoDeluxe encounters pixels that are differently colored from the original pixel you click.

Before using the Color Wand, adjust the *tolerance value* to tell PhotoDeluxe how similar color pixels must be in order to become part of the selection. Press Ctrl+K or choose File⇨Preferences⇨Cursors to display the Cursors dialog box, shown in Figure 9-3. Lower the Color Wand Tolerance value to make the Color Wand more discriminating — or less tolerant, if you will — so that it selects only pixels very close in color to the one you click with the Color Wand.

Figure 9-3:
Adjust the
Color Wand
Tolerance
value to
make the
Color Wand
more or
less dis-
criminating.

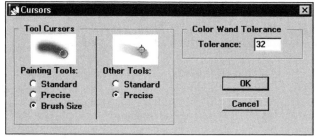

The top-left image in Color Plate 9-1 shows the results of using the default tolerance value, 32. The bottom-left image shows the selection outline created by doubling the tolerance value. In the right half of the color plate, I deleted the selected pixels to give you a better idea of the extent of the selections.

With the tool tolerance set at 64, PhotoDeluxe selects nearly all the sky pixels on the right side of the tower. Adding the remaining sky areas to the selection is a simple matter of clicking the Add button in the Selections palette and clicking again in each remaining sky area with the Color Wand. (See "Fine-tuning a selection outline," coming up soon, for more about adding to an existing selection.)

The Color Wand is especially useful for selecting complex objects set against solid-color backgrounds, like the buildings in my example. You can use the wand to easily select the background and then invert the selection to select all the buildings and other foreground elements instead. Check out "Inverting a selection outline," later in this chapter, for more about this technique.

The SmartSelect tool

An alternative to the Color Wand, the SmartSelect tool also can be helpful in selecting an area that's surrounded by differently colored pixels. As you drag along the edge of the element that you want to select, the SmartSelect tool automatically places the selection outline along the border between the element and the contrasting pixels that surround it.

Make sense? Didn't to me, either, until I tried out the tool for myself. So grab an image and take these steps:

1. **Choose the SmartSelect tool from the Selections palette.**

   When you select this tool, the SmartSelect options palette appears, as shown in Figure 9-4. By raising or lowering the values in the palette, you can adjust the performance of the tool. More on that in a moment.

Figure 9-4:
Raise or
lower these
values to
control the
SmartSelect
tool.

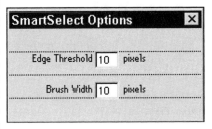

2. **Click the spot where you want the selection outline to begin.**

3. **Move the mouse along the edge of the area that you want to select.**

   Don't press the mouse button — just move your mouse so that the cursor follows the edge of the area. As you move the mouse, PhotoDeluxe searches for pixels that contrast those underneath your cursor. It then lays down a selection outline between those contrasting pixels and the pixels under your cursor. In Figure 9-5, you can see me in the act of using the SmartSelect tool to create a selection outline in the pie image shown earlier, in Figure 9-2. As I dragged along the perimeter of the pie, PhotoDeluxe placed the selection outline at the point where the pie pixels meet the plate pixels.

   Notice the little squares that appear every so often along the selection outline? These squares, labeled in Figure 9-5, are called _selection points_. If your selection outline ever gets off target, move your cursor over the most recent selection point and press Delete. Keep backing up over selection points and deleting them until you reach the spot where the selection outline went bad. Now move the mouse again to redraw the selection outline.

Selection point

Figure 9-5:
The
SmartSelect
tool in
action.

If the SmartSelect tool doesn't do a good job of finding the edge of the element, you can click to create your own selection points, which anchor the selection outline everywhere you click.

4. **Keep going until you reach the beginning of the outline and your cursor changes into the letters *Ok.***

5. **Click to complete the selection outline.**

Now that you understand the fundamentals, try playing with the two options in the SmartSelect options palette to fine-tune the tool's performance. Note that you must set these values before you start your drag with the SmartSelect tool; you can't change them in midstream:

- ✔ **Edge Threshold:** Change this value to make the tool more or less discriminating when it looks for contrasting pixels. If the area that you're trying to select contrasts only slightly from the background, raise the value to make the tool more sensitive. Lower the value if you want the tool to look for big shifts in contrast only.

- ✔ **Brush Width:** Adjust this option if the SmartSelect tool starts roaming too far from your cursor in its search for contrasting pixels or doesn't go far enough. Lower the value to restrict the tool to a narrower area; raise the value to give the tool more freedom. You can enter a value from 1 to 20.

If you previously used the Business Edition of PhotoDeluxe, you may be wondering what happened to the Feather option in the SmartSelect Options dialog box. I'm sorry to report that Version 4, like Versions 2 and 3, doesn't offer this feature. That means that you can't use the SmartSelect tool to create *feathered* selections (selections that gradually fade from full opacity to full transparency) as you can in the Business Edition. The good news is that you can still achieve some feathering effects by using the Effects⇨Feather command, which you can read about at the end of this chapter.

Freehand selection tools

With the Polygon and Trace tools, you can draw freehand selection outlines around the object you want to select. The two tools work a little differently from one another, but both require some degree of mouse coordination — a quality that I don't seem to have. If you're good at drawing, though, you may prefer these tools. Otherwise, you can use them to create a general selection outline and then use the techniques discussed later in this chapter to refine the outline.

✔ To create a selection outline with the Trace tool, just drag around the area that you want to select. If you let up on the mouse button before you come back to the spot where you began the selection outline, PhotoDeluxe automatically completes the outline by connecting the start and end points of your drag with a straight line.

   Press Ctrl+L to switch to the Trace tool in a nanosecond.

✔ The Polygon tool works like an advanced Trace tool. To draw a curved segment of your selection outline, drag with the Polygon tool as you do with the Trace tool. If you want to draw a straight segment, let up on the mouse button at the spot where you want that straight segment to start; then click at the spot where you want the segment to end. PhotoDeluxe creates the straight segment for you, which is a good thing — drawing a perfectly straight line with a mouse can be a challenge for the steadiest hand.

   To complete the selection outline, double-click. If you double-click anywhere but at the beginning of the selection outline, PhotoDeluxe automatically closes the selection outline with a straight segment.

   After your first click with the Polygon tool, you can't cancel out of the selection-drawing process. If you change your mind about that selection outline or want to start over, double-click to close the selection outline and then press Ctrl+D or click the None icon in the Selections palette to lose the selection outline.

Fine-tuning selection outlines

Unless you're selecting an entire layer, you probably won't create an exact selection outline on the first try. That's why PhotoDeluxe offers several ways to adjust the selection outline. Grab any selection tool but the Object Selection tool and tweak your outline as follows:

✔ **Select additional pixels:** Click the Add button in the Selections palette. Now you can start a second selection outline while keeping the first one intact. You can either create a totally separate outline or expand the existing one.

You can mix and match selection tools — draw a rectangular selection to select part of your image and then use the Color Wand to select another region, for example.

✔ **Deselect some currently selected pixels:** If your selection outline encompasses elements that you don't want selected, click the Reduce button in the Selections palette. Now your selection tools work in reverse. If you drag with the Oval tool, for example, PhotoDeluxe deselects any previously selected pixels that you enclose with your drag.

✔ **Move the selection outline within the same layer:** You can move the selection outline to another part of your image by Ctrl+Alt+Dragging inside the selection.

To move the selection outline in small increments, don't drag it. Instead, hold down the Ctrl and Alt keys and press an arrow key on your keyboard. Each press of an arrow key moves the outline one pixel in the direction of the arrow. Press Ctrl+Alt+Shift and an arrow key to move the outline ten pixels.

Be sure that you press Ctrl+Alt as you drag or press the arrow keys and that the Object Selection tool isn't active! Otherwise, you move the pixels inside the selection outline, not the outline itself.

Keep playing with selection outline until you get it right. If you make a bonehead selection move, click Undo or press Ctrl+Z right away to undo it.

Remember, no matter which technique you use, you select pixels on the active layer only. After you create a selection outline, though, you can transfer the outline to any other image layer by clicking the layer name in the Layers palette.

Inverting a selection outline

As I mentioned earlier in this chapter, sometimes you can get quicker selection results by selecting everything *except* the element that you want to edit and then inverting the selection. Inverting the selection reverses the selection outline so that pixels that were formerly selected are deselected, and vice versa.

If you haven't already feasted your eyes on Color Plate 9-1, take a look now. Can you imagine trying to select all those buildings and ornamental shapes with any of the selection tools? What a chore! But you can easily select the sky — a few clicks of the Color Wand should do the job — and then invert the selection to deselect the sky and select everything else.

To invert your selection, click the Invert button in the Selections palette or press Ctrl+I.

Rearranging Selected Pixels

Selecting is a neat trick, but the real fun starts when you manipulate the pixels inside the selection. You can put your head on someone else's body, duplicate that head to create a two-domed monster, and otherwise shove pixels around until even the photographer who snapped the picture wouldn't recognize the image.

The following sections explain how you can rotate, move, copy, and resize a selection. Note that image layers come into play during these operations, so if you haven't yet explored that topic in Chapter 11, you may find some of the information presented here a little difficult to grasp. If you can't quite figure out what's going on, take a quick glance through the basic layer information in Chapter 11 and then come back here.

Moving and copying selections

Just as you can move a paragraph from one page to another in a word-processing program, you can move pixels at whim, either relocating them within the same image or sending them to another image. Likewise, you can duplicate a selection as many times as you want — think of PhotoDeluxe as a copy machine with unlimited toner and no paper jams.

For small moving and copying jobs, you select the Move tool and then just drag the selection into place or press the arrow keys on your keyboard to nudge it a small distance. The next two sections explain how to do both.

However, if you're transferring selections between two images, you must have both images open at the same time — that can be a problem if you're working with large images, limited computer memory and free hard-drive space, or both. If PhotoDeluxe balks at keeping both images open, use the time-honored method of transferring and duplicating data: the Cut, Copy, and Paste commands. With this option, you need only one image open at a time. Look for details in the upcoming section "Using good old Cut, Copy, and Paste."

PhotoDeluxe treats your selection differently depending on what tools you used to create the selection outline and how you move or copy it. The differences can affect your future editing options, so pay close attention as you wade through all this moving and copying stuff.

Dragging a selection to a new home

Want to move a selected something from here to there? First, understand the ramifications. Whenever you move a selection, you rip a hole in your image where the moved pixels use to be. If you delete a selection from the bottom layer in an image, the image canvas shows through the hole; delete a selection from any other layer, and pixels on the underlying layer become visible through the hole.

As an example, look at the top image in Figure 9-6. This picture contains two image layers. The bottom layer contains the left rose, which sits amid a sea of gray and black. (You can see this image in the next section, in Figure 9-7.) The top layer holds the second rose all by itself — there are no surrounding pixels.

In the lower-left example of the figure, I moved that second rose, revealing the bottom rose image through the hole. To create the lower-right example, I merged the two rose layers, so that everything lives on the bottom layer of the image. When I moved the rose this time, the canvas became visible through the hole. The hole looks white because an empty canvas always appears white in print. (See Chapter 2 for more on that one.)

Figure 9-6:
Moving a
selection
reveals the
underlying
image layer
(bottom left)
or the image
canvas
(bottom
right).

With that disclaimer out of the way, the following steps explain how to move a selection around within an image, whether you want to relocate an entire layer or just part of it. You can use the same steps to move a selection from one image to another. Just open both images, place them side-by-side on-screen, and then work through the steps.

I recommend that you read through the rest of this section before trying these steps; you can mess things up if you don't understand the whole process.

1. Grab the Move tool by pressing Ctrl+G or clicking the Move icon in the Selections palette.

If the Object Selection tool is active, you must press Ctrl+G or choose Select⇨Selection Tools⇨Move. You can't click the icon in the Selections palette. Also, the Selections palette continues to show that the Object Selection tool is active, but it's not. You can tell for sure by looking at your mouse cursor — when the Move tool is active, the cursor looks like a four-headed arrow. When the Object Selection tool is active, your cursor looks like a standard mouse pointer.

Technically, you can skip this step altogether if you used the Object Selection tool to select an entire layer. Unless you activate the Move tool, though, you can't precisely position the selection using the handy technique described in the next step.

2. Drag or nudge the selection to its new home.

If you're moving a selection to another picture, drag the selection from one image window to the other.

For moving selections around in the same image, you can either drag or press the arrow keys to nudge the selection into place. Press an arrow key once to shift the selection one pixel in the direction of the arrow. Press Shift with an arrow key to move the selection 10 pixels. Remember, you can use this technique only if the Move tool is active.

If you're moving only some pixels on a layer, be aware that PhotoDeluxe treats your relocated pixels differently depending on whether you're moving your selection to another image or to a new position in the same image.

When you transplant a selection from Image A to Image B, PhotoDeluxe creates a new layer in Image B and puts the moved pixels on the layer. Because those pixels live on their own layer, you can reposition them or apply any other edits without affecting other parts of the image. See Chapter 11 to find out more about how all this layer stuff works.

PhotoDeluxe also creates a layer to hold the moved pixels when you move a selection in the same image, but the layer is temporary. If you open the Layers palette (View⇨Show Layers), you see the layer, called *Floating Layer.*

PhotoDeluxe displays the layer name in italics to remind you that the layer isn't permanent. You can either merge the floating layer with the underlying layer — a process known as *setting the layer down* — or turn it into a permanent layer.

If you set the layer down, you can't move the selection without creating a new hole in the image. By converting the floating layer to an official layer, you can continue to edit it separately from the rest of the image. Clicking your image with any selection tool but the Move tool automatically sets the layer down, so be careful.

Here's how to turn a floating layer into a permanent layer:

1. **Open the Layers palette by choosing View⇨Show Layers.**

2. **Drag the floating layer to the New Layer icon in the bottom-left corner of the palette.**

   You can also choose Make Layers from the Layers palette menu. (Click the arrow in the upper-right corner of the palette to open the menu.) Either way, PhotoDeluxe displays the Maker Layer dialog box.

3. **Enter a layer name into the Name box, if you like.**

   Leave the other options alone until you read about them in Chapter 11.

4. **Click OK or press Enter.**

Keep in mind, though, that each new layer you create adds to the size of your image file. If you're sure that you won't need to move the selection again in the future, reduce your image size by setting the floating layer down. You can use these options to merge the floater with the underlying layer:

- ✔ Click None in the Selections palette.
- ✔ Press Ctrl+D.
- ✔ Click the image with a selection tool other than the Move tool.

Copying a selection

Chapter 7 introduces you to one method of duplicating an element in your picture: using the Clone tool. The Clone tool is just the ticket for small jobs such as covering up a blemish with pixels copied from the surrounding area. But when you want to copy a larger element, such as the rose in the left example in Figure 9-7, the Clone tool is inefficient. PhotoDeluxe offers several select-and-copy options that get the job done more quickly.

Figure 9-7:
A single rose (left) becomes two (right). I selected the left rose, duplicated it by Alt+ Dragging with the Move tool, and then rotated the copy.

To copy a selection and transfer the copy to another picture, open both image windows. Activate the Move tool and then Alt+Drag the selection from one window to the other. You can use this technique to move a standard selection or an entire layer. PhotoDeluxe automatically puts the copy on a new layer — a real one, not a temporary, floating one.

If you want to create a copy and keep it in the same image, use these techniques:

✔ Choose Edit⇨Duplicate. PhotoDeluxe places the copy on a new, permanent layer just above the layer that holds the original pixels. The copy appears offset from the original so that you can see both the copy and the original. To relocate the duplicate, press Ctrl+G to select the Move tool and then drag or nudge the copy into place.

For some reason, you can't undo the Duplicate command. To get rid of an unwanted duplicate, either press the Delete key or drag the duplicate layer to the Trash icon in the Layers palette.

✔ For standard selections — that is, selections created with any tool but the Object Selection tool — you can Alt+Drag the selection with the Move tool, just as you can to copy a selection from one image to another.

You also can copy and nudge a selection by pressing Alt and an arrow key while the Move tool is active. This technique gets tricky, however. Each time you press Alt and an arrow key, you create a new duplicate and merge the previous copy with the underlying layer. If you want one copy only, press and hold the Alt key, press an arrow key once, and then release the Alt key. Now you can nudge the copy into place by pressing just the arrow keys.

Whether you Alt+Drag or Alt+nudge, PhotoDeluxe places the copy on a floating layer. You can manipulate the floating layer as you do when moving a selection (again, see the preceding section). Don't forget — if you click with any selection tool but the Move tool or otherwise get rid of the selection outline, you merge the floating layer with the underlying layer.

Using good old Cut, Copy, and Paste

Like almost every computer program, the PhotoDeluxe Edit menu offers the Cut, Copy, and Paste commands. These commands make use of the Windows Clipboard, a temporary holding tank for computer data. When you choose Cut, PhotoDeluxe lifts the selection out of your image and puts it into the Clipboard. Choose Copy, and PhotoDeluxe duplicates the selection and puts the copy on the Clipboard. To retrieve the selection from the Clipboard and put it into an image, you choose the Paste command.

Moving and copying selections via the Clipboard requires a few more steps than the methods covered in the preceding sections, but it offers a few advantages, too:

- ✔ You can move or copy a selection from one image to another without keeping both images open at the same time. If your computer is slow and has limited system resources, making PhotoDeluxe cranky when you open multiple photos, this may be the only way to move or copy selections.

- ✔ The Clipboard retains a copy of your selection even after you paste the selection. That means that you can keep pasting additional copies of the selection as many times as you like, right up until you close PhotoDeluxe or copy or cut something else to the Clipboard.

- ✔ You can use Cut, Copy, and Paste to copy or move a selection into other programs as well as into other PhotoDeluxe images. For example, you can paste a selection into a spreadsheet you're building in Microsoft Excel. (Alternatively, you can save the image and import it into the other program. Check the Help system for the program you're using to find information about the best procedure to follow.)

If you want to paste your selection into another program, you must turn on the Export Clipboard option. To toggle the option on and off, choose File➪Preferences➪Export Clipboard. A checkmark next to the option name means that the option is turned on. PhotoDeluxe still asks whether you want the Clipboard data to be available to other programs when you close your image — answer in the affirmative, or PhotoDeluxe dumps the Clipboard contents.

The following steps walk you through the process of moving or copying a selection from one image to another image. You can use these same steps to move or copy a selection inside the same image — just skip Step 3.

1. **Select the pixels that you want to move or copy.**

2. **Choose Edit➪Copy or Edit➪Cut.**

   For quicker results, press Ctrl+C to choose the Copy command; press Ctrl+X to choose Cut. You may as well commit these shortcuts to memory — you can use them in almost any program, not just PhotoDeluxe.

   However you choose the command, remember the following:

   - Copy duplicates the selection and leaves the original image intact.

   - Cut lifts the selection out of the image, leaving a hole. If the pixels you cut came from the bottom layer of an image, the image canvas peeks through the hole. If you cut a selection from any other image layer, the pixels on the underlying layer poke their heads through the hole. Cutting text from the Text layer does not leave a hole, however.

3. **Open the image that you want to paste the copy into.**

   You can close the first image if you want.

4. **Choose Edit➪Paste or press Ctrl+V.**

   PhotoDeluxe creates a new layer in your image and dumps the Clipboard contents onto the layer, positioning the pasted pixels smack dab in the center of the layer. The layer is selected automatically for you.

5. **Manipulate the pasted pixels to your heart's content.**

   Now you can edit the selection as you would pixels on any image layer. Use the techniques described in the preceding two sections to move your layer, if necessary. Check out Chapter 11 for the full story on layers, and see other sections of this chapter to find out how to resize, rotate, and do other fun stuff with selected layers.

   PhotoDeluxe doesn't let you undo the Paste command. If you don't like what you see after choosing the command, press Delete immediately. You also can drag the layer that contains the pasted selection to the Trash icon in the Layers palette.

Pasting selections into a selection

You may have noticed that the Edit menu contains a Paste Into command in addition to a Paste command. With Paste Into, you can paste the contents of the Clipboard into a selection outline. Why would you want to do that? Suppose that you want to put your face in the center of a daisy — think of the Anne Geddes portraits where babies appear framed by flowers.

First, you copy your face to the Clipboard. Then you select the area of the daisy that you want your face to occupy. When you choose the Paste Into command, PhotoDeluxe makes the selected daisy pixels transparent and places the pasted face on a floating layer. The face pixels then appear inside the original selection outline instead of the daisy pixels.

If you want, you can use the Move tool to reposition the face pixels so that another part of your mug shows through the selection outline. After you get your face properly framed, you can send the floating face pixels to a permanent layer or merge them with the underlying image. Do the latter, and the originally selected daisy pixels get trashed, as do any face pixels that didn't fit inside the selection outline. If you send the floating pixels to their own layer, however, PhotoDeluxe retains all face pixels and all daisy pixels. You can continue repositioning your face inside the daisy if necessary. If you decide that daisies don't become you, you can trash the face layer, bringing the original daisy pixels back into view.

To be honest, you can get essentially the same results by using the regular Paste command. You can delete the daisy pixels, paste the face pixels, and then move the face layer under the daisy layer, so that the face pixels show through the hole left by the deleted daisy pixels. After you paste, you can use the Move tool to tweak the positioning of your face pixels, just as when you use Paste Into.

The only difference between the two methods is that Paste Into can preserve all your original daisy pixels. But you have to remember to turn the floating face layer into a permanent layer if you want to retain those daisy pixels or to be able to reposition your face later.

Because you already have too much to remember, I recommend that you stick with the regular Paste command. If you think that you may want your original face or daisy image back some day, save a copy of each picture before you start your framing project.

Rotating and flipping selections

You can turn a selection on its ear, flipping it vertically or horizontally, as I did with the copied rose back in Figure 9-7. You also can spin a selection 90 degrees to the right, 90 degrees to the left, or to any degree you choose.

All commands related to this kind of selection gymnastics live on the Orientation menu. Here's a list of the things you can do:

- **Flip a selection horizontally:** Choose Orientation⇨Flip Horizontal or press Ctrl+[(left bracket).

- **Flip a selection vertically:** Choose Orientation⇨Flip Vertical or press Ctrl+] (right bracket).

✔ **Rotate a selection 90 degrees clockwise:** Choose Orientation⇨Rotate Right or press Ctrl+> (on most keyboards, you need to press Shift and the period key to access the > key).

✔ **Rotate a selection 90 degrees counterclockwise:** Choose Orientation⇨Rotate Left or press Ctrl+< (or Ctrl+Shift+period).

✔ **Rotate a selection to some other degree:** To accomplish this one, you need to tug a Rotate handle. The Rotate handles appear automatically when you select an entire layer using the Object Selection tool or paste a selection into an image from the Clipboard. Figure 9-8 shows you how the handles look.

Resize handle   Rotate handle

Figure 9-8: Drag the resize and rotate handles to manipulate an entire layer.

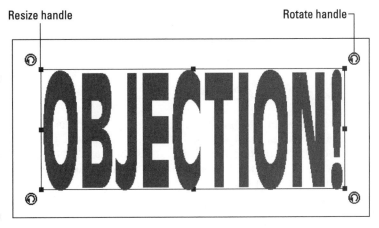

Don't see any rotate handles? Choose Orientation⇨Free Rotate or press Ctrl+4 to display them.

After you drag a Rotate handle, release the mouse button to see how your spun selection looks. If you're satisfied, click outside the selection outline or press Enter. If not, keep dragging the rotate handles until you get the selection positioned where you want it. You can click Undo at any time to do away with your last tug on a handle.

To give up on the whole rotating idea and get rid of the Rotate handles, press the Escape key (usually labeled Esc).

When you rotate or flip a selection, you're moving pixels, which means that you create a hole in your image. Of course, you may not always see that hole because the rotated or flipped selection completely fills it. For example, when you rotate a perfect circle, you simply move each pixel into a spot that another pixel previously occupied. Similarly, when you flip an entire layer, you don't wind up with a hole because the flipped layer occupies the same space as it did before.

If you created your selection with any tool other than the Object Selection tool, PhotoDeluxe ships your rotated or flipped pixels to a floating layer. The earlier section on moving pixels explains floating layers, so I won't blather on about them here. Just remember that you have the option of turning the floating layer into a permanent layer or setting the layer down, which merges the rotated pixels with the underlying layer.

To convert the floating layer into an official layer, drag it to the New Layer icon in the Layers palette or choose Make Layer from the Layers palette menu. To set the layer down, just get rid of the selection outline. Press Ctrl+D, click None in the Selections palette, or click with any selection tool but the Object Selection tool.

Avoid rotating the same area of any image more than once if possible. Multiple rotations can degrade your image quality.

Resizing selections

I almost hate to get into the subject of resizing selections because you can really destroy your image quality if you alter the dimensions of a selection very much. (For an explanation of why resizing can damage your picture, travel back to Chapter 3.) If you don't like what you see after you resize, hit that Undo button or press Ctrl+Z immediately to put things back the way they were.

The Resize handles, which you can see back in Figure 9-8, provide the key to resizing selections. To display the handles, choose Size⇨Free Resize or Size⇨Resize. If you choose either command when nothing is selected in your picture, PhotoDeluxe assumes that you want to resize the entire layer. You also can select a layer and display the resizing handles by clicking any element on the layer with the Object Selection tool.

What's the difference between Resize and Free Resize? Not much. Free Resize just makes you press a key as you drag to resize an image without distorting it. With Resize, you just drag.

PhotoDeluxe gives you the Free Resize controls when you select a layer by clicking it with the Object Selection tool. So that you don't have to remember two different sets of dragging techniques, I suggest that you always choose Free Resize when you need to display the handles for yourself.

The following list explains what you can do with the Free Resize handles:

- ✔ **Change the width of the selection:** Drag a side handle.
- ✔ **Change the height of the selection:** Drag a top-center or bottom-center handle.

✔ **Adjust width and height at the same time:** Drag a corner handle. You can enlarge or reduce both dimensions by different amounts, but you distort your image if you do.

✔ **Resize the selected area while retaining the original proportions:** Shift+Drag a corner handle. PhotoDeluxe controls your resizing to make sure that both width and height increase or decrease by the same amount.

✔ **Resize without moving the center of the selection:** Press Alt as you drag any resize handle. This method enables you to create interesting fun-house mirror effects. For even more ways to distort an image, see Chapter 15.

If you ever want to undo the last drag of a handle, click the Undo button or press Ctrl+Z. When you're done stretching or shrinking your selection, press Enter or click outside the selection box to make your changes official.

To abandon your resizing notions, press Esc any time before you click or press Enter.

Deleting a Selection

If you want to get rid of the pixels inside a selection, just press Delete. The Delete key works just like the Cut command, except that Delete doesn't send your selection to the Clipboard. Press Delete, and the selection is gone for good.

Assuming that you're working on the background layer, the empty image canvas appears where the deleted pixels used to be, as shown earlier, in the right example in Figure 9-6. When you delete pixels on any layer but the background image layer, however, you create a transparent hole in the layer. Pixels from the underlying image layer show through the hole, as in the left example in the figure.

Deleting or Filling a Feathered Selection

Feathering a selection makes the edges of a selection outline fuzzy, so that instead of a harsh transition between the selected and deselected pixels, you get a soft, gradual transition.

In PhotoDeluxe, you can feather your selection outline and then fill the selection or the deselected areas with a solid color. You also can delete either area.

Perhaps the most common use of this feature is to give a photograph a soft, fade-into-nothingness frame, as I did for the lovely specimen in Figure 9-9. Here in Indiana, we love our farm animals and feel that they deserve all the dignity they can get, even when sneering at the camera.

Figure 9-9: Such a lovely smile (left) deserves a special, feathered frame (right).

To create a similar result, first select the area that you want to fill or delete. (You can't select the entire image for this effect.) Next, choose Effects⇨ Feather to display the dialog box shown in Figure 9-10. In the option box in the top-left corner of the dialog box, enter a feather value to tell PhotoDeluxe how fuzzy you want to make the edges of the selection. Higher numbers increase the fuzziness of the selection. I used a value of 13 to create the effect in Figure 9-9.

To delete everything but the selection, as I did in the figure, click the Delete Background icon. To delete the selection and keep the background, choose the Delete Selection icon. In both cases, you get a hole in your image, just as when you move or rotate a selection. If you delete a selection on the bottom image layer, the image canvas appears; on any other image layer, the underlying layer shows through the hole.

Keep in mind that where the edges of the area you keep are the same color as the underlying area, you don't get a definitive boundary between the two. For example, in Figure 9-10, the light sky pixels at the top of the horse's head and the white background blend together.

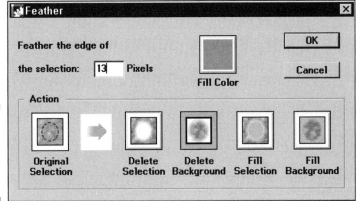

Figure 9-10:
You can fill
or delete a
feathered
selection.

If you want to pour a solid color into either the selection or the background, click the Fill Selection or Fill Background icon, respectively. Click the Fill Color swatch to display the Color Picker, where you can choose the color that you want to apply. (See Chapter 10 for more information about the Color Picker.) Click OK to apply the effect to your image.

Want to explore some other framing effects? Choose Effects⇨Extensis⇨ PhotoFrame to display a plug-in that enables you to create several kinds of frames as well as to frame your entire image. Chapter 14 provides details.

Part IV

Amazing Feats of Digital Trickery

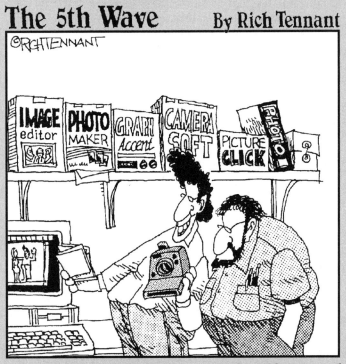

The 5th Wave   By Rich Tennant

"...and here's me with Cindy Crawford. And this is me with Madonna and Celine Dion..."

In this part . . .

One of the things I appreciate most about Adobe PhotoDeluxe 4 is that it enables me to express creative notions that I simply can't put forth using traditional art tools. An art class washout, I can't paint a decent bowl of fruit to save my life. When I sketch people, they get sticks for arms and legs, circles for hands and feet. And if you're thinking of giving me a lump of potter's clay and asking me to sculpt a little something, you'd better be prepared to go home with a thumbprint ashtray. But with PhotoDeluxe, I can create acceptable — and sometimes really terrific — works of photographic art with a fair amount of ease.

Regardless of whether you share my artistic limitations, this part of the book aims to inspire your creative side by introducing you to some of the more advanced options available in PhotoDeluxe. You find out how to build photographic collages using image layers, how to use some of the program's more interesting special-effects filters, and how to create eye-catching text. I've also included some ideas on how to use your image masterpieces.

If you are as inept as I am with traditional art tools, you'll be amazed at how PhotoDeluxe enables your artistic side to shine. And if you're the next Monet or Picasso, time spent in this digital art studio should advance your genius even further. The best part is that you don't have to inhale any smelly paint-thinner fumes or get clay underneath your fingernails in the pursuit of your art.

24-bit image

8-bit image

Color Plate 3-1:
A 24-bit image can contain approximately 16 million colors, resulting in life-like renditions of subtle color variations (top). Saving the image to the GIF format results in an 8-bit image, which can have a maximum of 256 colors. Such a limited supply of colors often results in splotchy images (bottom).

Color Plate 7-1:
My original daisy image (left) looked dark and dingy — hardly a happy floral specimen. Applying the Instant Fix filter brightened up the scene, but also altered the image colors too much for my taste (middle). By selecting just the daisy and making manual adjustments using the Brightness/Contrast and Color Balance filters, I created a bright, sunny flower that remains faithful to the original image colors (right).

Color Plate 7-2:
Increasing the Saturation value brought the faded colors of this feathered friend (left) back to life (right).

Color Plate 7-3:
To get rid of the pink cast in my snowman scene (left), I used the Color Balance command, increasing the amount of green and blue and decreasing the amount of red.

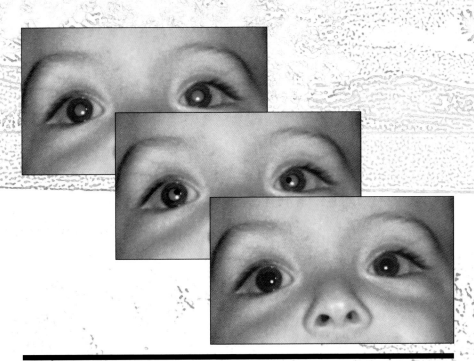

Color Plate 8-1:
A camera flash reflecting in a subject's eyes causes the eerie red-eye phenomena (top). The Remove Red Eye filter doesn't do a terrific job of correcting the condition (middle); you get much better results using the Selection Fill command (bottom).

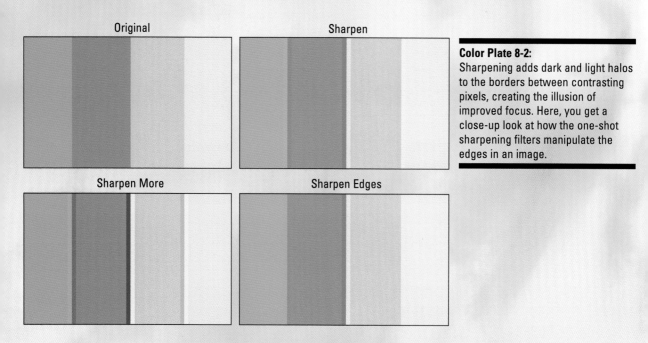

Original

Sharpen

Sharpen More

Sharpen Edges

Color Plate 8-2:
Sharpening adds dark and light halos to the borders between contrasting pixels, creating the illusion of improved focus. Here, you get a close-up look at how the one-shot sharpening filters manipulate the edges in an image.

Color Plate 8-3:
With the Unsharp Mask filter, you can adjust the intensity of the sharpening halos by changing the Amount value and adjust the area affected by the halos by changing the Radius value. Here, you see the effects of applying the filter at two different Amount and Radius values. I used a Threshold setting of 0 in all four examples.

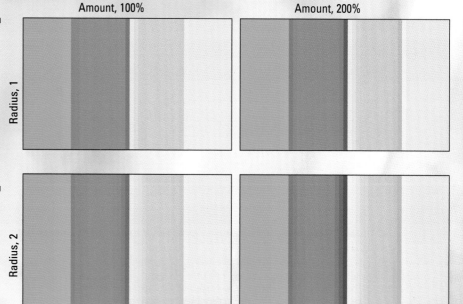

Amount, 100%

Amount, 200%

Radius, 1

Radius, 2

Color Plate 8-4:

My original feather image (center) begged for some sharpening. The Sharpen filter (top left) didn't do enough, while Sharpen More (top right) went too far. Sharpen Edges (bottom left) gave me a sharp background and a blurry feather. With Unsharp Mask, I was able to generate just the right amount of sharpening for both feather and background (bottom right). The inset areas give you close-up view of the different sharpening effects.

Figure 9-1:
To select an intricate subject against a plain background, use the Color Wand to select the background and then invert the selection. I clicked just to the right of the tower using a Tolerance value of 32 (top) and 64 (bottom). In the right images, I deleted the selection to show how cleanly the tower was separated from the sky. With a few more clicks, I could easily select other portions of the sky to finish the job.

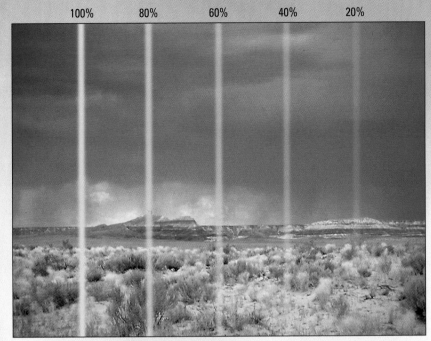

100%   80%   60%   40%   20%

Color Plate 10-1:
Press a number key to make your brush strokes more or less transparent. I dabbed at this desert image using five different opacity values.

Color Plate 10-2:
Dragging along the beak with the Smudge tool, I gave an already overdecorated bird a digital nose job and then added a few eyelashes for good measure.

Color Plate 10-3:
I filled the original pumpkin (center) with the blue-green pattern shown in the background of this image, varying the blend mode to create different effects. Starting at top left and going clockwise, the blend modes used are Normal, Color, Darken, Difference, Overlay, and Lighten.

Original

Fill, Normal

Fill, Color

Hue, +100

Color Plate 10-4:
Craving a new kind of grape, I selected the purple ones in the top left image and filled the selection with orange, using the Normal blend mode (top right). The result is a flat, unappetizing blob. Applying a green fill using the Color mode (bottom left) delivered more natural results, as did simply shifting the Hue value (bottom right).

Color Plate 11-1:
I combined elements from these six images, photographed on a recent trip to China, into the collage shown in Color Plate 11-2.

Color Plate 11-2:
Image layers expand your creative possibilities enormously. This collage features six image layers and three text layers, with the lower right image from Color Plate 11-1 serving as the background layer.

Color Plate 12-1:
By using a special technique outlined in Chapter 12, you can work around the limitations of the Text tool and create special text effects like these.

Color Plate 13-1:
I took a rather boring paddleboat image and created more interesting versions by applying the Negative filter (top right) and the Solarize filter (bottom left). To create a variation of the Negative effect, I blended the Negative image with the original using the Difference layer blend mode (bottom right).

Color Plate 13-2:
A car this cool deserves more than an ordinary photographic treatment (top). Selecting
everything but the car and applying the Color to Black/White command spices things up a
bit (middle). To create the antique photograph effect (bottom), I applied the command to
the whole image and then applied a light tint by using the Selection Fill command with the
blend mode set to Color.

Color Plate 13-3:
To correct an overexposed, ugly sky (left), I selected the sky area and applied the Clouds filter, using two shades of blue as the foreground and background colors (right).

Original

Find Edges

Color Plate 13-4:
Applying three different edge-based effects filters results in three interesting takes on the original downtown scene.

Glowing Edges

Neon Glow, Difference

Original

Funnel

Bas Relief

Shear, Negative

Color Plate 13-5:
Experiment with the special effects filters to create unusual backgrounds for images. I started with the top-left image and created three psychedelic backgrounds using the Funnel filter (top right), followed by Bas Relief (bottom left), and then Shear and Negative (bottom right).

Chapter 10

Open Up Your Paint Box

- -

In This Chapter

▶ Choosing your paint color

▶ Dabbing at pixels with the Brush tool

▶ Adjusting the size and opacity of your paint strokes

▶ Painting perfectly straight lines

▶ Smearing colors with the Smudge tool

▶ Filling a selection with a pattern or color

▶ Experimenting with blend modes

▶ Creating a gradient fill

- -

*I*f you've ever taken an oil painting class, you may be aware that many items in the typical paint box are, shall we say, user-unfriendly. Inhale too many paint-thinner fumes or absentmindedly chew on a brush handle that's coated with certain pigments, and you can do some serious damage to your health. Some people even speculate that one reason Van Gogh went bonkers and divested himself of his ear was that he ingested too much toxic paint.

Thankfully, digital painting is less hazardous to your health. No toxins are involved, unless you count that major mug of caffeine I see on your cup warmer. True, trying to paint just the right stroke with a mouse can sometimes lead to mental anguish, but I don't think you're at risk of severing any body parts. Hey, put those scissors down! You're going to want that ear later, really!

This chapter shows you how to work with the two major PhotoDeluxe painting tools: the Brush and Line tools. You also learn how to dump a whole bucketful of paint onto the canvas using the Selection Fill command, smear colors around your image using the Smudge tool, and perform a few other painting tricks as well.

Painting without Pain

As you ply the Brush, Line, or other painting tools, keep the following tips in mind to get the results you want with a minimum of effort and stress:

- ✔ **Paint on a separate layer.** Create a new layer by clicking the New Layer icon in the Layers palette (View➪Show Layers). If you hate what you paint, you can simply delete the layer and start over — you haven't damaged your original image. To find out more about editing on a layer, read Chapter 11.

- ✔ **Select before you paint.** PhotoDeluxe confines your paint strokes to the boundaries of the selection so that you can't mistakenly paint over pixels that you didn't intend to color. Chapter 9 explains how to select parts of your image.

- ✔ **Set the paint tool cursors to Brush Size.** Select this option in the Painting Tools section of the Cursors dialog box (Ctrl+K). Your cursor then gives you a better idea of the size and shape of the brush you're using. For precise painting in small areas, press the Cap Locks key to toggle between the Brush Size cursor and the Precise cursor, a tiny crosshair cursor. For more about changing cursor styles, see Chapter 2.

Picking a Paint Color

You can carry two colors of paint in your PhotoDeluxe paint box at a time:

- ✔ The *foreground color* is the primary color. The Brush and Line tools always apply the foreground color. Some special effects also involve the foreground color.

- ✔ The *background color* is a minor role-player. It's used only when you apply some special effects, such as the Clouds and Bas Relief filters, both covered in Chapter 13.

To set the foreground or background color, choose Effects➪Choose Colors. The Color Picker dialog box, shown in Figure 10-1, rushes onto the stage.

Most times, you'll be successful in selecting your colors from this dialog box. If you run into trouble, you can order a custom color from the Windows system color picker. The next two sections explain both options.

Figure 10-1:
Click in the
Available
Colors
preview or
on a color
swatch to
set the fore-
ground or
background
color.

Working in the Color Picker dialog box

If you upgraded to Version 4 from Version 2, the Color Picker dialog box
offers some new features to help you nail down just the right shade of paint.
Here's what you need to know to go color-hunting:

✔ The Foreground and Background swatches show the currently selected
foreground and background colors. Click the radio button for the color
that you want to change. (Don't click the icon itself, or you open the
Windows color picker.)

✔ Select a color by clicking it in the Available Colors preview at the bottom
of the dialog box or by clicking a swatch in the Color Swatches area.

You can switch the Available Colors display from the default, full-color
spectrum to a grayscale spectrum or a spectrum that fades from the
foreground color to the background color. Click the icons to the right
of the preview or Shift+Click the preview itself to display a different
spectrum.

✔ If you want your paint color to exactly match an existing image color,
move your cursor into the image window and click the color in the image.

✔ Having trouble selecting the exact color you need? Open the Windows
system color picker by clicking the Foreground or Background color
swatch, depending on which color you want to change. The Windows
color picker gives you some additional tools for specifying a color. The
next section explains how to use them.

✔ After you track down the perfect shade, click OK to close the dialog box
and get on with your painting.

If you choose a color that doesn't already have a color swatch in the Color Picker dialog box, you can create a swatch by clicking the Add Swatch button. The next time you need the same color, just click its swatch.

You can add as many as eight swatches. After that, you must delete an existing swatch to add a new swatch. To remove a swatch, click it and then click Remove Swatch.

The Windows system color picker

While you're working in the PhotoDeluxe Color Picker dialog box, you can take a side trip to the Windows system color picker, which offers a few advanced tools for color creation. Click the Foreground or Background swatch in the Color Picker dialog box to open the Windows Color dialog box, as shown in Figure 10-2. Initially, you see just the left side of the dialog box.

Color field ⌐   Lightness slider ⌐

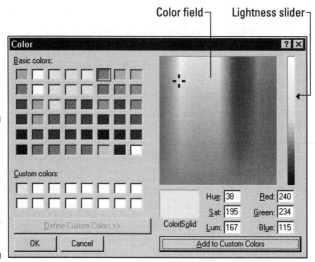

Figure 10-2:
The Windows color picker offers more ways to select your paint colors.

If you see the color of your dreams in one of the Basic Colors swatches, click it and click OK to return to the PhotoDeluxe Color Picker dialog box. Otherwise, click the Define Custom Colors button to display the hidden half of the dialog box. (The button becomes unavailable after you click it, as shown in the figure.)

The right side of the dialog box is a bit formidable, but not so difficult when you know how it works. The next section explains the basics of color-picking; the section after that provides tips for selecting colors for a Web page.

Defining a custom color

You define a custom color using three methods:

✔ Drag the cursor inside the color field to select a basic hue; drag the lightness slider to adjust the amount of black and white in the color. Both controls are labeled in Figure 10-2.

✔ Enter values into the Red, Green, and Blue option boxes to define a color based on the RGB color model, which mixes red, green, and blue light to create colors. A value of 255 indicates full-intensity color. Full-strength red, green, and blue make white. See Chapter 5 for more about RGB and its print counterpart, CMYK.

✔ Enter values into the Hue, Sat, and Lum boxes to define the color according to another color model, HSL. The Hue value reflects the basic color; Sat indicates the *saturation,* or intensity, of color; and Lum (luminosity) indicates the *brightness.*

Most people find the first option easiest. In fact, you have my permission to ignore the RGB and HSL values altogether unless you want to be able to create the exact same color later. As you define a color using the color field and lightness slider, Windows automatically enters the corresponding RGB and HSL values. Jot down either set of values and the next time you open the Color dialog box, you can enter those same values for a perfect color match.

Better yet, click the Add to Custom Colors button to add a swatch for the color to the Custom Colors area on the left side of the dialog box. Now you can just click the swatch to reselect the color. You can add as many as 16 swatches. To replace an existing swatch with a new one, click the existing swatch, define the new color, and click the Add to Custom Colors button.

Remember that you can also create swatches for your custom colors in the PhotoDeluxe Color Picker dialog box. Then you don't have to open the Windows color picker to use the color later; you just click the swatch in the Color Picker dialog box.

Choosing Web-safe colors

If you're picking a color to use in an image that you plan to put on a Web page, you may want to limit yourself to a 256-color palette known as a *Web-safe palette.* The Color/Solid swatch at the bottom of the Windows Color dialog box helps you do so.

First, some background: A computer monitor can display a finite number of solid colors. It displays other colors by blending — or *dithering* — the available solid colors. Dithered colors appear blotchy or speckled on-screen, although they print fine.

A typical monitor can be set to display anywhere from 256 to 16 million solid colors. The Web-safe palette ensures that your colors look good even on monitors set to the very lowest color display. Color Plate 3-1 illustrates the difference between an image that contains 16 million colors and one with just 256.

To choose Web-safe colors in the Windows Color dialog box, take these steps:

1. **Set your monitor to display a maximum of 256 colors.**

   You can make this change on the Settings tab of the Windows Display Properties dialog box. (Right-click the Windows desktop to display the dialog box.) You may also be able to change the display through a dialog box specific to your monitor or video card, depending on your computer.

2. **Pick your color.**

   The preceding sections explain how to select a color and also how to get to the Windows Color dialog box via the PhotoDeluxe Color Picker dialog box.

3. **Inspect the Color/Solid swatch.**

   The Color side of the box shows the closest shade your monitor can produce by blending two of the 256 colors in its palette. The Solid side shows the closest solid color you can achieve within the 256-color spectrum. (Unless you set your monitor to display fewer than the maximum number of colors, you won't see any difference between the two halves of the Color/Solid box. I was running my monitor at 16 million colors when I captured the screen shown in Figure 10-2, and as you can see, the Color and Solid swatches are identical.)

4. **If the Color side of the box looks dreadful, double-click the Solid side to select the closest solid color.**

   From here, everything works the same as described in the preceding two sections.

Introducing the Painting Tools

Like most people, I use PhotoDeluxe to repair photographic images, not to paint masterpieces from scratch, which is why I rarely pick up the Brush or Line tools. These tools come in handy on occasion — for example, to repair a portion of a border that you accidentally deleted or dab a spot of color onto a scratch or other image defect. But as a general rule, the Brush and Line tools are more for creative expression than for fixing everyday images.

Of course, I might feel differently about these tools if I possessed any painting skills at all. If you're talented at painting with traditional tools, I suspect that you'll have a blast with the digital variety.

Whether you're making a small image correction or painting the masterpiece of the century, the following sections explain everything you need to know to ply the Brush and Line tools.

If you're really interested in digital painting, invest in a graphics tablet. With a tablet, you can use a pen-like stylus to paint or draw, dragging the stylus across the tablet as you would a pencil. Not only do you enjoy a more natural painting or drawing experience, you also get much better control than you do with a mouse. For the same reasons, tablets also make performing precise or complicated touch-up jobs with other editing tools much easier, too. The best new is that you don't have to spend very much to get a decent tablet. For example, you can get a Wacom Graphire tablet, which comes with both a stylus and a cordless mouse, for about $100. The Graphire tablet itself is about the same size as a regular mouse pad.

Painting with the Brush tool

To paint freehand brush strokes, choose Tools⇨Brush or press Ctrl+J. That's right, J, as in, um . . . hmmm. Not sure where they got that one from. At any rate, just drag with the Brush tool to lay down a paint stroke. You can adjust the width, softness, and opacity of your stroke as outlined in the next two sections.

To paint a perfectly straight line, click at the spot where you want the line to start and Shift+Click at the spot where you want the line to end. Click at a second location to add another straight segment to the line.

If you want to create a perfectly horizontal or vertical line, press the mouse button to set the start of the line — press, don't click — and then Shift+Drag to create the line.

Choosing a brush tip

When you first select the Brush tool, PhotoDeluxe displays the Brushes palette shown in Figure 10-3. You also see a similar palette when you work with the Clone, Eraser, and Smudge tools. By clicking icons in the palette, you can change the size and softness of your paint strokes and also open the Color Picker dialog box to change the paint color quickly.

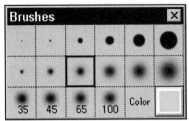

Figure 10-3:
Change the
size and
shape of
your brush
here.

Here's your field guide to this tiny but essential palette:

- The circular icons represent the available brushes. Click an icon to select a brush.

- Icons in the top two rows reflect the actual size of the brush. The smallest brush is just one pixel. Brushes in the last row of the palette are too large to show at their actual size. The number beneath the brush icon indicates the size of the brush in pixels.

- Choose a brush from the top row to paint hard-edged strokes, as if you were drawing with a pen. The other brushes paint soft-edged strokes, more like those you get with a traditional paintbrush.

- Click the Color swatch to open the Color Picker dialog box and change your paint color. You can read more about selecting colors in the preceding sections of this chapter.

- You can relocate the palette on-screen by dragging its title bar.

- Close the palette by clicking the Close button on the title bar. When you do, PhotoDeluxe puts away both the palette and the Brush tool.

You can change your cursor so that it reflects the size of your brush tip. Press Ctrl+K to open the Cursors dialog box and choose Brush Size under the Painting Tools options. You also can press the Caps Lock key to toggle back and forth between a brush-size cursor and a cross-hair cursor without opening the dialog box. (If you're zoomed out from your image and working with a small brush size, PhotoDeluxe surrounds the brush cursor with crosshairs so that you can see the cursor more easily.)

Adjusting opacity

When you work with the Brush, Line, Clone, and Eraser tools, you can vary the tool's opacity setting. If you're painting with the Brush tool, for example, you can paint strokes that are fully opaque, or you can make your strokes translucent, so that some of the underlying pixels show through. Figure 10-4 and Color Plate 10-1 offer a look at the same stroke at different opacity levels.

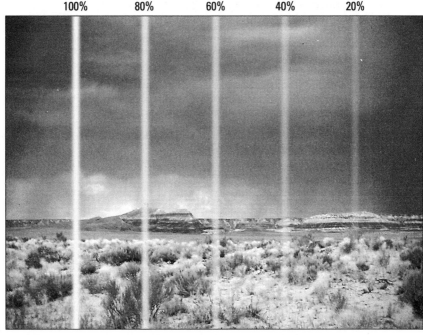

Figure 10-4:
Lowering
the opacity
of the Brush
tool makes
underlying
image pixels
visible
through
your paint
strokes.

Adjusting the tool opacity is as easy as pressing a number key. (If you're using your numeric keyboard, be sure that you turn on the Num Lock function.) Press 0 for fully opaque strokes. Press 9 for 90 percent opacity, 8 for 80 percent, and so on. The opacity settings don't transfer from one tool to another; you set the value for each tool independently. If you set the Brush tool at 50 percent opacity, for example, the other tools aren't also automatically set to 50 percent opacity.

PhotoDeluxe leaves it up to you to remember what opacity value you chose — the value isn't indicated in the Brushes palette or anywhere else. Furthermore, the value you set for a tool remains in force until you press another number key while the tool is selected. If a tool doesn't alter your image in the way that you expected, the opacity setting may be the cause.

Painting straight lines

You can paint a perfectly straight line by Shift+Dragging or Shift+Clicking with the Brush tool. When you use this technique, however, you're limited to the brush sizes available in the Brushes palette. If you want to paint a line of some other size, you need the Line tool; choose Tools⇨Line to activate the tool.

Using the Line tool couldn't be simpler — you just drag to create your line. Before you drag, though, establish the line characteristics as follows:

✔ Set the line thickness by entering a Line Width value in the Line Tool Options dialog box, as shown in Figure 10-5.

✔ Change the line color by clicking the Color icon and selecting the color from the Color Picker dialog box. Like the Brush tool, the Line tool applies the Foreground color.

✔ Set the line opacity by pressing a number key — 0 for full opacity, 9 for 90 percent opacity, and so on.

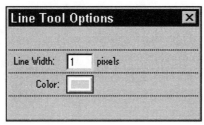

Figure 10-5:
Set your line
width and
color here.

Press Shift before or during your drag to constrain your line to an angle that's an increment of 45 degrees. To envision this feature, imagine a 360-degree circle. If you put your tool cursor in the middle of the circle and try to Shift+Drag to the outside edge of the circle, PhotoDeluxe allows you to drag only to the 0-degree point on the top of the circle, the 45-degree point, the 90-degree point, the 135-degree point, and so on.

Although you can't draw soft-edged lines with the Line tool, you can fuzz up the edges of an existing line. Here's the secret, courtesy of astute technical editor, Hew Hamilton: Select your line and apply the Feather command to it (Effects⇨Feather). Set the color in the Feather dialog box to be the same as the original line color and set the feathering value according to how soft you want to make the edges of the line. Click the Fill Selection icon and click OK. Voilà — fuzzy line. (Chapter 9 explains the Feather command in detail.)

Dragging Your Finger through Wet Paint

The Smudge tool takes you back to the fun of yesteryear, when your kindergarten teacher introduced you to the fine art of finger painting. When you drag with this tool, you smear your image pixels together, creating an effect that looks as if you dragged your paw through wet paint.

As you can see from Color Plate 10-2 and Figure 10-6, you can create some fairly entertaining effects with the Smudge tool. In the right image in the figure and color plate, I gave an unsuspecting feathered friend a makeover by dragging from the middle of the beak toward the edge of the picture. Just to make the poor bird look even sillier, I added a few long eyelashes by dragging outward from the dark rim around the eye. I do hope that all the Audubon Society members out there will forgive me.

To mess up your own images, choose Tools⇨Smudge to select the Smudge tool and display the Smudges palette, which works just like the Brushes palette described earlier in this chapter. Click an icon to select a brush for the Smudge tool and then drag to smudge or Shift+Drag to smudge in a straight line.

You can control the impact of the Smudge tool by pressing a number key before you drag. You get a full-pressure smudge when you press 0, which means that the tool smears a color from the spot where you begin dragging to the spot where you release the mouse button. At lower pressure, the color is smeared for only a portion of your drag. Press 1 for 10 percent pressure, 2 for 20 percent, and so on.

If you use the Smudge tool at full pressure and/or with a large brush, PhotoDeluxe may take a few moments to complete the smudge effect. Don't panic if nothing happens right away when you let up on the mouse button. Give the effect a second or two to materialize.

Figure 10-6: A few swipes of the Smudge tool made this bird's beak and eyelashes grow.

Painting with a Power Roller

If you have a large area to color, don't waste your time scrubbing at it with the Brush or Line tool. PhotoDeluxe offers two tools that paint as many pixels as you want at one time: the Selection Fill command and the Color Change tool. I describe both tools in the next page or so, but here's an up-front disclosure: I don't recommend the Color Change tool because it's not terribly precise. You usually wind up either painting more pixels than you intended or not coloring all the ones you did want to paint.

Using the Selection Fill command

The Selection Fill command fills a selected area with either a solid color or a predefined pattern. Take these steps to flood your selection:

1. **Select the area that you want to fill.**

   If you need help, check out Chapter 9.

2. **Press Ctrl+9 or choose Effects⇨Selection Fill.**

   PhotoDeluxe opens the Selection Fill dialog box, as shown in Figure 10-7.

Figure 10-7: Use the Selection Fill command to paint selected pixels with a solid color or multicolor pattern.

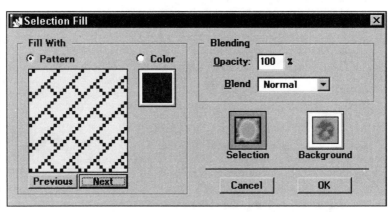

3. **Choose a fill type by clicking the Pattern or Color radio button.**

   For a solid color fill, select the Color radio button. Then click the color swatch to open the Color Picker dialog box and choose your fill color. Click OK to return to the Selection Fill dialog box after you pick your color.

   To fill the selection with a pattern provided by PhotoDeluxe, select the Pattern radio button. Click the Previous and Next buttons to preview the available patterns.

You can create a custom pattern by using the Define Pattern command. The next section explains how.

4. **Enter the fill opacity in the Opacity option box.**

Keep the fill opacity at 100 to completely cover all selected pixels with the fill. Lowering the value makes your fill translucent, so that you can see underlying pixels through it. The lower the value, the more transparent your fill becomes.

5. **Choose a blend mode from the Blend menu.**

The blend options determine how PhotoDeluxe blends your fill pixels with your original image pixels. Each mode creates a different effect; you can explore the possibilities in Color Plate 10-3 and read more about these options later in this chapter's "Blending pixels in cruel and unusual ways."

6. **Click the Selection icon to fill the selection, or click the Background icon to fill the deselected area.**

7. **Click OK or press Enter.**

If you don't like the results of the fill, press Ctrl+Z or click the Undo button. Unfortunately, you can't preview the effects of your settings inside the Selection Fill dialog box, so filling is sometimes a matter of trial and error.

You can fill a selection with the foreground color in a snap by pressing Alt+Delete. Your color is applied at 100 percent opacity and with the Normal blend mode in force.

Filling a selection with a custom pattern

If none of the patterns available in the Selection Fill dialog box amuses you, you can fill a selection with your own patterns. In Figure 10-8, I filled a canvas with a custom pattern created from the bird image in Figure 10-6.

To create a custom pattern and fill a selection with it, open the image that contains the area that you want to use as the basis for your pattern. Keep in mind that you can turn only rectangular areas into patterns. After opening your image, take these steps:

1. **Choose the Rectangle selection tool.**

Press Ctrl+M to do it in a flash.

2. **Select the area that you want to use as the basis for your pattern.**

3. **Choose Effects➪Define Pattern.**

PhotoDeluxe turns your selection into a pattern and stores the pattern with the prefab ones.

   4. **Select the area that you want to fill with the pattern.**

       This time, your selection can be any shape.

   5. **Choose Effects⊅Selection Fill.**

       Your custom pattern should appear in the pattern preview area.

   6. **Click the Pattern button, set the remaining fill options, and click OK or press Enter.**

       See the preceding section for details about all the available fill options. PhotoDeluxe fills the selected area with the pattern, repeating the pattern as many times as necessary.

Figure 10-8:
You can fill a selection with your own custom patterns by using the Define Pattern and Selection Fill commands.

PhotoDeluxe can remember only one custom pattern at a time. If you create a second pattern, the program chucks the first one from the Selection Fill dialog box. Also, PhotoDeluxe doesn't save any custom patterns when you shut down the program. If you want to reuse a pattern in a future editing session, perform this saving routine immediately after you draw the initial selection outline to create your pattern:

   1. **Press Ctrl+C to copy the selection to the Clipboard.**

   2. **Choose File⊅New and click OK to create a new image.**

       PhotoDeluxe automatically sizes the new image to match the size and resolution of the image on the Clipboard.

   3. **Press Ctrl+V to paste the pattern into the new image.**

   4. **Save the image as usual.**

To fill a selection with the pattern, open the pattern, press Ctrl+A to select the entire image, and apply the Define Pattern command. Remember that choosing the Define Pattern command deletes the current custom pattern in the Selection Fill dialog box.

Blending pixels in cruel and unusual ways

When you fill a selection using the Selection Fill command, you can choose from six different blend modes. *Blend modes* control how PhotoDeluxe mixes the fill pixels with the pixels inside the selection. Color Plate 10-3 illustrates how you can vary the effects of the Selection Fill command by using different blend modes.

To create the different pumpkins, I started with the original pumpkin image in the center of the color plate. I selected the pumpkin "skin" — everything but the eyes, nose, mouth, and stem — using the SmartSelect tool. Then I filled the skin with one of the patterns available in the Selection Fill dialog box. The pattern appears in the background of the color plate.

The following list explains the different blend modes. After you get past the first two modes, things get a little complicated. Truthfully, predicting how the blend modes will affect your image isn't easy, so don't worry if you don't understand what's going on. Just experiment until you get results that you like. Don't forget that you can vary the effect of a blend mode by adjusting the Opacity value in the Selection Fill dialog box.

To make these explanations a little simpler, I refer to the original image pixels as the *base pixels* and the color or pattern applied by the Selection Fill command as the *fill pixels:*

- ✔ **Normal:** If you choose this mode, the fill pixels completely obscure the base pixels. I used this mode for the top-left pumpkin in Color Plate 10-3. All highlights and shadows from the original pumpkin are lost. (For a look at the Normal mode when used with a solid color fill, see the top-right image in Color Plate 10-4.)

- ✔ **Color:** This mode applies the hue and saturation of the fill pixels but takes its brightness cue from the base pixels. The result is a fill that retains the original shadows and highlights of the image. In the top-right pumpkin in Color Plate 10-3, for example, you can still see the ribbing in the pumpkin skin.

If you want to change the color of an image element in a way that looks natural, the Color mode is one good option. Take a look at Color Plate 10-4 for further proof.

✔ **Lighten and Darken:** These modes apply the fill depending on the brightness of both the blend and fill pixels. With Lighten, the fill is applied only if it is brighter than the base pixels. With Darken, the fill is applied only if it is darker than the base pixels. PhotoDeluxe analyzes each base pixel and its corresponding fill pixel individually, and then applies the fill accordingly.

When PhotoDeluxe evaluates the brightness of the pixels, however, it considers the brightness of the red, green, and blue components of each pixel, not the overall brightness of the pixel. (Remember, images that you edit in PhotoDeluxe are based on the RGB color model, which mixes colors using red, green, and blue light.) For that reason, figuring out what effect you'll get with Lighten and Darken isn't as easy as you might expect, as illustrated by the examples in Color Plate 10-3. The pumpkin to the left of the original pumpkin illustrates the results of the Lighten mode; the pumpkin to the right of the original illustrates the Darken mode.

✔ **Difference:** Ready to have your mind totally boggled? With the Difference mode, PhotoDeluxe first evaluates the brightness values for the red, green, and blue components of each fill pixel and each base pixel. Then, for each pixel, the program subtracts the fill values from the base values, depending on which one has the greater values. Don't even try to make sense of it — just keep in mind that the Difference mode gives you an inverted effect, similar to a photo negative, but more colorful. I used this mode to create the bottom-right pumpkin in Color Plate 10-3.

✔ **Overlay:** Every bit as challenging as Difference, Overlay multiplies the base pixel information by the fill pixel information if the base pixel is darker than the fill pixel. If the base pixel is lighter, Overlay multiplies the inverse of the base pixel and blend pixel. And if you can understand *that,* please use your mind for something more important than image editing.

In practical terms — albeit not crystal-clear terms — Overlay applies your fill color or pattern in a way that retains the highlights and shadows from both the fill pixels and the base pixels. When you want to replace the color of an image with another color, try the Overlay mode if you can't get the effect you want with the Color mode.

These same blend modes are available in the Layer Options dialog box, where you can specify how you want PhotoDeluxe to mix the pixels in one layer with another layer. (For information about working with layers, see Chapter 11.) In fact, if you want to experiment with blend modes, the Layer Options dialog box is a better place to do it than the Selection Fill dialog box. You can preview the effects of the selected blend mode from inside the Layer Options dialog box; the Selection Fill dialog box has no preview option.

To take this road to blend-mode nirvana, draw your selection outline, create a new layer, and fill the selection by applying the Selection Fill command with the blend mode set to Normal. Double-click the new layer in the Layers palette to open the Layer Options dialog box, where you can set the layer opacity and blend mode. You can take this same approach when you paint with the Brush or Line tools.

Trying the Color Change tool

Note the name of this section. I chose the headline because I think that after you try the Color Change tool once, you're likely to abandon it in favor of the more capable and precise Selection Fill command, explained in the preceding sections.

The Color Change command works like a combination of the Color Wand and the Selection Fill command. Color Change selects an area of the image and then fills the selection for you. Unfortunately, you can't accurately predict which pixels will be selected and recolored in most cases. Furthermore, the command is a bit awkward to use, as you can discover for yourself by following these steps:

1. **Choose Tools⇨Color Change.**

   PhotoDeluxe activates the Color Change tool and displays the diminutive Color Change palette, shown in Figure 10-9.

Figure 10-9: Click the Color icon to set the replacement fill color.

2. **Click the Color swatch to change the fill color (optional).**

   The Color swatch opens the Color Picker dialog box, where you can select a new fill color as explained in "Picking a Paint Color" earlier in this chapter.

3. **Press a number key to set the tool opacity.**

   Press 0 to make your fill completely opaque; 9 for 90 percent opacity; 8 for 80 percent opacity; and so on.

4. **In your image, click the color that you want to replace with the fill color.**

PhotoDeluxe selects all adjacent pixels that are similar in color to the pixel you clicked, just as if you clicked with the Color Wand. Then — before you can say "Stop, that's not the area I wanted to select!" — PhotoDeluxe fills the selection.

You do have the power to vary the sensitivity of the Color Change tool, as you can with the Color Wand. In fact, you use the same control as when you adjust the Color Wand. Press Ctrl+K to open the Cursors dialog box and adjust the Color Wand Tolerance value. Lower the value to make the Color Change tool more selective; raise the value to include a greater spectrum of colors in the selection.

When you work with the Color Wand, you rarely get the selection outline just right the first time; the same is true with the Color Change tool. But with the Color Change tool, you don't have the opportunity to refine the selection before the fill is applied. In Figure 10-10, I set the Color Change tool opacity to 100 percent, chose light gray as my fill color, and clicked at the spot on the collar marked by the Paint Can cursor (the standard cursor for the Color Change tool). By clicking a few pixels away, I could fill an entirely different area of the collar.

Figure 10-10:
The Color Change tool selects and fills an area with one click, but is often imprecise.

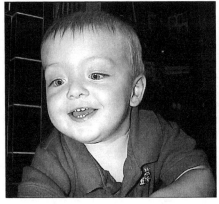 

If the Color Change tool alters too few pixels, you can keep clicking to fill more areas. If too many pixels were changed, you have to click Undo and start the whole procedure over. Because it's difficult (at best) to gauge which pixels the Color Change tool will select, I suggest that you avoid this option. Instead, create an exact selection using the Selection tools discussed in Chapter 9 and then apply your fill using the Selection Fill command explained earlier in this chapter. You get more control over the selection and you also get the advantage of the blend and opacity options available in the Selection Fill dialog box.

Replacing One Color with Another

When you want to change the color of something in your picture, you have several options. Some work better than others, as illustrated in Color Plate 10-4. I decided to create a new type of grape, so I selected the grapes in the original image (top left) and then filled the selection three different ways:

✔ In the top-right image, I applied the Selection Fill command with the Blend mode set to Normal, the Opacity value set at 100 percent, and orange as my fill color. The result is a solid expanse of flat color — hardly a natural-looking effect. Forget this option. You get the same unhappy results if you paint over the grapes with the Brush or Line tools set to 100 percent opacity, by the way.

✔ To create the glowing green grapes in the bottom-left image, I once again used the Selection Fill command. But this time I chose green as the fill color, set the Blend mode to Color, and the Opacity value to 100 percent. Because the Color mode retains the brightness values of the original grapes, you don't lose any image details and you achieve more lifelike results. Another possibility is to choose the Overlay mode, which retains the brightness values of both the grapes and the fill color.

You can get the same results by painting with the Brush tool on a new layer. Select the grapes, create a new layer immediately above the grape layer, set the layer blend mode to Color or Overlay in the Layer Options dialog box, and then paint inside your selection. See Chapter 11 for more information about layers.

✔ In the bottom-right example in Color Plate 10-4, I selected the grapes, chose the Quality⇨Hue/Saturation command, and adjusted the Hue value in the Hue/Saturation dialog box. (You can read more about this dialog box in Chapter 7, in the section that discusses color saturation.)

To understand how Hue works, think of a *color wheel* — a circular graph on which every color is mapped out. Red is situated at the 0-degree position on the circle, green at 120 degrees, and blue at 240 degrees. When you change the Hue value, you move so many degrees around the color wheel.

Suppose that you select a blue pixel. If you raise the Hue value to 120, your pixel becomes red. Blue occupies the 240-degree mark on the color wheel, and 240 degrees plus 120 degrees equals 360 degrees — or 0 degrees, whichever way you want to look at things. (A circle is 360 degrees total, for all those who skipped math class.) Either way, you get a red pixel because red lives at 0 degrees.

Note how the shadows and highlights in the grapes were affected differently when I adjusted the Hue value and when I applied a fill using the Color blend mode. In the Color mode example (bottom left in Color Plate 10-4), all pixels are some shade of green. In the Hue example (bottom right), the areas that were dark on the original grapes become almost black.

If you want to make subtle color changes, you can also give the Quality⇨Color Balance command a whirl. Using this command or its twin, Effects⇨Variations, you can adjust the amount of red, green, and blue in your color. See Chapter 7 to explore Color Balance and Variations fully. For color shifts that are totally unrealistic, check out the special-effects color filters discussed in Chapter 13.

Whichever color-changing technique you use, remember that you can adjust the effect by playing with opacity. If you apply your new color on a layer, raise or lower the Opacity value in the Layer Options dialog box to make the new color more or less transparent. If you apply the new color by using the Selection Fill dialog box, adjust the Opacity value in the Selection Fill dialog box.

Creating a Gradient Fill

A gradient fill? Sounds like something you pour on a driveway to repair cracks, doesn't it? Well, in the ever-odd world of digital nomenclature, a *gradient* refers to a gradual transition from one color to another. If you fill a selection with a black to white gradient — *apply a gradient fill,* in techie terms — you get something like the image in Figure 10-11.

Figure 10-11:
A black-to-white circular gradient.

Gradient fills are great for spicing up a boring background. If your image features an object set against a plain white background, for example, you can apply the gradient to the background to add some depth and interest to the background.

The following steps explain how to create a simple gradient fill:

1. **Select the area that you want to fill.**

   Alternatively, select the background. The Gradient Fill command enables you to fill either the selected or the deselected area.

2. **Press Ctrl+8 or choose Effects⇨Gradient Fill to open the Gradient Fill dialog box (see Figure 10-12).**

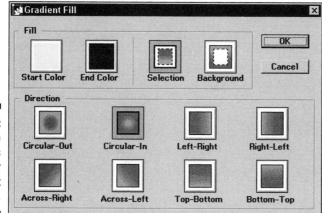

Figure 10-12: Set the style and colors of your gradient fill here.

3. **Set the start and end colors of the gradient.**

   Click the Start Color icon to display the Color Picker dialog box and choose the initial gradient color. Click the End Color icon to select the other gradient color. (If you need help using the Color Picker, see "Picking a Paint Color," earlier in this chapter.)

4. **Specify whether you want to fill the selected pixels or deselected pixels.**

   To fill pixels inside the selection outline, click the Selection icon. To fill pixels outside the outline, click the Background icon.

5. **Choose a gradient direction.**

   Click one of the eight icons at the bottom of the dialog box to choose the style and direction of the gradient.

6. **Click OK or press Enter.**

For some fun special effects, try creating your gradient fill on a separate layer from the rest of the image. Reduce the layer opacity to something less than 100 percent, so the underlying image remains visible, and blend the gradient with the underlying image using one of the layer blend modes covered a few pages ago. See Chapter 11 for the complete scoop on layers.

Chapter 11

Better Living through Layers

*I*f you want to become proficient at image editing, this chapter is a must-read. Here you find out about the professional's secret weapon: layers. By taking advantage of layers, you can save yourself an enormous amount of time and heartache. Just as important, you can explore a whole spectrum of creative effects that are impossible to achieve without layers.

In other words, don't miss this chapter!

Peering through Layers

After such a glowing introduction, you're no doubt drooling over the concept of layers — except maybe you're not really sure what a layer *is*.

Perhaps an analogy can help. Imagine that instead of creating a digital image, you're creating transparencies to use with an overhead projector. You know — those old-fashioned sheets of clear acetate that people relied on before whiz-bang multimedia presentations came into vogue.

Anyway, you put an image of a house on one transparency. The house image is completely *opaque* (solidly colored) and covers the middle of the transparency; the rest of the sheet is clear. On another transparency, you put an image of a peaceful mountainside. That image covers the whole sheet and, like the house, is fully opaque.

If you put the house transparency on top of the mountain transparency and project the two images, the result is a scene of a house set against a mountain backdrop. The mountain image is visible where the house transparency is clear. If you reverse the order of the two transparencies, however, the mountain image totally obscures the house image.

Now suppose that you want to add a third transparency with some notations about urban sprawl and the decay of our natural resources or something like that. You pick up a marker and start scribbling on a new sheet of acetate. But instead of writing *environment,* you mistakenly write *enviroment.* No problem — you just trash that sheet of acetate and grab a new one. You haven't damaged your house image or your mountain image in any way.

Fine, you think, but what does all this have to do with digital images? Well, image layers are like digital sheets of acetate. Every image starts out with two layers: one for regular image pixels and another reserved solely for text that you create with the Text tool.

You can create as many additional image layers as you like. You can put different image elements on different layers, just as you put that house, mountain, and text on different transparencies. And just as with overhead transparencies, empty areas of a layer allow elements from underlying layers to show through.

Fine again, you say. But why would you want to compartmentalize your various picture elements this way? Here are just a few reasons:

- ✔ **You can edit one element without affecting the rest of the image.** If you want to change the color of your house image, for example, you can paint on the house layer without fear that you'll spill some paint on the text or mountain image.

- ✔ **You can experiment freely.** If you want to try out a special effect, for example, you can apply the effect on a duplicate of your original layer. If you don't like the results, you just delete the layer. Your original image isn't affected in the least.

- ✔ **You can shuffle layer order to combine image elements in different ways.** You can put your house layer on top of your mountain layer, so that you create the house-on-a-mountainside image. Swap layers, and the mountain obscures the house.

- ✔ **You can reposition elements on one layer with respect to elements on other layers.** If all the elements are on a single layer, you can't move any of them without leaving background-colored holes in the image. (See Chapter 9 for details on that issue.)

✔ **You can adjust layer opacity to expand creative possibilities even further.** For example, if you have your mountain layer stacked on top of your house layer and reduce the opacity of the mountain layer to just 50 percent, you see a faint house image through your mountain image.

✔ **You can create interesting special effects using layer blend modes.** *Blend modes* control how pixels on one layer mix with pixels on the underlying layer. You can find out more about blend modes in Chapter 10 and see examples of blend mode effects in Color Plate 10-3.

The rest of this chapter explores these and other ways to take advantage of layers. Although working with layers may seem like the long way to do things at first, after you compare editing with layers to editing without them, you'll never again want to be caught layerless.

Working with the Layers Palette

The key to creating, arranging, and editing layers is the Layers palette, shown in Figure 11-1. To display the palette, choose View➪Show Layers. If the palette obscures your image, you can relocate the palette by dragging its title bar. You also can drag a corner of the palette to resize it.

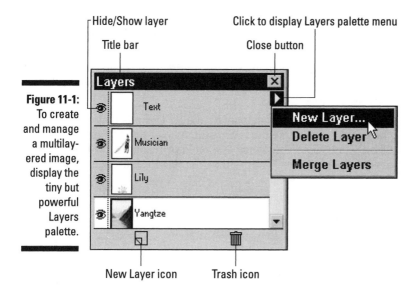

Figure 11-1: To create and manage a multilayered image, display the tiny but powerful Layers palette.

Hide/Show layer

Title bar

Click to display Layers palette menu

Close button

New Layer icon   Trash icon

For such a small creature, the palette offers loads of options for creating and managing layers. Later sections in this chapter offer more details about various aspects of the palette, but here's an introduction:

✔ The palette lists all layers in your image. To the left of a layer name, you see a thumbnail representation of the layer contents. By default, every image contains a background layer, called Layer 0, and a text layer, called (oddly enough) the Text layer.

✔ Only one layer is *active* — affected by your edits — at a time. The name of the active layer appears highlighted in the palette. (In Figure 11-1, the Yangtze layer is active.) To make a different image layer active, click its name.

If you want to activate the Text layer, you need to haul out the Object Selection tool and click the actual text in the image. Chapter 12 provides more information on the Text layer.

✔ Click the eyeball icon to the left of a layer name to hide the layer contents. Click again to bring the layer back into view. To hide all layers but one, Alt+Click the eyeball next to the layer that you want to see. Alt+Click the eyeball again to redisplay all layers.

Hidden layers do not print. That fact can come in handy if you want to print two versions of a picture, one including certain layers and another without those layers.

✔ Click the right-pointing arrow in the upper-right corner of the palette to display the palette menu. The menu, shown in Figure 11-1, contains commands for managing layers.

You don't need to visit the menu to choose the New Layer and Delete Layer commands. Instead, click the New Layer and Trash icons at the bottom of the palette.

✔ Double-click a layer name to display the Layer Options dialog box. In the dialog box, you can rename the layer, adjust layer opacity, and choose a layer blend mode. See "Making Layer Elements Transparent" and "Fooling Around with Blend Modes" later in this chapter for more information.

Creating New Layers

When you open an image for the first time, PhotoDeluxe automatically generates two layers. The bottom layer, called Layer 0, holds your image pixels. The top layer, the Text layer, waits to collect any text that you create with the Text tool (explained in Chapter 12).

If you want to create more layers, you have several options:

✔ Click the New Layer icon (labeled in Figure 11-1) or choose New Layer from the palette menu. PhotoDeluxe displays the New Layer dialog box, shown in Figure 11-2. Here, you can give your layer a name, set the opacity of the layer, and choose a layer blend mode. You can revisit this dialog box at any time by double-clicking the layer name in the Layers palette, so don't worry if you're not sure just yet what opacity or blend mode you want to use.

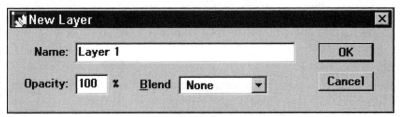

Figure 11-2:
Give your new layer a name here.

After you click OK, PhotoDeluxe adds your new layer directly above the layer that was active when you clicked the New Layer icon or chose the New Layer command. The new layer is now the active layer.

✔ Want to bypass the New Layer dialog box? Alt+Click the New Layer icon. PhotoDeluxe creates a new layer using 100 percent as the Opacity value and Normal as the blend mode. The new layer is assigned a name — Layer 1, Layer 2, and so on, depending on how many layers already exist in your image.

✔ To copy the contents of an entire layer to a new layer, drag the layer name to the New Layer icon. PhotoDeluxe puts the duplicate layer directly above the original.

You also create a new layer when you use the Paste command to paste a selection that you copied or cut to the Windows Clipboard. If you drag and drop a selection or paste a selection with the Paste Into command, the selection goes on a temporary layer, called a *floating layer.* To turn the floating layer into a permanent layer, drag the Floating Layer item in the Layers palette to the New Layer icon or choose Make Layer from the palette menu. You can get a full explanation of these bewildering possibilities in Chapter 9.

PhotoDeluxe accepts as many as 99 layers per image, but remember that every layer you add increases the size of your image file and the amount of RAM and scratch disk space PhotoDeluxe needs to process your edits. (The scratch disk is explained in Chapter 2.) If your computer starts complaining about overload, either delete some of your layers or merge all your layers together, as described in "Gluing layers together," later in this chapter.

Shuffling Layer Order

In the Layers palette, you see the names of all layers in your picture. PhotoDeluxe lists the names according to their positions in the image. The Text layer is always the top layer of any image, even if you don't create any text.

Although you can't move the Text layer, you can rearrange other layers to combine image elements in different ways. For example, both images in Figure 11-3 contain three image layers: one for the Yangtze River scene, one for the lily, and one for the musician. The river image is the bottom layer in both images.

Figure 11-3: Swapping the stacking order of the lily and musician layers creates two different scenes.

In the left example, I placed the musician layer on top of the lily layer, so that the musician appears to be standing in front of the lily, with his feet resting on the lily petals. In the right example, I switched the two layers so that the lily layer is the top layer and the musician layer is the middle layer. Now the musician appears to be standing amid the lily petals at the back of the image. I didn't move the musician or the lily in the image frame to come up with these images — I merely rearranged the order of the two layers.

You can shuffle the order of your layers by using the following techniques:

✔ Drag the layer names in the Layers palette. Click the name of the layer that you want to move and then drag it up or down to the position you want the layer to occupy. As you drag, your cursor changes into a clenched fist to show that you grasped the layer correctly, as shown in Figure 11-4. A heavy black line indicates where the layer will be dropped if you release the mouse button.

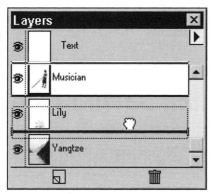

Figure 11-4:
Drag a layer
up or down
the list to
change its
placement
in the layer
stacking
order.

✔ Grab the Object Selection tool and click any element on the layer that
you want to move. (PhotoDeluxe doesn't select the layer if you click a
transparent area.) Then click the Stacking Order button in the image
window, labeled in Figure 11-5, to display a menu containing four
options:

- Send to Back sends your layer to the bottom of the stack.

- Send Back One moves the layer down one level.

- Bring Forward One moves the layer up one position.

- Bring to Front places the layer at the top of the layer stack.

Stacking Order button

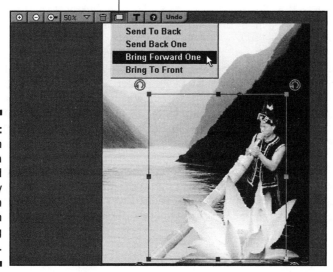

Figure 11-5:
You also can
reposition a
selected
layer by
choosing an
option from
the Stacking
Order menu.

Even though you can't change the position of the Text layer, you can use the technique I discuss in Chapter 12 to turn text into a regular image layer. After you make the conversion, you can shift words around at will.

Trashing, Merging, and Saving Layers

PhotoDeluxe insists that every image contain at least one layer for image pixels and one layer for text pixels. But aside from that restriction, you're in control of the layer switchboard.

You can add new layers by following the instructions found earlier in this chapter, in the section "Creating New Layers." You also can delete layers at will and keep your layers independent or merge them into one happy family when you save your picture. The next three sections tell you how to take care of these layer-management tasks.

Deleting a layer

To get rid of a layer in your image, take any of these roads:

- ✔ Open the Layers palette (View➪Show Layers) and drag the layer name to the Trash icon at the bottom of the palette. (See Figure 11-1 for a look at the palette and icon.)

- ✔ Click the layer name in the Layers palette and then click the Trash icon.

- ✔ Switch to the Object Selection tool, if it's not currently active, and then click a layer element in the image window or click the layer name in the Layers palette. When you select the layer using these methods, you can delete the layer by clicking the Trash button in the image window (next to the Stacking Order button back in Figure 11-5), pressing Delete, or clicking the Trash icon in the Layers palette.

When you delete a layer, you dump all pixels on the layer. If you want to reduce the number of layers in the image without destroying any image elements, use the Merge Layers command, discussed next.

Also remember that hidden layers don't print, so you don't need to delete a layer just to create a version of your picture that doesn't include stuff on that layer. Just click the eyeball icon next to the layer name in the palette and then send your picture off to printing camp. Click the eyeball again to bring the layer back into view.

Gluing Layers Together

Because every layer you add to an image increases the image file size, merge layers together whenever possible. When you merge layers, they become permanently fused together, so that all elements from the individual layers reside on the same layer. Unfortunately, layer merging is an all-or-nothing proposition. You either merge all your image pixels together or keep them on separate layers. You can't merge only two layers in a four-layer image, for example. The only layer that always retains its independence is the Text layer.

Merging layers is called *flattening the image* in image-editing parlance.

After you flatten your image, you lose the ability to move, resize, and otherwise manipulate the individual image elements without affecting the rest of the image. Before you flatten, you may want to make a copy of the layered image in case you're ever interested in working with the separate layers again. Be sure to save your image in the native PhotoDeluxe format, PDD. (The Photoshop format, PSD, also retains layers but isn't the best option for saving works in progress, for reasons Chapter 4 explains.)

When you're really ready to take away layer independence, open the Layers palette menu by clicking the arrowhead near the top-right corner of the palette (refer to Figure 11-1). Choose Merge Layers to smush those layers together.

Saving layered images

I know that I just mentioned this two short paragraphs ago, but the file-saving issue is so important that it bears repeating. When you save a picture, you *must* save it in the PhotoDeluxe native format, PDD, or the Adobe Photoshop format, PSD. Choose any other format, and PhotoDeluxe merges image layers without any advance notice. In this case, even the Text layer gets merged.

Save in the PDD format unless you need to open the file in Photoshop or want to take advantage of the special text technique that I discuss in the next chapter. Although Photoshop retains image layers, it converts the Text layer into a standard image layer, so you can't go back and edit your text in PhotoDeluxe easily. In addition, PhotoDeluxe can work with PDD files much more quickly than files saved in other formats. Chapter 4 can fill you in on these and other file-saving issues.

Creating See-Through Layers

You can change a layer's opacity to make an element on one layer appear to fade into the layer below. In Figure 11-6, I used this trick to give the musician and lily a ghostly appearance. The image contains three layers: The musician occupies the top layer, the lily the middle layer, and the background the bottom layer. I set the layer opacity for both the lily layer and the musician layer at 50 percent and left the background image set to full opacity.

Figure 11-6: I turned the lily and musician into ghosts of their former selves by reducing the layer opacity to 50 percent.

The following steps explain how to alter the opacity of any layer except the Text layer. Chapter 12 explains how to create translucent text:

1. **Double-click the layer name in the Layers palette.**

   PhotoDeluxe displays the Layer Options dialog box, which looks just like the New Layer dialog box shown in Figure 11-2, except for the name on the title bar.

2. **Enter a value in the Opacity option box.**

   Double-click the box and type in a new value. After you double-click the box, you also can press the up- and down-arrows to raise or lower the value one step. A value of 100 percent makes your layer perfectly opaque, so that any pixels on the layer completely obscure any pixels on underlying layers. Any value less than 100 percent makes the layer pixels translucent, so that the underlying pixels become visible.

As you change the value, PhotoDeluxe displays the effect in the image window, so you can play around with different values until you get the look you want.

3. Click OK or press Enter.

These steps affect all pixels on the layer. The next section explains how you can make just some parts of a layer more or less opaque.

Fading a Portion of a Layer

Want to make just some areas on a layer translucent? You have two options: To make the areas completely transparent, select the areas that you want to change (see Chapter 9 for help) and then press Delete. If you want to control how transparent your pixels become, introduce yourself to the Eraser tool.

The Eraser tool is one of the coolest weapons in the PhotoDeluxe arsenal. When you drag over a portion of your image with the Eraser, PhotoDeluxe completely or partially erases the pixels you touch, depending on the tool setting you choose. You can use the Eraser to change the opacity of pixels on any layer except the Text layer. (See Chapter 12 for more about text.)

Figure 11-7 offers an example. In this image, the musician image is on the top layer, with the lily image on the layer immediately below. The right image catches me in the act of erasing the musician's leg. Wherever the Eraser tip touches the leg, PhotoDeluxe makes the pixels transparent, allowing the underlying lily image to show through.

Here's how to use the Eraser:

1. Press Ctrl+E or choose Tools⊅Eraser.

PhotoDeluxe activates the tool and displays the Eraser palette, which is just like the Brushes palette that appears when you work with the Brush tool. (For details, see Chapter 10.)

2. Choose a brush from the Eraser palette.

Again, review Chapter 10 to understand your options here.

Don't forget that you can set your cursor to reflect the actual size of the brush you choose. Press Ctrl+K to open the Cursors dialog box, choose the Brush Size option in the Painting Tools section of the dialog box, and click OK. For more about cursor options, see Chapter 2.

3. Set the Eraser opacity.

If you want to make pixels completely transparent, press 0. Press any other number from 1 to 9 to make the pixels partially transparent. Press 1 for 10 percent opacity, 2 for 20 percent opacity, and so on.

4. Click or drag over the pixels you want to erase.

Figure 11-7: Rub the Eraser tool over image pixels to make them transparent.

If you erase pixels on the bottom layer of your image, you reveal the image canvas. By default, the canvas appears white, which may fool you into thinking that the erased areas aren't really transparent. But if you open the Background Options dialog box (choose File➪Preferences➪Image Background) and change the background display to one of the checkerboard options, you can see that you are indeed making the pixels transparent, not white. Keep in mind, though, that transparent areas appear white when you print your picture or place it in a program other than PhotoDeluxe.

Fooling Around with Blend Modes

Blend modes enable you to mix the pixels in one layer with the pixels in another layer in a variety of ways to create special effects. When you work with multilayered images, you have access to the same blend modes available in the Selection Fill dialog box. You can see examples of the effects that each mode creates in Color Plate 10-3 and read more about each mode in Chapter 10.

You can set the layer blend mode in two ways:

✔ When you create a new layer, select a mode from the Blend drop-down list in the New Layer dialog box. (See "Creating New Layers," earlier in this chapter, for more information about adding layers.)

✔ To change the blend mode for an existing layer, double-click the layer name in the Layers palette to open the Layer Options dialog box. Choose the blend mode from the Blend drop-down list.

While you're inside either the New Layer dialog box or the Layer Options dialog box, you can see how your image appears with a particular blend mode selected. Play around with the different modes until you're happy with the effect and then click OK or press Enter to close the dialog box.

Creating a Multilayered Collage

To get a better understanding of how to put all the advantages of layers to use, take a look at Color Plates 11-1 and 11-2. In Color Plate 11-1, you see a collection of images that I shot on a recent trip to China. Color Plate 11-2 shows the collage that I created by layering all those individual elements.

The following list explains how I combined the elements into the collage. Reviewing these tactics can give you some ideas about how to build your own multilayered masterpiece:

✔ First, I opened each individual image and did any necessary color correction, sharpening, and so on.

✔ I wanted to keep all my original images intact in case I needed them again in the future, so I saved each corrected image under a new name, as explained in Chapter 4.

✔ Working on the duplicate images, I selected the portion of the image that I wanted to use in the collage. In most cases, I relied on the SmartSelect tool as the primary selection tool. (See Chapter 9 for a review of selection tools.)

✔ One by one, I copied and pasted the selected elements into the Yangtze River image.

✔ After pasting in each element, I moved it into position using the techniques discussed in Chapter 9. I resized a few image elements — but only slightly, because too much resizing can damage image quality, as explained in Chapter 3. I slightly rotated the lily image and kept all the other images at their original orientation.

✔ Using the Eraser tool with a soft, fuzzy brush and an opacity value of 50 percent, I nipped at the edges of the stone lion's feet to create a softer transition between the lion's paws and the background water. I did the same thing along the bottom and right corner of the golden statue image so that the statue appears to be tucked behind the mountain and sunk into the water. I set the Eraser opacity at 50 percent when erasing along the water edge and 100 percent when rubbing along the mountain edge.

I also dragged the Eraser over the inside leg of the musician. Originally, the leg obscured the lily petals rather than the other way around. (The left image in Figure 11-3 shows the original appearance of the two layers.) By erasing the leg pixels, I brought the lily pixels back into view so that the musician appears to be perched inside the flower.

✔ I created the shadowed text, which actually includes three separate components: a block of red text, a block of black text, and a drop shadow. You can find out how to create similar text effects in Chapter 12.

✔ For all layers, I set the layer opacity to 100 percent and the blend mode to Normal.

The collage would have been impossible to create without using layers. Sure, I could have pasted all the image elements directly onto the river image. But without layers, I wouldn't have been able to position, size, and erase the elements as I did in the multilayered version. For maximum creative potential, layers are without a doubt the image-editor's best friend.

Chapter 12

Text Expressions

"*A* picture is worth 1,000 words," says the old adage, and you'll get no argument from me on that one. But on occasion, you need 1,001, 1,002, or even 1,003 words. That's the time to pick up the Text tool. Using the Text tool, you can add captions, callouts, or other words of wisdom to your images.

This chapter shows you how to create simple text using the Text tool and the special Text layer that PhotoDeluxe reserves for your pithy phrases. You also find out how to work around some inherent limitations in the Text tool and create some special text effects, such as the examples in Color Plate 12-1.

Laying Down Language

Because of the way PhotoDeluxe designed the Text layer, you can create only a few text effects with the Text tool. Later sections in this chapter show you how to work around the Text tool's limitations and expand your text artistry. But whether you want the most basic or most advanced effects, you always start by using the Text tool to create your initial text elements. Here's how to type on your image:

1. **Click the T button at the top of the image window.**

   (Take a look ahead at Figure 12-2 if you have trouble locating the button.) You also can choose Tools⇨Text or press Ctrl+T instead of clicking the button. Either way, PhotoDeluxe activates the Text tool and opens the Text Tool dialog box, which is shown in Figure 12-1.

Text-entry box

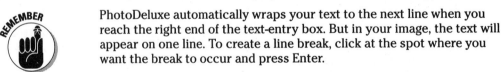

Figure 12-1:
Type your
text into the
Text Tool
dialog box.

2. **Type your text in the text-entry box.**

   When you first open the dialog box, you should see a blinking line, otherwise known as the *text-insertion cursor,* in the text-entry box. If you don't, click in the box to display the cursor. You can then type your text.

   PhotoDeluxe automatically wraps your text to the next line when you reach the right end of the text-entry box. But in your image, the text will appear on one line. To create a line break, click at the spot where you want the break to occur and press Enter.

   If you want to add several lines of text to your picture, you may want to create each line on separate trips to the Text Tool dialog box. That way, you can adjust the color, positioning, and other attributes of each line individually.

3. **Select the font and type size.**

   When you choose a font from the Font drop-down list, your text appears in that font inside the text box. PhotoDeluxe does not show the text at its actual size, however. You can change the size — or any text formatting, for that matter — down the road, so just pick an approximate size on your first trip to the dialog box.

   Type size is measured in *points,* the traditional unit of measurement for type. One inch equals roughly 72 points.

4. **Choose an Alignment option.**

These options determine whether your text runs horizontally across the image, like normal book text, or vertically. In addition, if you enter multiple lines of text, the options also control how the rows of text align with respect to each other. For example, if you click the first alignment option in the top row, text lines are aligned by the left edge.

The top three alignment options apply left alignment, centered alignment, and right alignment, respectively. The bottom three options orient your text into columns, so that it runs vertically on the page rather than horizontally. Here, you can opt for top, centered, or bottom alignment.

5. **Set the text color.**

The Color swatch shows the current color. To change the color, click the swatch and choose a color from the Color Picker dialog box. (Refer to Chapter 10 for help.)

6. **Set the text opacity.**

If you upgraded to PhotoDeluxe 4 from Version 2 or the Business Edition, you'll appreciate the Transparency option in the dialog box. Adobe added this option to Version 3 and carried it over to Version 4, making the task of fading text into the rest of your picture as easy as it always should have been.

To create fully opaque text, set the Transparency value to 0. Raise the value to create translucent text. You can either drag the Transparency slider bar or enter a number in the option box to set the value. PhotoDeluxe doesn't offer a preview of the transparency effect in the image window or in the dialog box, but you can easily change the value later, so guesstimate for now.

7. **Click OK.**

PhotoDeluxe creates your text, places it on the special Text layer, and then selects the text and the Object Selection tool automatically. While the text is selected, you can resize, rotate, or reposition it. See the next section for how-tos.

You can create as many blocks of text as you like, just repeat the steps to add more text. If you screw up and type something incorrectly, the next section explains the easiest way to fix things.

Editing Text

You can revise your text at any time. You can open the Text Tool dialog box to fix spelling mistakes or other problems, and you also can use the Object Selection tool to relocate your text.

However, you retain full text-editing privileges only for pictures that you save in the native PhotoDeluxe format, PDD. Save your picture in the Photoshop format, PSD, and PhotoDeluxe sends the contents of the Text layer to a regular image layer. (This conversion actually comes in handy for creating text effects, as you find out in the next section.) When you open the new PSD image, you can continue manipulating some aspects of your text, such as opacity, but you can't correct typos via the Text Tool dialog box.

Saving to other file formats limits you even further. PhotoDeluxe merges text and image pixels together, so when you open the saved picture, your text pixels work like normal image pixels. You can edit text separately from the rest of the picture only if you draw a selection outline around each and every character. And, as with images saved in the Photoshop format, you can't alter the text via the Text Tool dialog box.

In other words, until you're 100 percent sure you won't ever want to eat your words, always save your picture in the PhotoDeluxe format. You can then edit every aspect of your text as necessary.

To alter text, first click it with the Object Selection tool. PhotoDeluxe surrounds the text with a solid selection outline, just as when you select a layer with the tool. The Resize and Rotate handles appear as usual. (If you just exited the Text Tool dialog box, the text should already be selected.) You can see the outline and handles in Figure 12-2.

After selecting your text, you can do the following:

- **Change the actual words or characters:** Double-click inside the selection outline to redisplay the Text Tool dialog box (or use one of the other three methods for opening the dialog box). PhotoDeluxe displays the existing text in the text-entry box. Drag over the characters you want to delete and then press Delete or type replacement characters.

- **Change text font, color, alignment, or transparency:** Again, revisit the Text Tool dialog box.

- **Resize or distort text:** Drag a Resize handle, labeled in Figure 11-2. (Check out Chapter 9 for all your handle-dragging options.) You also can open the Text Tool dialog box and enter a new value in the Size option box.

- **Rotate text:** Tug a Rotate handle, also labeled in the figure. With text, you can't use the Rotate Right and Rotate Left commands to spin the selection 90 degrees, as you can with an ordinary selection.

Rotate handle

Text-tool button   Selection outline   Resize handle

Figure 12-2:
Drag the
Rotate and
Resize
handles to
enlarge,
shrink, or
spin your
text.

✔ **Flip text:** PhotoDeluxe doesn't let you apply the Flip Horizontal or Flip
Vertical commands to text, either, but you can drag a Resize handle to
flip your words. Drag a right Resize handle past a left Resize handle (or
vice versa) to flip the text horizontally. Drag a top handle past a bottom
handle to flip the text vertically.

✔ **Move text:** Put your cursor inside the selection outline and then drag
the text. Unfortunately, you can't nudge the selection into place using
the arrow keys as you can a regular selection, and you can't drag text
from one image window to another. If you want to move text from image
to image, use the Edit⇨Cut and Edit⇨Paste commands, both described
in Chapter 9.

✔ **Duplicate text:** Choose Edit⇨Duplicate. PhotoDeluxe copies the text and
offsets the copy so that you can see it clearly. Alternatively, you can use
the Copy command to put a copy of the text on the Windows Clipboard
and then choose Paste to dump the copy from the Clipboard into the
active image. You can't, however, use the Alt+Drag method of copying
regular selections to copy text.

✔ **Delete text:** Just press Delete to wipe out a selected text block.

Creating Special Text Effects

With all the powerful special effects that PhotoDeluxe lays at your feet, you'd think that you'd be able to produce some pretty impressive text. Well, you can — but only if you know a secret trick to free your text from the Text layer.

Using this method, you turn text into ordinary image pixels that live on an ordinary image layer. After that, you can do just about anything you want with your text, from painting on it to filling it with an image. Color Plate 12-1 shows some examples of typographical treatments for inspiration; the following sections give you specific instructions to start you on your text adventure.

Basic recipe for cooler text

Before you can explore advanced text effects, you have to help your text escape from the Text layer to a regular image layer. Here's how:

1. **Use the Text tool to create your text as usual.**

   The first part of this chapter explains how.

   Double-check your text to make sure that the words are spelled correctly. After you complete the rest of these steps, you can't use the Text Tool dialog box to edit individual words or change the font or text alignment.

   Also, set the text opacity to 100 percent. You can lower the opacity later, but you can't increase it. You can alter text size and color later, so don't concern yourself with those text characteristics too much.

2. **Choose File⇨Export⇨File Format to open the Export dialog box.**

3. **Deselect the Flatten Image check box in the dialog box.**

4. **Select Photoshop 3.0 & 4.0 (*.PSD) from the Save As drop-down list.**

5. **Enter a filename, select your storage locations, and click Save.**

   See Chapter 4 if you need help negotiating these exporting steps.

   PhotoDeluxe saves your image in the Photoshop format. In the process, everything on the Text layer gets relocated to a new, ordinary image layer. The on-screen image, the PDD version, pretends not to notice.

6. **Close the on-screen image (the PDD version).**

   You don't need to bother saving this version unless you want to retain a backup that contains the official Text layer. If you do, save the image in the PDD format.

7. Open the PSD version of the image.

After you open the image, take a look at the Layers palette. Magic! The official Text layer is empty, but all the text you created is intact on the new layer.

What your liberated text can do

Transporting your text to a regular image layer opens up a zillion creative possibilities — maybe more.

Before you can explore those possibilities, though, you first have to select the characters that you want to change, just as you select other elements of your image before editing them. Because the text pixels are all by their lonesomes on the layer, your selection job is easy:

- ✔ If you want to select just one or two characters, make the text layer — the one you just created, not the official Text layer — active. Then click each character with the Color Wand, making sure to click the Add icon in the Selections palette before you start.

- ✔ To select many characters, use the Color Wand to select the background instead of the text. After you select the background, invert the selection by clicking the Invert icon in the Selections palette or pressing Ctrl+I. Now the text characters, and not the background, are selected.

- ✔ Want to select each and every character? Select the text layer by clicking its name in the Layers palette or by clicking any character with the Object Selection tool. Alternatively, you can click the All button in the Selections palette, press Ctrl+A, or choose Select⇨All. (Keep in mind that the method you choose affects which kinds of edits you can apply, just as it does for any other image layer. Check out Chapter 9 for specifics.)

After you select your text, you can do all the following and more:

- ✔ Use the fill commands and Brush tool to paint the text or fill it with a gradient or pattern. See Chapter 10 for details.

- ✔ Apply the Outline command to create effects like the one in the top example in Color Plate 12-1. I applied the Outline command twice, once to create the white outline and once to create the dark purple outline. The next section provides specifics.

- ✔ Make an image appear inside your text, as I did in the middle image in Color Plate 12-1. Read about this effect in the "Image-filled text" section later in this chapter.

✔ Fade your text into the underlying image. Just double-click the layer name in the Layers palette and adjust the Opacity value. In the bottom image in Color Plate 12-1, for example, I reduced the opacity of the text to 90 percent so that the underlying money image was visible through the letters.

✔ Control how the text pixels blend with the image pixels by changing the Blend modes in the Layer Options dialog box. Chapter 10 explains blend modes.

✔ Apply any special effect, from a distortion filter to a color-effects filter. The bottom image in Color Plate 12-1 shows the results of applying the Effects➪Distort➪Sphere command to my text.

✔ Get rid of any jagged edges that you sometimes get with large text by applying a slight blur with the Effects➪Soften command. I used this trick to smooth out the edges of all the text examples in Color Plate 12-1. Inside the Soften dialog box, use the lowest Radius value that smoothes the text edges. Too high a Radius value creates fuzzy text.

✔ On the other hand, maybe you *want* a fuzzy-text effect. If so, use the Soften filter with a high Radius value. Your text appears as if you sprayed it on your image with an airbrush.

✔ Put a shadow behind the text to help separate it from the rest of the image, as shown in the middle example in Color Plate 12-1. The next section gives you the step-by-step.

✔ Place the text in any position in the image stacking order. You can use your text as the background layer of the image, sandwich it between two other image layers, or put it at the very top of the image.

✔ You can spread the individual characters in your text farther apart or closer together — both of which are known as *kerning* in the typesetting world. Just select the character that you want to move, press Ctrl+G to select the Move tool, and nudge the character with the arrow keys.

In other words, you're king of the text hill. So let your imagination rule, and never again be limited to the boring effects you can create with the standard PhotoDeluxe Text layer. Text layer? We don't need no stinkin' Text layer!

Shadowed and outlined text

Figures 12-3 and 12-4 offer an illustration of two easy text effects. In Figure 12-3, I applied the Outline command twice put a double-line border around each character. Figure 12-4 shows a shadow that I added by applying the

Drop Shadow command. (The next section explains how I created the text interior.)

Figure 12-3:
I created a double outline by applying the Outline command twice.

Figure 12-4:
Filling the text with an image and adding a drop shadow gives the text an entirely different attitude.

To apply an outline or shadow to your text — or both — follow these easy steps:

1. **Create a new image with your text on a regular layer, as outlined in the preceding steps.**

2. **Select all the text by clicking a character with the Object Selection tool.**

   To apply effects to just one character, use one of the other selection tools to separate it from its neighbors.

3. **Choose Effects⇨Drop Shadow to add a shadow; choose Effects⇨ Outline to outline the text.**

   Flip back to the end of Chapter 7 to find out how to select your shadow options and how to adjust your shadow after you create it. That chapter also explains the Outline command.

Image-filled text

Want to unleash some really eye-catching text? Fill your text with an image, as I did in Figure 12-4 and the middle example in Color Plate 12-1. Here, I filled the text characters with an image of all kinds of currency. To create a similar effect, take these steps:

1. **Open the image that you want to use as your text interior (the *fill*).**

2. **Create your text by using the Text tool.**

3. **Save the image in the Photoshop format (PSD) to send the text to its own, free-wheeling image layer.**

   Follow the steps earlier in this chapter in "Basic recipe for cooler text."

4. **Open the newly created PSD version of the picture.**

5. **In the Layers palette, click the name of the text layer to make it active.**

   The layer you want is not the official PhotoDeluxe Text layer, but the new layer that the program created when you saved to the PSD format.

6. **Click the layer background with the Color Wand.**

7. **Click the name of the layer that holds the image that you want to use as the fill.**

   PhotoDeluxe transfers the selection outline that you created in Step 6 to the image layer.

8. **Press Delete.**

   Everything outside the selection outline leaps off the digital cliff. You now have a layer of original text and the layer left behind when you deleted the background. Assuming that your original layer is set to 100 percent opacity, it completely obscures the text on the layer below. If you want to check for yourself that the text-filled image is in fact there, click the eyeball icon next to the original text layer in the Layers palette.

9. **Drag the original text layer to the Trash icon.**

   Your image-filled text comes into view and remains selected. If you want to apply other effects, you're one step ahead.

Chapter 13

Wild and Wooly Pixel Adventures

· ·

In This Chapter

▶ Sending reality out the window

▶ Giving pixels a dye job

▶ Sucking the color out of a picture

▶ Putting color into the cheeks of grayscale images

▶ Creating faux clouds, stars, and beams of light

▶ Creating psychedelic backgrounds via multiple filters

· ·

*O*ne of the things I appreciate most about PhotoDeluxe is that it offers many of the same great special-effects filters found in Adobe's higher-end (and much higher-priced) image editor, Photoshop. Playing with these ilters is like sipping expensive French champagne for the price of a wine cooler.

Of course, with PhotoDeluxe, the servings of special effects aren't as generous as in Photoshop. But as this chapter proves, you get more than enough to make you a little tipsy with power. You can create wacky color effects, bend and twist your image, and even turn a dull, overcast sky into an expanse of brilliant blue dotted with fluffy white clouds. In short, with a few selections from the Effects menu, you can give your pixels a night they'll never forget.

Throwing Colors to the Wind

PhotoDeluxe offers several filters that shift the colors in your image. Chapter 10 introduces you to the Hue/Saturation filter, which sends pixels on a trip around the color wheel, and Chapter 7 explains the Color Balance and Variations filters, which adjust the balance of different color components in your image. You can see examples of the Hue/Saturation filter in Color Plate 10-4 and the Color Balance filter in Color Plate 7-3.

For more bizarre color effects, though, try the following filters, all found on the Effects menu:

- ✔ **Negative:** This filter inverts colors to create an effect similar to a photographic negative. The top-right image in Color Plate 13-1 shows how the filter changed my original paddleboat image (top left).

- ✔ **Stylize⇨Solarize:** This filter produces an effect similar to what happens if you expose film to light during the development process, if that rings any bells for you. If not, see the bottom-left image of Color Plate 13-1. The Solarize filter can make your image look a little dark, so you may want to tweak the brightness and contrast after applying the filter, as I did for the Color Plate example.

- ✔ **Artistic⇨Posterize:** Posterize reduces your image to just a few brightness levels. You can use this command to achieve a comic-book-like effect. By adjusting the Levels value in the Posterize dialog box, you control the allowable number of brightness values. The lower the Levels value, the more dramatic the effect.

Before applying these filters, you can expand the realm of creative possibilities by copying your entire image to a new layer. Apply the filter to the new layer and try different layer blend modes to mix the filtered layer with the underlying image. Using this technique, you can create many variations on the basic filter effect. In the lower-right image in Color Plate 13-1, for example, I applied the Negative filter to the new layer and then blended the filtered layer with the underlying image, using the Difference blend mode. The result is a bolder, more colorful version of the Negative filter. (For more about layers and blend modes, check out Chapter 11.)

Playing with Gray

Bright, eye-popping colors are in vogue today, but don't overlook the power of black-and-white images. As anyone who has ever seen an Ansel Adams photograph can attest, a black-and-white image can be every bit as arresting as a color image.

In the image-editing world, what most folks call a black-and-white photograph is known as a *grayscale* image. That's because the image is made up of many different shades of gray — typically 256. A true black-and-white image contains just two colors, pure black and pure white.

The following sections explain how PhotoDeluxe handles grayscale images and give you the step-by-step for creating the two grayscale effects shown in Color Plate 13-2.

Real gray versus faux gray

PhotoDeluxe treats grayscale images differently than most graphics programs. These differences are important, so pay attention:

- When you open an image in PhotoDeluxe, the program determines whether the file was saved in the native PhotoDeluxe format, PDD. If not, PhotoDeluxe creates a copy of the image, converts the copy to the PDD format, and opens the copy for you to work on. In other words, any image you see on-screen is a PDD image. (For more on this PDD stuff, see Chapter 1.)

  PDD images are *always* full-color RGB images, regardless of whether the original image was full-color, grayscale, black-and-white, or whatever. That doesn't mean that PhotoDeluxe adds colors to your image that weren't there before. What it does mean is that *you* can add any colors you want. Suppose that you open a 256-color, grayscale image that somebody gave you. PhotoDeluxe converts the grayscale image to the PDD format, converting the image to the RGB color model in the process. Now that the image is an RGB picture, you can stroke on red paint, or blue, or green, or any other color. You're no longer bound by the original 256-color limitation.

- In addition, the Effects⇨Color to Black/White command doesn't create a true grayscale image. PhotoDeluxe merely desaturates your colors so that they all appear gray; your actual image remains a full-color RGB image.

- If you need a true, 256-colors-or-fewer grayscale image — for example, to open the image in a program that only supports true grayscale files — use the File⇨Export⇨Grayscale File command to save the picture. See the next section for details.

The PhotoDeluxe approach seems a little odd if you're used to working with other image editors, where grayscale means 256 shades of gray, period. But the PhotoDeluxe take on gray actually comes in handy for creating certain effects.

Turning gray

To make your image go gray, use one of the following commands, depending on what type of grayscale picture you want to create:

- **Effects⇨Color to Black/White:** As discussed in the preceding section, this command creates a grayscale effect by desaturating your image. Your picture remains an RGB image. Use this option unless someone tells you that they need a true grayscale image.

✔ **File⇨Export⇨Grayscale File:** This command makes a copy of your image, converts all colors according to a 256-color grayscale spectrum, and saves the 256-color copy to disk as a true grayscale image. Your on-screen image is unaffected.

If you watch the File Information box at the bottom of the PhotoDeluxe program window, you can see clear-cut evidence of the differences between these two operations. When you apply Color to Black/White, the image file size doesn't change one whit. If you choose Export⇨Grayscale File, the number changes by a bunch of whits. PhotoDeluxe limits your image to just 256 colors, which reduces the file size. The Color to Black/White desaturates image colors but doesn't change the total *number* of colors your image can contain, so the file size remains steady.

Although Grayscale has it all over Color to Black/White in terms of file size, Color to Black/White enables you to create effects that you can't achieve with files you save via the Grayscale command. You can make just a portion of your image gray, as I did in Color Plate 13-2. The top image is the original image. I selected the car and then inverted the selection so that the background was selected. Then I applied the Color to Black/White command to the background only, creating the middle image in the color plate. Desaturating the background in this way adds extra emphasis to the subject.

Colorizing a grayscale image

One other benefit of the PhotoDeluxe approach to grayscale conversions is that you can add color back into an image at any time. This feature enables you to colorize grayscale images to create a variety of effects, including the antique photograph effect shown in the bottom image in Color Plate 13-2. To create a similar effect, take these steps:

1. **Press Ctrl+A or click the All button in the Selections palette to select your entire image.**

   This step assumes that you have only one image layer plus the Text layer. If you have more layers, merge them by choosing Merge Layers in the Layers palette menu. For more information about layers, see Chapter 11.

2. **Choose Effects⇨Color to Black/White.**

3. **Click the New Layer icon in the Layers palette.**

   PhotoDeluxe creates a new layer. The selection outline that you created in Step 1 shifts to the new layer.

4. **Choose Effects⇨Selection Fill to open the Selection Fill dialog box.**

   Chapter 9 explains this dialog box in detail if you need help.

5. **Set the fill color to a shade of rusty yellow that looks like what you see in antique photographs.**

6. **Choose the Fill Selection option, set the Opacity value to 50 percent, and set the Blend mode to Color.**

   Play with the Opacity value until you get the amount of coloring you want. Also experiment with using the Overlay blend mode instead of the Color mode.

7. **Click OK.**

   Your image now appears as though it's peering through a rusty yellow window. If you're not satisfied with the effect, double-click the name of the yellow layer in the Layers palette to open the Layer Options dialog box, where you can adjust the opacity and blend mode further.

Turning Cloudy Skies Blue

Many a picture has been spoiled by nature's refusal to provide an idyllic blue sky. The left image in Color Plate 13-3 is a case in point. I took this picture on a day so cloudy that the sky actually looks white in the image. With the help of the Effects⇨Render⇨Clouds command, however, you can turn gray skies blue and even add puffy clouds, as I did in the right image in the color plate.

To create a similar change to your sky, click this way:

1. **Select the sky.**

   Chapter 9 describes different selection techniques.

2. **Choose Effects⇨Choose Colors to select your sky and cloud colors.**

   In the next step, PhotoDeluxe creates your new sky by blending the foreground and background colors that you choose in this step. I find that using a light and dark shade of blue, rather than blue and pure white, works best. (Chapter 10 explains how to select the foreground and background colors.)

3. **Choose Effects⇨Render⇨Clouds.**

   PhotoDeluxe fills the selection with a random pattern based on your foreground and background colors.

   If your clouds look harsh or unnatural, choose Effects⇨Blur⇨Soften to blur them slightly. Raise the Radius value in the Soften dialog box until things look better.

For otherworldly clouds, choose Clouds Texture from the Render submenu instead of Clouds. The Clouds Texture filter blends the cloud image with the underlying image using the Difference blend mode.

Seeing Stars and Spotlights

Version 4 includes two new filters, Lens Flare and Lighting Effects. I don't think you'll have much use for either, but they're new and bound to attract attention, so I figured I'd better explain them. I was afraid that if I left you to explore these two on your own, you might get so discouraged that you'd throw in the mouse for good. Lens Flare and Lighting Effects are among the least intuitive filters in all of PhotoDeluxe.

If you have an hour to spare or just want to know how to do something that your neighbor can't, read the next two sections, which explain both filters. Otherwise, skip to something else and don't look back.

Adding a ring of light

Lens Flare simulates the ring-of-light effect that sometimes occurs when stray light hits a camera lens from a certain angle. The right example in Figure 13-1 shows a flare that I added to the original space scene on the left.

Professional photographers work hard to *avoid* lens flare, but if you want to add one to your picture, choose Effects⇨Render⇨Lens Flare to open the dialog box shown in Figure 13-2. Drag the crosshair cursor in the preview area to position the center of the flare. You can change the style and brightness of the flare by using the options above and below the preview. Unfortunately, you can't preview the effect in the image window, and getting a clear idea of how the flare will look from the dialog box preview is difficult. So, make a guess, click OK to apply the filter, and then click Undo or press Ctrl+Z immediately if you don't like what you see.

Figure 13-1:
I used the Lens Flare filter to add a starburst effect (right) to a space scene (left).

Figure 13-2:
Drag the
crosshair to
the spot
where you
want to
create the
flare.

Putting a subject in the spotlight

Lighting Effects shoots beams of light across your image, as if you hung your picture on a wall and then focused a spotlight, flashlight, or other lighting source on it. Figure 13-3 offers an example. The left image shows my original daylight scene taken at the Coliseum in Rome. In the right image, I applied the Lighting Effects filter, setting the filter options to create the illusion that somebody trained a spotlight on the area in the bottom-right corner of the scene. As you can see, the filter not only shines a light on one area, but also casts shadows over other areas. In this example, the filtered image appears to be a night scene.

On the surface, Lighting Effects seems as though it would come in handy on all sorts of occasions. The problem is, getting the lighting options set just right is very difficult, and you can't preview the effect on your image while choosing those options. So you usually wind up spending a lot of time creating a lighting setup, applying the filter, hitting the Undo button, and then trudging off to try again.

To try the filter for yourself, choose Effects⇨Render⇨Lighting Effects. PhotoDeluxe displays the Lighting Effects dialog box, shown in Figure 13-4. Be afraid. Be very afraid. Also be prepared to twiddle your thumbs for a while as you experiment: The Lighting Effects filter takes longer to apply than most other filters.

Figure 13-3:
I lit my
original
image (left)
with a single
spotlight
(right).

Light distance control

Light source

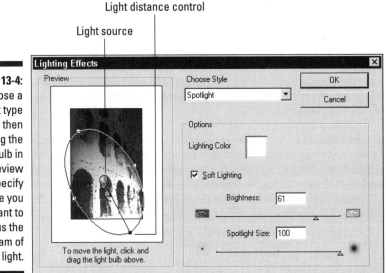

Figure 13-4:
Choose a
light type
and then
drag the
light bulb in
the preview
to specify
where you
want to
focus the
beam of
light.

The options on the right side of the dialog box are easy enough to understand. You select a type of light from the Style drop-down list and then adjust the color, softness, size, and brightness of the light beam. But when you shift your attention to the preview on the left side of the dialog box, things become less clear. Here, you position the light source and aim the light as follows:

✔ Drag the light bulb to light a different area. The circle around the light bulb indicates the extent of the area that will be lit. For some light types, you get more than one bulb and can position each one independently.

✔ Drag one of the four squares around the circle to change the direction of the light or enlarge or reduce the size of the area that you want to light.

✔ See the square at the end of the line that extends from the light bulb — the one labeled Light Distance Control in Figure 13-4? Drag that square in and out to move the light source closer and farther away. Imagine moving a flashlight closer to or farther from an object in a darkened room, and you get the idea.

✔ After you set your lights, click OK to apply the filter. Not quite right? Click Undo, reopen the dialog box, and fiddle with the settings some more. PhotoDeluxe remembers the settings that you just applied so that you don't have to start from scratch. I used the settings shown in Figure 13-4 to create the effect in the right image in Figure 13-3.

For safety's sake, don't apply this filter directly to your image. Instead, drag the layer that contains the subject you want to light to the New Layer icon in the Layer dialog box. PhotoDeluxe copies the layer and makes the copy active. Apply the filter to the copied layer only. If you later change your picture in a way that requires different light sources or settings, you can just trash the copied layer to get rid of the original lights.

Tracing Edges with Color

Several filters on the Effects menu apply color treatments based on the *edges* in your image — areas where light pixels meet dark. Color Plate 13-4 shows the results of applying three of these filters to the original city scene. The following list explains each effect:

✔ **Stylize⇨Find Edges:** This command searches out areas of contrast. Then it colors low-contrast areas with white and emphasizes edges with dark outlines. The top-right image in Color Plate 13-4 offers an example.

✔ **Stylize⇨Glowing Edges:** A variation of Find Edges, this filter turns low-contrast areas dark and highlights edges with white — so that the edges in your image "glow." When you choose this command, PhotoDeluxe displays a dialog box in which you can adjust the width and brightness of the glowing edges. You can also adjust the sensitivity of the filter by playing with the Smoothness control. If you use a high Smoothness value, the filter applies the glowing effect only to major edges (areas of highest contrast). A lower value finds more edges and thus gives you more glowing lines. In the bottom-left image of Color Plate 13-4, I applied the filter using an Edge Width value of 5, Edge Brightness value of 6, and Smoothness value of 5.

✔ **Artistic⇨Neon Glow:** This animal is a bit difficult to explain, but in essence, it repaints your image using the current foreground and background colors. Then it adds glowing highlights to edges in the scene, creating a neon-like appearance.

Choosing the Neon Glow command brings up a dialog box with several options. Drag the Glow Size slider to adjust the thickness of the glow. Negative values give you an inverted photograph effect. The Glow Brightness value determines the opacity of the glow. Higher values make more of your original image detail visible. Click the Glow Color swatch to choose a color for the edge glow.

Predicting the outcome of this filter is difficult at best. So just play around until you arrive at an effect that makes you happy, and don't forget to experiment with blending a filtered version of your image with the original, using the layer blend modes discussed in Chapter 11. Copy your entire image to a new layer, apply the filter to the new layer, and then select your blend mode and layer opacity in the Layer Options dialog box. In the bottom-right image of Color Plate 13-4, I blended the filtered image with the original using the Difference blend mode at 100 percent opacity. I used dark blue and pale yellow as my foreground and background colors, set the Glow Brightness to 28, the Glow Size to 14, and the Glow Color to red.

Blurring the Focus

Filters on the Effects⇨Blur menu do just what the name implies: blur the image to create the illusion of soft focus. For the most part, I rely on the blur filters only to create special effects. But on occasion, they come in handy for corrective editing as well. For example, applying a slight blur can lessen the jagged appearance that sometimes results from overcompressing an image. And blurring the background of an image, as I did in the car images in Color Plate 13-2, lends more emphasis to the foreground subject and even makes the focus of the subject seem sharper by comparison.

For corrective blurring, turn to the Soften command. Soften enables you to specify just how blurry you want the scene to become — just raise or lower the radius value in the Soften dialog box. The Blur and Blur More commands each apply a set amount of blurring, giving you no control at all.

The remaining blur filters, Circular and Motion, send your pixels on a wild ride. You can use both filters to give your image a sense of motion, as I did in Figure 13-5. In this image, I selected everything but the elephant figurine. I then applied the Circular filter to create that "world spinning out of control" look shown in the top image in the figure. In the bottom example, I instead applied the Motion filter. Motion also shifts selected pixels but sends them in a straight line instead of a circle.

Figure 13-5:
I applied the
Circular
filter to
everything
but the ele-
phant in the
top image.
In the
bottom
image, I
applied the
Motion filter
instead.

Both filters enable you to play with the blurring effect by adjusting some fairly complex dialog box controls. Figure 13-6 shows the options for each filter. In the Circular dialog box, shown on the left in Figure 13-6, you have the following options:

Figure 13-6:
You can
adjust the
effects cre-
ated by the
Circular and
Motion Blur
filters in
these dialog
boxes.

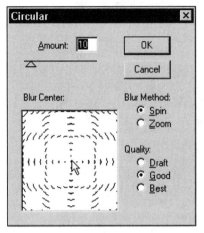 

✔ Specify the direction of the blur by clicking the Zoom or Spin radio button. With Spin, the blur rotates around a central point, as in the top image back in Figure 13-5. Zoom blurs the pixels from the edge of the image inward. The effect is similar to what you see when you look through a camera viewfinder and zoom in on a subject.

✔ Relocate the origin of the blur by dragging the center point inside the Blur Center grid, as I'm doing in Figure 13-6, or clicking in the grid. By default, the blur starts from the center of your image. Only selected pixels get blurred, however.

✔ Adjust the amount of blurring by raising or lowering the Amount value.

✔ The Quality options determine how well and how quickly PhotoDeluxe applies the filter. Best creates the smoothest-looking blur but takes the longest to apply. Draft produces the least smooth blur but takes the least time to process. Good falls somewhere in the middle on both counts.

You have fewer options when applying the Motion filter. In the Motion Blur dialog box, set the direction of the blur by entering an Angle value or by clicking on the circle next to the option box, as shown in Figure 13-6. A value of 0 or 180 gives you a perfectly horizontal blur, for example. Raise or lower the Distance value to increase or decrease the amount of blurring. Higher values create a more dramatic blur.

Turning Images into Colorful Backgrounds

Need an interesting background to liven up a boring product shot or portrait? Open a colorful picture — just about any scene will do — and then turn it into an eye-catching background by applying special effects filters. Color Plate 13-5 shows three backgrounds that I created from an ordinary field-of-flowers image (top left). Here's how I created each background:

- ✔ To produce the top-right image, I applied the Effects⇨Distort⇨Funnel filter to the original image with the Rectangular to Polar option selected. You can find out more about the Funnel filter and other Distort filters in Chapter 15.

- ✔ To create the bottom-left image, I applied the Effects⇨Sketch⇨Bas Relief filter to the top-right image. I set the Detail value to 13, the Smoothness value to 3, and the Light Direction value to Bottom. Because Bas Relief colors your image with the current foreground and background colors, I selected sky blue as my foreground color and pale yellow as the background color before applying the filter.

- ✔ Taking things a few steps further, I distorted the bottom-right image by using the Effects⇨Distort⇨Shear filter. (Chapter 15 describes this filter in detail.) Then I chose the Effects⇨Negative command to invert all colors in the image.

By applying filter on top of filter, you can create an unlimited variety of effects. To add even more possibilities to your repertoire, apply special-effects filters on a layer separate from the rest of the image and then blend the effects layer with the image layer, using the blend modes discussed in Chapter 10.

Putting Your Picture in a Frame

After you finish editing your image, you may want to give it a snazzy frame to help set the right tone for the picture. Chapter 7 shows you how to create a few very simple frames. PhotoDeluxe also gives you two options for framing your pictures more elaborately:

- ✔ The PhotoDeluxe program CD contains a variety of frames. To use them, put the CD in your CD-ROM drive, click the Cards & More Guided Activities button, choose Labels & Frames, and then choose Frames. Follow the on-screen prompts to select and apply a frame.

- ✔ The Extensis PhotoFrame plug-in enables you to create other cool framing effects. For two examples, see Figure 13-7. The old-time effects are perfect for this old-time photograph, which captured my older sister and me performing some odd Christmas ritual that evidently required us to wear t-shirts and bad pants. I'm a bit blurry because I'm doing a little holiday dance to entertain the relatives. But you just can't let a little blur stop you from taking the opportunity to embarrass your siblings when you get the chance, you know?

PhotoFrame offers three framing effects: CameraEdge, WaterColor, and SoftCircle. I used CameraEdge on the left image in Figure 13-7 and WaterColor on the right image. The SoftCircle filter creates a feathered, circular frame much like the one shown at the end of Chapter 9, which I created with the PhotoDeluxe Feather command.

Before you apply a PhotoFrame filter, create a new layer to hold your frame so that you can just delete the layer if you ever want to remove the frame. Then select the new layer and choose Effects⇨Extensis⇨PhotoFrame. You see the dialog box shown in Figure 13-8.

Figure 13-7:
Two framing effects created by using the Extensis PhotoFrame plug-in.

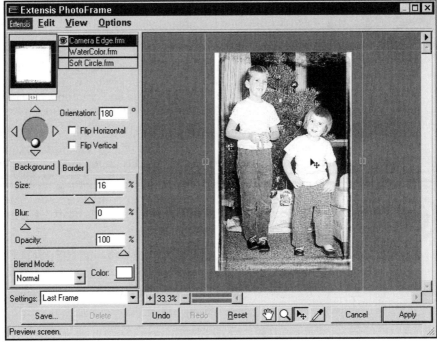

Figure 13-8:
The
PhotoFrame
dialog box
offers
countless
controls for
building
your custom
frame.

You can explore the options easily enough on your own, but here are some basics to get you started:

✔ The Zoom buttons, Zoom tool, and Hand tool at the bottom of the dialog box work similarly to those in an image window. Click with the Zoom tool to zoom in, Alt+Click to zoom out. Drag with the Hand tool to pull a hidden portion of the image into view. (You don't have to hold down the spacebar as you do in an image window.)

✔ You can apply the three frame effects together or individually. To toggle an effect on and off, click the eyeball next to its name at the top of the dialog box. If the eyeball is visible, the effect is applied.

✔ If you choose the CameraEdge filter, you can vary the look of the frame by changing the options on the Background and Border tabs. Change the angle and layout of the frame by using the Orientation options just above the tabs.

Additionally, you can adjust the placement of the frame with respect to your image. Click the Move tool icon at the bottom of the dialog box and move your cursor inside the preview area. A selection outline with four square handles appears around the frame. Drag inside the outline to move the frame. Drag the square handles to change the size and shape of the frame.

✔ The SoftCircle effect applies the feathered frame around the center of the image (or the selected area, if you draw a selection outline before you choose the PhotoFrame command). Unfortunately, you can't move the frame from this position, which means that sometimes the frame may hide a part of your image that you prefer to show. You can, however, move the layer that holds the frame after you exit the dialog box. (I'm assuming that you took my advice and created a new layer before opening the dialog box.) See Chapter 9 for details about moving layers.

✔ Click the Undo button at the bottom of the dialog box to undo the last adjustment. Click the Reset button to change all the dialog box settings back to the way they were when you first opened the dialog box.

✔ If you create an effect that you really like, click the Save button and save your settings. You're asked to give your settings a name; type in the name and click OK. To use those same settings again later, just select the name from the Settings pop-up menu.

✔ To apply the frame and exit the dialog box, click the Apply button.

Chapter 14

Projects for a Rainy Day

· ·

In This Chapter

▶ Adding your picture to stationery

▶ Inserting images into a spreadsheet, multimedia presentation, or word-processor document

▶ Jazzing up your pictures with clip art

▶ Morphing clip art graphics

▶ Creating 3-D objects using your photos

▶ Slapping your mug on everything but the kitchen sink

· ·

*A*fter hours of sweat-inducing labor, you sit back to survey the magnificent image you created. Now what? Well, you could do the obvious: Print three dozen copies and pass them out to every friend and family member you can find. But frankly, in this age of digital media, prints are just a tad dull. For some really fun and a few practical ways to use that image, browse through the ideas in this chapter. (See Chapter 6 for more on-screen uses for your pictures.)

Putting Your Face on a Letter

Guided Activities are easy to use for the most part, but PhotoDeluxe sometimes doesn't fully explain each step. I'm, therefore, including a detailed example to help you get a better idea of what happens as you work your way through a Guided Activities project. The following steps show you how to create personalized stationery. After you complete this project, you should be able to figure out the other Guided Activities on your own.

Before you take the first step, do any cropping, color correcting, or other necessary editing and then save the image in the PDD format. (You can have your image open or not.)

1. **Put the PhotoDeluxe program CD in your CD-ROM drive.**

2. **Click the Cards & More Guided Activities button.**

3. **Click the Pages & Certificates icon and then click Stationery in the drop-down menu.**

   PhotoDeluxe displays the Stationery Guided Activities tabs.

4. **Click the Choose Stationery tab and then click the Choose Stationery icon on the tab.**

   The Templates organizer window opens, showing thumbnail previews of the available stationery designs. In this organizer window, you can't create, rename, or remove albums as you can in the My Photos organizer. If you click the Find Photos button, you can search for a design by keyword, but PhotoDeluxe doesn't provide many designs, so you can probably scroll through the thumbnails faster than you can do a search via Find Photos. (For more about the Find Photos feature, see Chapter 4.)

5. **Double-click a thumbnail or drag it to an empty spot in the image-editing area.**

   PhotoDeluxe opens the stationery template in a standard image window, as shown in Figure 14-1.

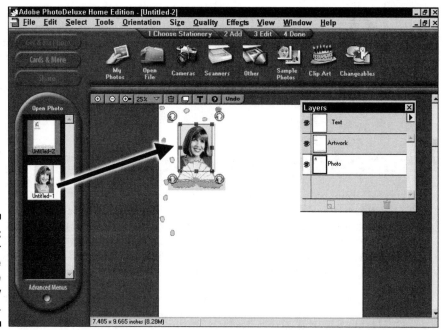

Figure 14-1:
Drag your image into the Stationery template.

6. Click the Add tab and select the photo you want to use.

PhotoDeluxe displays the same project tab you see if you use the Guided Activities to open an image. You can use the icons to open your image or use the standard image-opening procedures offered up in Chapter 1 (File⇨Open and so forth). If the image that you want to use is already open, just double-click its thumbnail or drag the thumbnail onto the page, as illustrated in Figure 14-1.

PhotoDeluxe sizes your image to fit the template *unless* you drag a thumbnail to into the template and drop the thumbnail somewhere other than where the design calls for the picture to be placed. In that case, your picture gets inserted at its original size.

Either way, PhotoDeluxe pastes the image into a separate layer, just like any other selection you paste. (See Chapter 9 for more information.) The only difference is that the image goes on the layer *underneath* the template layer, not above it. PhotoDeluxe automatically selects the image and displays the Resize and Rotate handles, as shown in Figure 14-1.

You can also add clip art to your stationery if you want. Just click the Clip Art icon on the project tab and double-click the thumbnail for the clip art you want to use. Check out the section "Pasting Clip Art into Your Image," later in this chapter, for more details about clip art.

7. Size and position the image as needed.

Use the techniques discussed in Chapter 9 to tweak the image. You can't change the size of the frame that surrounds your picture, but you can enlarge or reduce the picture itself and move the image around in the frame.

8. Click Done.

What about that Edit tab that lives between the Add and Done tab? Skip it. If you click the tab, PhotoDeluxe just tells you to click the Done tab if you want to make other changes to the image.

But whether you click both tabs or just Done, you're not really finished with your stationery. You still have to add any text to the page. If you decide *not* to add any text, click Done and skip to Step 10.

9. Add or edit the text.

To add text, click the Text tool button in the image window or press Ctrl+T and type away. Chapter 12 explains the ins and outs of creating text.

Some templates contain placeholder text to show you where to put your text. To replace the placeholder text, double-click it with the Object Selection tool, which opens the Text Tool dialog box. You can then enter your own text, change the font, or otherwise modify the text.

To resize or rotate text, click it with the Object Selection tool and then drag the Resize or Rotate handles, as described in Chapter 9. Click inside the selection outline and drag to move the text around.

10. Choose View⇨Show Layers to look at the Layers palette.

Your image contains three or more layers, depending on the template you selected. You need to see what's where before you move on. The Text layer contains any prefab text plus any text that you add; another layer holds the template artwork; and one or more additional layers hold images that you add. (If you need help understanding layers, see Chapter 11.)

11. Delete any extra Photo layers.

Some templates include several layers for photos. Typically, you get one layer for each image the template design includes. PhotoDeluxe names these layers *Photo* in the Layers palette. On occasion, you may wind up with empty image layers. Even though they don't contain any images, those layers enlarge the image file size, so review the Layers palette and delete any empty photo layers.

To do this, Alt+Click the eyeball next to any Photo layer in the Layers palette. (Alt+Clicking hides every layer but the layer you click.) If the layer is empty, delete it by dragging the layer to the Trash icon at the bottom of the palette. Sometimes, the layer contains text that tells you where a picture goes. If you didn't add a picture to that layer, you can delete the layer.

Keep Alt+Clicking all the Photo layers' eyeballs until you've inspected each one. To bring all layers back into view, Alt+Click again on the last eyeball you clicked.

If you change your mind and want to add an additional image, just do so as you normally add photos to an image.

12. Save the image.

If you want to preserve the individual stationery layers, save the card in the PDD file format. You can read more about saving images and the PDD format in Chapter 4.

Be sure to click the Done tab as instructed in Step 8 before you save, or PhotoDeluxe merges all layers during the save process.

You can't delete or edit the Artwork layer, but if you just want to use the template layout and not the artwork, here's a workaround: Click the Artwork layer's eyeball in the Layers palette to hide the layer and then save the image in any format except PDD or PSD. Other formats don't save hidden layers (but other formats also merge all image layers, so be sure that you don't need the visible layers to remain separate). Next, close the on-screen image and open the one you just saved. No more artwork!

If you ever need more input than the Guided Activities panels provide, enable the Assistant Drawer, which slides out from the right side of the program window to explain each step in a bit more detail. Choose File⇨Preferences⇨ Show Assistant Drawer to toggle the Assistant Drawer on and off.

Importing Images into Other Documents

You can easily add an image to a spreadsheet, word-processor document, multimedia presentation, or any other document. The following steps give you generic instructions for adding images to a Microsoft Word 2000 document. The process should be nearly identical for almost any other spreadsheet, word processor, or multimedia program.

1. **Prepare your image.**

   Do all your retouching and resizing in PhotoDeluxe.

2. **Save the image in a file format that can be recognized by the other program.**

   Microsoft Word can work with files saved in the TIFF, GIF, and JPEG formats, among others. Most programs can work with these same file formats, but check the help system to find out what format your program recommends.

   If you have a choice of formats, choose TIFF for print documents. For Web use, pick GIF or JPEG. For multimedia presentations, JPEG usually works best. (You can explore these formats in Chapters 4 and 6.)

3. **Open the document to which you want to add the image.**

4. **Choose Insert⇨Picture⇨From File.**

   You use this same command to add pictures in Microsoft Excel as well as in some other Microsoft programs. If you're using some other program, check the help system for information about importing files or adding graphics.

   After you choose the command in Word, the Import dialog box opens. This dialog box works like a regular old Open dialog box. Locate the image file that you want to add and click the Insert button. (In other programs, the button may be named Open or Import or something like that.)

You can also use the standard Cut, Copy, and Paste commands to copy or move an image from PhotoDeluxe into most programs. For information about this approach, see Chapter 9.

Pasting Clip Art into Your Image

Along with sample photos and project templates, the PhotoDeluxe program CD contains a selection of clip-art graphics that you can add to your photos. In Figure 14-2, for example, I added some clip art to mark special occasions on a calendar that I created by using the Calendar Guided Activity.

PhotoDeluxe offers three different types of clip art: regular old clip art, like the stuff shown in Figure 14-2; Changeables clip art, which you can alter before putting it in your image; and 3-D clip art, which enables you to put your picture onto a 3-D object. The next sections explain how to work with all three types of clip art.

Adding regular clip art

Most Guided Activities include a step where you can add clip art to your projects. You usually do this on the Add tab, as shown back in Figure 14-2. You can add as many pieces of clip art as you want while you're at the Add stage of the game.

Figure 14-2:
While creating a calendar using a Guided Activity, I added some clip art to highlight special days.

To put a piece of clip art in an image when you're not using a Guided Activity, take these steps:

1. **Open the image that you want to decorate and put the PhotoDeluxe CD in your CD-ROM drive.**

2. **Choose File⇨Open Special⇨Clip Art.**

   The Clip Art organizer window opens, displaying thumbnails of the available graphics. You can read more about this organizer window in Chapter 1.

3. **Drag a thumbnail into the image window.**

   PhotoDeluxe puts the clip art on a new layer. You can resize, move, and rotate the clip art using the Object Selection tool, just as you do any layer. See Chapter 9 for details. You can also adjust the opacity of the art and blend it with the underlying image using layer blend modes. For more about these options, book a flight to Chapter 11.

Want to open a piece of clip art in its own image window? Double-click the graphic's thumbnail or drag the thumbnail to an empty part of the image-editing area instead of into an open image window.

Adding morphable clip art

Like its predecessor, PhotoDeluxe 4 includes a special brand of clip art called Changeables. You can adjust the shape, design, and color of Changeables graphics before adding them to your photos.

Slip the PhotoDeluxe program CD in your CD-ROM drive and choose File⇨Open Special⇨Changeables to display thumbnails for the Changeables graphics. Drag a thumbnail into an image window to add the graphic to an existing picture. To put the graphic into its own image window, double-click the thumbnail or drag it to an empty spot in the image-editing area. Either way, PhotoDeluxe displays the Changeables dialog box, which has controls for altering the graphic, as shown in Figure 14-3.

The controls differ depending upon the graphic. For the dog shown in the figure, for example, you can adjust the shape and color of the dog, move the tail into various stages of wagging, and even make the dog appear to be panting. (Sorry, you can't add doggie drool.) Play around with the controls to see what's possible and click OK when you're happy with the graphic. PhotoDeluxe adds the graphic to its own layer, so you can resize, reshape, and otherwise manipulate the art as you do any layer.

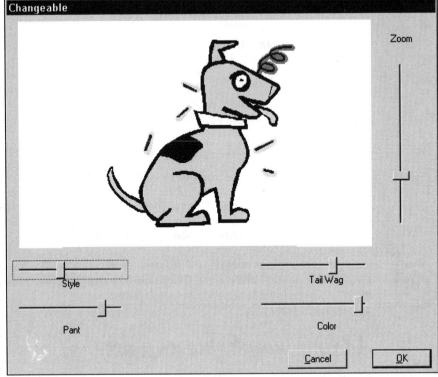

Figure 14-3:
With
Changeables,
you can
vary the
shape,
color, and
other
aspects of a
piece of
clip art.

Going into the third dimension

PhotoDeluxe now incorporates a program called Kazoo, which you can use to put your picture on a 3-D object and then spin and rotate your creation in 3-D space. You can even e-mail your 3-D image along with a Kazoo viewer to friends so that they can see what you've made.

Personally, I don't think that you'll have much use for this feature except to entertain your kids. For one thing, you get a very limited choice of 3-D objects, although you can download additional objects from the Kazoo Web site (www.kazoo3D.com). More important, 3-D imaging puts a huge strain on your computer. Unless you use a really powerful system, processing the 3-D objects takes a while, which kind of takes the fun out of things.

Still want to try out the 3-D feature? Put the PhotoDeluxe program CD in your CD-ROM drive and take these steps:

1. **Click the Cards & More Guided Activities button.**

2. **Click the 3D Activities icon and choose Create 3D Clip Art from the drop-down menu.**

3. **Follow the instructions on the project tabs to create your 3-D object and display it in the Kazoo 3D window.**

   The window appears as shown in Figure 14-4. To see your object from all sides, click the Rotate, Roll, and Move buttons and drag in the window. To zoom in, click the Zoom button and drag up in the window; drag down to zoom out. You can also change the look of the object by choosing a different option from the Style menu and then clicking the Preview button.

Figure 14-4: You manipulate a 3-D object in the Kazoo 3D window.

4. **Click OK to save the object in the Kazoo file format (file extension .kzp).**

5. **Click Done to close the Guided Activity.**

To view the object in PhotoDeluxe, take Steps 1 and 2 but choose View 3D Clip Art instead of Create 3D Clip Art from the drop-down menu. For more information about using the viewer and e-mailing your object and the viewer, visit the Kazoo Web site.

A more useful application of the 3-D feature enables you to add one of the 3-D objects to an image. After you place the object in your image, it becomes a 2-D object — meaning that you can't spin it in space as you can the 3-D version. But you can spin the object *before* you put it in the picture to choose which side of the object appears on in the picture. To try this option, choose Create 3D Artwork from the drop-down menu and follow the screen prompts.

Creating T-Shirts, Mugs, and More

With more and more consumers getting into digital imaging, more and more companies are offering products that you can use to display your digital artwork. Kodak, Epson, Hewlett-Packard, and others offer special paper stock for creating greeting cards, business cards, postcards, stickers, name badges, and other print media. Some manufacturers even offer special transfer paper that you can use to put your pictures on T-shirts or other cloth items, such as quilt squares. PhotoDeluxe provides Guided Activities that walk you through the steps of preparing your pictures for these special projects.

If you don't want to invest in special printer media, don't have a good printer, or if you need to create a large quantity of customized pieces, have your items printed at a commercial printer or quick-print shop such as Kinko's. The Adobe ActiveShare Web site, which Chapter 6 explains, offers online services of this sort, so you really don't even have to leave home to get the job done. Is this a great world or what?

Part V

The Part of Tens

The 5th Wave   By Rich Tennant

CRICHTENNANT

"SOFTWARE SUPPORT SAYS WHATEVER WE DO, DON'T ANYONE START TO RUN."

In this part . . .

This part of the book is like a strong blast of information espresso. Containing scads of hints, tips, and suggestions that you can digest in mere moments, the chapters in this part give you a quick jolt that leaves you refreshed, awakened, and heady with newfound knowledge.

You not only find the answers to the most frequently asked questions about Adobe PhotoDeluxe 4, but also get a rundown of PhotoDeluxe keyboard shortcuts and a look at ten great distortion filters. I've condensed everything so that even the quickest swig of text can have a big impact on your image-editing prowess.

In fact, this part is the perfect pick-me-up if you find yourself nodding off during your next office meeting. While your boss drones on about some meaningless subject, you can sneak glances at these pages (being careful to look up periodically and nod in thoughtful agreement, of course). Before that meeting is done, you can soak up a bunch of great information without anyone being the wiser — but you.

Chapter 15

Ten Ways to Wreak Havoc on an Image

*M*any chapters in this book show you how to make subtle improvements to your images — to enhance, rather than alter, the original scene. In this chapter, you're invited to toss reality to the wind and explore some of the more entertaining special effects in the PhotoDeluxe bag of tricks.

This chapter introduces you to the seven filters on the Effects⇨Distort sub-menu and their counterparts on the Size menu, all of which enable you to bend, stretch, warp, and otherwise distort your image. Applied with a light touch, these filters are the perfect partner in crime when you want to make a despised coworker or neighbor look silly — not that I'm advocating such treachery, of course. Taken to their extreme, the filters remove any semblance of the original photograph and lead to some interesting pixel productions.

Throughout this chapter, I use the highly decorated specimen shown in Figure 15-1 as a subject. This same feathered friend gets an application of the Smudge tool back in Chapter 10, and I suppose I should pick on some other creature for this chapter. But given that face and those feathers, this bird surely takes some ridicule from the rest of the animal kingdom already, so what harm could a little more digital foolishness do?

Figure 15-1:
A well-decorated bird agrees to be distorted in the name of art.

Effects⇨Distort⇨Funnel

For complete obliteration of your image, you can't top the Funnel filter. The PhotoDeluxe help system says that this filter makes your image appear as if it were either reflected in a curved mirror or wrapped around the inside of a funnel. I think this description is a little off but can't come up with anything better.

When you choose the Funnel filter, PhotoDeluxe displays a dialog box containing two options: Rectangular to Polar or Polar to Rectangular. Huh? What does that have to do with a funnel? Or a mirror? Actually, nothing. Adobe took the Funnel filter directly from Photoshop, where the filter is called the Polar Coordinates filter. They changed the filter name but not the dialog box option names.

At any rate, if you select the Rectangular to Polar option, you get the image-going-down-a-funnel look shown in the left half of Figure 15-2. Select Polar to Rectangular, and you get the gooey mess shown in the right-hand image.

Figure 15-2:
The results
of the
Funnel filter
using the
Rectangular
to Polar
setting (left)
and the
Polar to
Rectangular
setting
(right).

Effects⇨Distort⇨Pinch

If you want to make someone look really goofy, give the Pinch filter a go. When you select the filter, PhotoDeluxe displays a dialog box containing a single option: Amount. Positive Amount values pinch the image inward, creating that shrunken-head look you see in the left half of Figure 15-3. Negative values pinch pixels outward, creating the fish-eye lens effect shown in the right image.

Figure 15-3:
I applied the
Pinch filter
with a posi-
tive Amount
value (left)
and a nega-
tive Amount
value (right).

Effects⇨Distort⇨Pond Ripple

The Pond Ripple filter does pretty much what the name implies: creates the illusion that your image is reflected in a pond and you just threw a stone into the water. You control the rippling waters using these filter options:

- ✔ **Amount**: Enter a positive value to create ripples that protrude above the surface of the image. Negative values invert the ripples.

- ✔ **Ridges:** Adjust this value to control how many ripples are created. High values give you lots of sharp, tightly spaced ripples; low values produce softer, more watery-looking ripples.

- ✔ **Style:** This option determines how PhotoDeluxe shifts your pixels around the image. You have three choices:

  - • **Pond Ripples** moves pixels outward from the center and rotates them around the center of the image — which, technical blather aside, creates your classic, stone-in-a-pond effect. I used this option with an Amount value of 100 and a Ridge value of 5 to create the left image in Figure 15-4.

  - • **Out From Center** moves pixels outward but doesn't spin them around. I'm not sure what real-world analogy to apply to this effect, so just take a gander at the right image in Figure 15-4 to get the general idea. I used the same Amount and Ridge values as in the left image (100 and 5, respectively) but changed the Style option to Out From Center to create this effect.

  - • **Around Center** rotates pixels in alternating directions around the center of the image but doesn't move them outward. The result is a ripple that has a zigzag look to it.

Figure 15-4:
The bird gets submerged in water via the Pond Ripple filter, which I applied using the Pond Ripples style (left) and the Around Center style (right).

Effects⇨Distort⇨Ripple

For another watery effect, dive into the Ripple filter (yuk, yuk). With this filter, the water washes over the picture in parallel rather than circular ripples.

Inside the Ripple filter dialog box, adjust the Amount value to change the magnitude or width of the ripples. The Size value affects the length of the ripples. Figure 15-5 shows the results of two Ripple filter settings. To create the left image, I used an Amount value of 400 and selected Medium for the Size option. For the right image, I set the Size option to Small and cranked the Amount value all the way up to the maximum, 999. With this second set of values, the effect looks more like textured glass than watery ripples.

Figure 15-5: An under-water effect (left) and a textured-glass effect (right), both courtesy of the Ripple filter.

Effects⇨Distort⇨Shear

If you want a little more control over how your image is distorted, try the Shear filter. You can distort your image according to a free-form curve of your own making, creating effects like those shown in Figure 15-6. You use the grid in the bottom-left corner of the Shear dialog box, shown in Figure 15-7, to bend and twist your image.

Figure 15-6:
I applied the Shear filter with the Wrap Around option (left) and the Repeat Edge Pixels option (right).

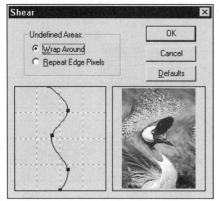

Figure 15-7:
Create a custom curve in the Shear dialog box to distort your image at will.

Initially, the grid contains a vertical line containing two *control points* (the little black squares). The top control point represents the top of your image and the bottom point represents the bottom of your image. To manipulate your image, do any of the following:

✔ Drag a control point to move the corresponding area of your image.

✔ Click anywhere on the line or in the grid to add new control points. PhotoDeluxe automatically redraws the line to accommodate the new control point. You can add as many control points as you want.

✔ To delete a control point, drag it out of the grid area.

✔ To get rid of all your custom control points, click the Defaults button. The original, two-point vertical line is restored, and your image appears as it did before you opened the Shear dialog box.

When you distort an image this way, gaps may appear along the edges of the image. The two options at the top of the dialog box determine how PhotoDeluxe fills in those gaps. If you choose the Wrap Around option, PhotoDeluxe fills the gaps on one side of the image with pixels that were shoved off the opposite side by the distortion, as in the left image in Figure 15-6. If you choose Repeat Edge Pixels, PhotoDeluxe simply repeats pixels from the edge of the selection as many times as necessary to fill the gap. The result is typically a striped effect, as shown in the right image of Figure 15-6.

Effects⇨Distort⇨Sphere

Figure 15-8 shows effects produced by the Sphere filter, which is a close cousin of the Pinch filter discussed earlier in this chapter. The Sphere dialog box provides two options for adjusting the effect: Mode and Amount.

Figure 15-8: The result of applying the Sphere filter using the Normal mode (left) and the Vertical Only mode (right).

✔ Select Normal from the Mode drop-down list to wrap your image around the inside or outside of a perfect sphere.

Enter a positive Amount value to wrap the image around the outside of the sphere, as I did in the left example in Figure 15-9; enter a negative value to wrap around the inside of the sphere. As you can see from the example in the figure, applying Sphere with a positive Amount value produces similar results to applying the Pinch filter with a negative value. (See the right image back in Figure 15-3.) Likewise, applying Sphere with a negative Amount value generates almost the same effect as applying Pinch with a positive Amount value. (See the left image back in Figure 15-3.) The difference is that the Sphere filter maps your pixels around a true sphere, whereas Pinch maps them on a sort of rounded cone.

✔ Choose Vertical Only or Horizontal Only from the Mode drop-down list to wrap your image on the inside or outside of a vertical or horizontal cylinder, respectively. Again, a positive Amount value puts your image on the outside of the cylinder, and a negative value puts the image on the inside of the cylinder. The right example in Figure 15-8 shows the results of selecting the Vertical Only option with an Amount value of –100.

The Sphere filter can distort only elliptical areas of an image. When you choose the command, PhotoDeluxe applies the distortion to the largest elliptical region within the bounds of your image or selection. The rest of the image is unaffected, which usually creates a distinct boundary between distorted and undistorted pixels. If you don't like that effect, use the Pinch filter instead of Sphere.

Effects➪Distort➪Twirl

Not for those prone to motion sickness, Twirl spins the center of the image around in circles while leaving the sides in place. Figure 15-9 offers two illustrations.

You control the extent and direction of the twirling by adjusting the Angle value inside the Twirl dialog box. Enter a positive value to rotate pixels in a clockwise direction; enter a negative value to spin them counterclockwise. You can enter values as high or low as 999 or –999. At these extreme values, you create a geometric spiral pattern that has little to do with your original image, as verified by the left example in Figure 15-9, where I used a value of +999. Use lower Angle values to create a more subtle twisting of your subject, as I did in the opposite example. An Angle value of –40 created just a slight counterclockwise rotation of the head and neck pixels.

If you want to create a spiral effect, apply the filter several times using an Angle value in the 100 or 200 range. You get a smoother spiral by applying the filter repeatedly at smaller values than by applying it once at a high value.

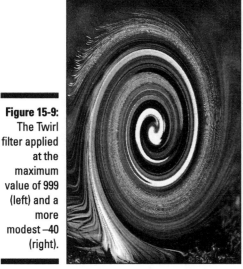 

Figure 15-9:
The Twirl filter applied at the maximum value of 999 (left) and a more modest –40 (right).

Size⇨*Distort*

If none of the filters on the Effects⇨Distort menu suits your fancy, check out the distortion options on the Size menu: Distort, Perspective, and Free Resize.

With Distort, you can skew your image as I did in Figure 15-10. After you choose the filter, PhotoDeluxe displays the black Resize handles around the selection. The handles work just as they do when you resize a selection except that you can drag the corner handles independently of each other, enabling you to distort the image.

After you tug a handle, PhotoDeluxe previews the effect in the image window. The preview can take several seconds to appear, so be patient. If you don't like the results, press Ctrl+Z or click the Undo button to undo your last drag. To apply the transformation for good, click inside the selection outline or press Enter. To cancel out of the distortion anytime before applying it, press Esc.

If you drag a handle off the canvas, a portion of your image disappears from view — you've stretched that area so that it no longer fits on the canvas. However, the pixels are still intact. To display them, use Size⇨Canvas Size to enlarge the canvas. Alternatively, you can move the image around on the canvas by dragging with the Move tool after you apply the transformation.

Figure 15-10:
The Distort filter enables you to skew your image by dragging a corner handle.

As long as you save the image in the native PhotoDeluxe format (PDD), any hidden pixels are retained. If you save to another format, any pixels not on the canvas are clipped away.

Size⇨Perspective

Perspective works similarly to Distort. When you drag a corner Resize handle after choosing the Perspective command, however, the opposite handle moves in tandem to create a perspective effect, as shown in Figure 15-11. I dragged a bottom handle inward and a top handle outward to achieve the effect in the figure.

For more tips on using the Perspective command, read the preceding section. All the hints for using Distort apply to Perspective as well.

Size⇨Free Resize

With Free Resize, you can resize your image without regard to the original image proportions. You can make an image tall and skinny, as I did in the left example in Figure 15-12, or short and fat, as in the right example.

Figure 15-11:
You can simulate perspective effects by using Perspective.

Figure 15-12:
I used the Free Resize command to stretch the image vertically only (left) and horizontally only (right).

Once again, you shape the image by dragging the Resize handles that appear when you choose the command. Drag a top or bottom handle to alter the vertical dimensions of the image; drag a side handle to stretch or shrink the image horizontally. To reshape the image in both directions at the same time, drag a corner handle.

For more information about using Free Resize, read the Size⇨Distort section earlier in this chapter. The tips presented there apply to Free Resize as well. For more information on working with the Resize handles, see Chapter 9.

Chapter 16

Top Ten PhotoDeluxe Brain Teasers

• •

In This Chapter

▶ Responding to scratch disk and out-of-memory errors

▶ Solving paint and edit tool weirdness

▶ Understanding why images look different on your monitor than they do on paper

▶ Discovering why images deteriorate in quality as you increase the print size

▶ Using your image in a brochure, spreadsheet, or other document

▶ Printing several pictures on one page

▶ Getting on-screen colors to match printed colors — sort of, anyway

• •

*E*ver hear the expression, "Ask a simple question, get a simple answer?" Well, this chapter gives you simple answers to *tough* questions. These stumpers can keep you scratching your head and saying "huh?" for hours — or however long it takes to find a neighborhood teen that can assist you.

The questions posed (and answered) in this chapter trip up almost every newcomer to image editing and PhotoDeluxe. You, however, have the answers right at your fingertips, unlike all the poor slobs who weren't clever enough to buy this book. So while those folks are transfixed by confusion, you can turn out one terrific image after another. Heck, you may even find yourself with enough spare time to enjoy a long walk with that local teenager. Mind you, that experience may also leave you scratching your head and saying, "Huh?" but at least you'll get to enjoy some fresh air and exercise.

What's a scratch disk?

While processing images, PhotoDeluxe uses a portion of your hard disk to temporarily store data. Adobe calls this hard-disk storage area the *scratch disk*. If your hard disk has limited free space, PhotoDeluxe may display a whiny little message about the scratch disk and refuse to carry out your commands. You need to delete some files on your hard disk to correct the problem. For more on this subject, check out Chapter 2.

My computer has mega-RAM, so why does PhotoDeluxe say "not enough memory?"

On average, the amount of memory (RAM) PhotoDeluxe needs to process a picture is about three times the image file size, so even a well-equipped computer can choke on large images.

Many times when PhotoDeluxe complains about memory, however, the problem isn't RAM but scratch disk space. You need at least as much scratch disk space as you have memory because PhotoDeluxe sometimes moves everything that's currently stored in RAM to the scratch disk while carrying out a command. If you have 64MB of RAM but only 40MB of scratch disk space, the program limits itself to 40MB of RAM so that it doesn't get into trouble if it needs to dump data to the scratch disk. For more information on memory issues, check out Chapter 2.

Why isn't the Brush/Line/Smudge/ Eraser/Clone tool working?

One great thing about PhotoDeluxe editing tools is that you can vary their impact. You can adjust the opacity of strokes you apply with the Paint, Line, Clone, and Eraser tools, and you can set the Smudge tool to smudge pixels over a shorter or greater distance. To adjust the tools, just press a number key. Press 0 for full opacity or full-intensity smudging; press 9 for 90 percent opacity/smudging, and so on.

On the downside, PhotoDeluxe gives you no on-screen indication of what tool setting is in force. If a tool isn't working the way you expected, you may have forgotten that you changed the opacity or smudge setting. Also remember that tools affect selected areas only, no matter what the setting. Chapters 9, 10, and 11 provide details.

Why do images look worse enlarged?

Each image starts life with a specific number of pixels. When you enlarge an image, one of two things has to happen:

  ✔ The number of pixels stays the same, and the existing pixels grow to cover the expanded image area. If the pixels get too big, your image looks jagged because the individual pixels become more noticeable.

> ✔ The software adds pixels to fill the gaps, an answer that usually results
> in blotchy or blurry pictures. The software can only guess at the color
> and brightness of the pixels that it adds, and even the smartest editing
> program doesn't get it right very often.

The moral of the story: To preserve the best image quality, avoid enlarging
images. If enlarging is a must, don't resize by more than 25 percent. For more
about this subject, refer to Chapter 3.

Why do my pictures look great on-screen, but terrible when I print them?

The problem is most likely that your image resolution is adequate for screen
display but not high enough for good print reproduction. Most printers do
their best work with an image resolution in the range of 250 to 300 pixels per
inch. A monitor needs far fewer pixels to generate an acceptable image. For
the complete story on resolution and how it affects image quality, check out
Chapter 3.

Why does my image print at one size and display at another size on-screen?

On-screen image size depends on the monitor display setting, which is measured in pixels, just like a digital photo. A monitor devotes one screen pixel
to each image pixel, so if you set the monitor display to 640 pixels horizontally by 480 pixels vertically, an image that's 640 wide by 480 pixels tall fills
the screen.

Now suppose that you prepare a picture for printing, setting the print size at
4 inches by 4 inches and the resolution at 200 ppi. That gives you a grand
total of 800 pixels horizontally and 800 pixels vertically. Display that image on
a screen that's 640 pixels wide by 480 pixels tall fills the screen.

For more insights on sizing images for the screen, flip to Chapter 6.

How do I print several pictures on one page?

To print multiple copies of the same image on one page, choose File⇨Print
Multiple. Select a paper size, click Print, and PhotoDeluxe automatically
prints however many copies of the picture fit on the page.

Printing several different images on one page takes a little more work. The easiest option is to create a new image, setting the width and height to match your page size and choosing a Resolution value appropriate for printing. Next, open each image you want to print and copy it into the new image. (Remember, though, that PhotoDeluxe changes the resolution of the moved image to match that of its new home.)

How do I put a PhotoDeluxe image into a brochure or other document?

After preparing your image in PhotoDeluxe, save the image in a format that can be read by the program you're using to create the document. In that program, check the help system to find out what command you use to import the image.

Alternatively, select the entire image in PhotoDeluxe, choose Edit➪Copy, switch to the other program, and choose Edit➪Paste. For more information, see Chapters 9 and 14.

Why don't printed colors match screen colors?

This problem occurs because monitors can create a broader spectrum of colors than printers can. If an on-screen color is beyond the printer's capabilities, the printer substitutes the closest available color.

PhotoDeluxe provides a tool to help get printer and monitor in sync: Choose File➪Adjust Color Printing to give it a whirl. Chapter 5 explains this and other tips for achieving better color matching.

How do I save an image in a format other than PDD?

In PhotoDeluxe, the File➪Save command lets you save images in the native PhotoDeluxe format (PDD) only. To save in some other image format, choose File➪Export➪File Format, or, to create a GIF image, File➪Export➪GIF89a Export. Chapter 4 explains file formats and other saving issues.

Chapter 17

Ten PhotoDeluxe Shortcuts

. . . .

In This Chapter

▶ Performing vital file functions: opening, closing, printing, and saving

▶ Undoing your mistakes

▶ Picking up the selection tools and drawing selection outlines

▶ Zooming in for a closer look — and zooming back out to get the big picture

▶ Adjusting cursor appearance and resetting the Tolerance value

▶ Varying the opacity of your tool strokes

▶ Adjusting brightness, contrast, saturation, and color balance

▶ Using the arrow keys to nudge things into just the right position

. . . .

So much time, so little to do — that's the story of my life.

No, wait, that's somebody else's life. My life is "So *much* to do, and not a prayer of getting it all done before this week's *Buffy, the Vampire Slayer.*"

If you, too, feel the pressure of a ticking clock, you'll appreciate the keyboard shortcuts listed in this chapter. Instead of clicking through menus, you can access commands and tools by pressing a few keys or clicking once on an icon or button. You not only save time, but you also save arm strength because you don't have to reach for the mouse so often.

Commit these shortcuts to memory and you can finish in plenty of time to watch the Buffster kick vampire keister *and* have enough energy left to lift some potato chips out of the bag and into your mouth. No need to thank me — helping people lead more artful, fulfilled lives is just part of my job.

Opening, closing, printing, and saving

Here's a batch of shortcuts that you can use every day:

- ✔ **Open an existing image:** Press Ctrl+O.
- ✔ **Save an image:** After you finish destroying . . . er, I mean, editing . . . your image, save it in a flash by press Ctrl+S. The first time you save an image, PhotoDeluxe asks you to give the image a name, specify a storage location, and provide a few other saving instructions. Thereafter, pressing Ctrl+S saves the image without all that fuss.

  You can't use this shortcut to save in a format other than PDD, the native file format. Instead, you must choose File⇨Export⇨File Format.
- ✔ **Open the Print dialog box:** Print dialog box: Press Ctrl+P.
- ✔ **Close an image**: Press Ctrl+W or just click the close button at the top of the image window.

You can find a bundle of other opening, closing, and saving tips in Chapters 1 and 4, if you're so inclined. More printing info is yours for the taking in Chapter 5.

Undoing bonehead moves

Ah, now here's a shortcut you should never be without. In fact, if you remember only one shortcut in this chapter, pick this one. If you screw up and do something you didn't mean to do — or you just don't like the results of something you *did* mean to do — whack the Ctrl key and the Z key. Alternatively, click the Undo button at the top of the image window.

You have to choose Undo immediately after you make a mistake. If you choose another command or take some other editing action, you lose your opportunity to Undo. The exception is choosing the Print command: You can print your image and then undo the move you made just before you printed the image.

You can also choose File⇨Revert to Last Saved to restore your image to the way it appeared immediately after you last saved it using the File⇨Save command. Chapter 7 offers more details.

Selecting and deselecting stuff

To limit the effects of your edits to a certain portion of your image, select that area before you make your changes. Use these shortcuts to breeze through selection chores, and turn to Chapter 9 for the complete scoop on selecting:

- ✔ **Select the entire image:** Press Ctrl+A or click the All button in the Selections palette.

- ✔ **Cancel a selection outline:** Press Ctrl+D or click None in the Selections palette.

- ✔ **Invert the selection outline:** Press Ctrl+I or click Invert in the Selections palette.

- ✔ **Activate the Rectangle tool:** Press Ctrl+M.

- ✔ **Activate the Color Wand:** Press Ctrl+F.

- ✔ **Activate the Trace tool:** Press Ctrl+L.

- ✔ **Activate the Move tool:** Press Ctrl+G.

- ✔ **Relocate a selection outline:** After selecting the Move tool, Ctrl+Alt+Drag inside the selection outline to move the outline large distances. Press the arrow keys to nudge the outline a few pixels.

Zooming in and out

Want to zoom in for a closer look at your pixels? Press Ctrl+Plus Key. (Some keyboards require you to press Ctrl+Shift+Plus Key.) To zoom out, press Ctrl+Minus Key. Chapter 1 offers more details about viewing your images on-screen.

Opening the Cursors dialog box

The Cursors dialog box is Grand Central Station for choosing how your cursors appear on-screen and for setting the *tolerance* (sensitivity) of the Color Wand and the Color Change tool. To get to the dialog box quickly, press Ctrl+K.

Activating painting and editing tools

Some of the more popular painting and editing tools are also available at the press of a key or click of a button:

- ✔ **Brush tool:** Press Ctrl+J.
- ✔ **Text tool:** Press Ctrl+T or click the T button on the image window.
- ✔ **Eraser tool:** Press Ctrl+E.
- ✔ **Selection Fill:** Press Ctrl+9 after creating a selection outline.
- ✔ **Gradient Fill:** Press Ctrl+8 after creating a selection outline.

To paint a straight line with the Brush tool, Shift+Drag or click at the spot where you want the line to begin and Shift+Click at the spot where you want it to end. This trick works with the Eraser tool, too. Pressing Shift as you drag with the Line tool constrains your line to 45-degree angles.

Adjusting tool opacity or pressure

You can control the opacity of the Brush, Eraser, Line, and Clone tools by pressing the number keys. Press 0 to create strokes that are completely opaque, press 9 to switch to 90 percent opacity, 8 to choose 80 percent opacity, and so on.

If you're using the Smudge tool, pressing the number keys changes the pressure of the tool, which dictates how far PhotoDeluxe smudges the pixels that you drag across. Press 0 to smudge for the entire length of your drag. Lower settings smudge pixels for only a portion of the drag. See Chapter 10 for additional information about all these tools.

Applying image correction filters

Use these shortcuts to access commands that correct common image problems. Chapter 7 provides details about using these photo-enhancement features.

- ✔ **Color Balance:** Press Ctrl+Y.
- ✔ **Brightness/Contrast:** Press Ctrl+B.
- ✔ **Hue/Saturation:** Press Ctrl+U.

Copying, moving, and pasting selections

To choose the always popular Cut, Copy, and Paste commands, covered thoroughly in Chapter 9, use these shortcuts:

- ✔ **Cut:** Press Ctrl+X.
- ✔ **Copy:** Press Ctrl+C.
- ✔ **Paste:** Press Ctrl+V.

Nudging selected pixels into place

When the Move tool is selected, you can nudge a selection into place by pressing the arrow keys. Press an arrow key once to nudge the selection one pixel in the direction of the arrow. Press Shift and an arrow key to nudge the selection ten pixels. More information about moving selections around your image awaits you in Chapter 9.

Appendix

Installing PhotoDeluxe

● ●

*P*hotoDeluxe provides a program installer that eases the process of putting the program on your system. Still, you need to make a few choices along the way, which the following steps help you do.

If you received PhotoDeluxe with a digital camera, printer, or scanner, your installation may work a little differently than outlined here. Your copy of PhotoDeluxe may also include some options that the standard version doesn't offer. Consider this chapter a general guideline and don't panic if what you see on-screen doesn't match exactly what I describe here. Check your camera, printer, or scanner manual for special installation instructions:

1. **Shut down all open programs except Windows.**

2. **Put the PhotoDeluxe CD-ROM in your CD-ROM drive.**

   If the PhotoDeluxe installation program doesn't appear after a few seconds, click Start⇨Run and enter the following into the text box: **D:\autoplay.exe**. (If your CD-ROM drive is set up to use some other drive letter than D, enter that letter rather than D.) Then click OK.

3. **Select the country where you bought the program and click Next.**

4. **Study the software license agreement and click Accept.**

5. **Click the ReadMe & Guides button.**

   In the window that appears, you can read last-minute information about installing and using PhotoDeluxe. Click the window close button after you read the documentation.

6. **Click the Install button, read the Welcome screen, and click Next.**

7. **In the Setup Type dialog box, click the Custom option.**

   You're a big kid now; you can decide for yourself which PhotoDeluxe components you want to install.

8. **Review the installation location at the bottom of the dialog box.**

   To the left of the Browse button, PhotoDeluxe shows the drive and folder where it plans to put the program files. Unless you have good reason to change the location, leave well enough alone. If you do need to change the location, click Browse, specify the folder and drive, and click OK.

9. **Click Next.**

   A window shows you the programs that you can install. By default, all three programs are selected for installation. (The check mark in the box indicates that the program will be installed.)

10. **Click the Adobe ActiveShare 1.2 Files check box to deselect it.**

    For reasons that you can explore in Chapter 6, I don't recommend installing ActiveShare. If you have a version of Acrobat later than Version 4.0, deselect that program, too.

11. **Click Next and enter your name, rank, and program serial number.**

12. **Click Next to review the information you just entered.**

13. **Click Yes to verify that everything is correct; click No to go back and change something.**

    After you click Yes, PhotoDeluxe displays a summary of all your installation choices.

14. **Click Back to change your installation options or click Next to begin installation.**

After the PhotoDeluxe files are installed, other installation dialog boxes may appear, depending on what options you selected in Step 10. Follow the on-screen prompts and select the default options unless you know what you're doing and have good reason to fool around with things.

When all files are installed, PhotoDeluxe asks whether you want to register the program via modem. If you do, click Finish and follow the on-screen prompts. To skip the registration, deselect the Registration check box and click Finish. The installer launches a small multimedia player window and begins a multimedia introduction to the program. If you're not interested, click the close button in the player window (the little X in the upper-right corner).

Finally, the installer announces that you need to restart your computer before you use PhotoDeluxe. If you don't want to register just yet, click the No option and click the Finish button. Otherwise, click Yes and click the Finish button. When your computer comes back to life, your newly installed program(s) appear on the Windows Start menu and a PhotoDeluxe program icon appears on the Windows desktop. Choose the program from the menu or double-click the icon to start playing with your new toy.

Index

Notes

Notes

Notes

Notes

Notes

Notes

SPECIAL OFFER FOR IDG BOOKS READERS

FREE GIFT!

FREE

IDG Books/PC WORLD CD Wallet

and a Sample Issue of

PC WORLD

THE #1 MONTHLY COMPUTER MAGAZINE

How to order your sample issue and FREE CD Wallet:

✉ Cut and mail the coupon today!

☎ Call us at 1-800-395-5763
Fax us at 1-415-882-0936

☛ Order online at
www.pcworld.com/subscribe/idgbooks

ORDER TODAY!

FREE GIFT/SAMPLE ISSUE COUPON

Cut coupon and mail to: PC World, 501 Second Street, San Francisco, CA 94107

YES! Please rush my FREE CD wallet and my FREE sample issue of PC WORLD! If I like PC WORLD, I'll honor your invoice and receive 11 more issues (12 in all) for just $19.97—that's 72% off the newsstand rate.

NO COST EXAMINATION GUARANTEE.
If I decide PC WORLD is not for me, I'll write "cancel" on the invoice and owe nothing. The sample issue and CD wallet are mine to keep, no matter what.

PC WORLD

Name _____

Company _____

Address _____

City _____ State ____ Zip _____

Email _____

Offer valid in the U.S. only. Mexican orders please send $39.97 USD. Canadian orders send $39.97, plus 7% GST (#R124669680). Other countries send $65.97. Savings based on annual newsstand rate of $71.88 .

SPECIAL OFFER FOR IDG BOOKS READERS

Get the Most from Your PC!

Every issue of PC World is packed
with the latest information to help
you make the most of your PC.

- Top 100 PC and Product Ratings
- Hot PC News
- How Tos, Tips, & Tricks
- Buyers' Guides
- Consumer Watch
- Hardware and Software Previews
- Internet & Multimedia Special Reports
- Upgrade Guides
- Monthly @Home Section

YOUR FREE GIFT!

As a special
bonus with your
order, you will
receive the
IDG Books/
PC WORLD
CD wallet,
perfect for transporting
and protecting your CD collection.

SEND TODAY

for your sample issue
and FREE IDG Books/PC WORLD CD Wallet!

How to order your sample issue and FREE CD Wallet:

✉ Cut and mail the coupon today!
Mail to: PC World, 501 Second Street, San Francisco, CA 94107

☎ Call us at 1-800-395-5763
Fax us at 1-415-882-0936

☛ Order online at www.pcworld.com/subscribe/idgbooks

PC WORLD

Discover Dummies Online!

The Dummies Web Site is your fun and friendly online resource for the latest information about *For Dummies*® books and your favorite topics. The Web site is the place to communicate with us, exchange ideas with other *For Dummies* readers, chat with authors, and have fun!

Ten Fun and Useful Things You Can Do at www.dummies.com

1. Win free *For Dummies* books and more!
2. Register your book and be entered in a prize drawing.
3. Meet your favorite authors through the IDG Books Worldwide Author Chat Series.
4. Exchange helpful information with other *For Dummies* readers.
5. Discover other great *For Dummies* books you must have!
6. Purchase Dummieswear® exclusively from our Web site.
7. Buy *For Dummies* books online.
8. Talk to us. Make comments, ask questions, get answers!
9. Download free software.
10. Find additional useful resources from authors.

Link directly to these ten fun and useful things at
http://www.dummies.com/10useful

For other technology titles from IDG Books Worldwide, go to
www.idgbooks.com

Not on the Web yet? It's easy to get started with *Dummies 101*®: *The Internet For Windows*® *98* or *The Internet For Dummies*® at local retailers everywhere.

Find other *For Dummies* books on these topics:
Business • Career • Databases • Food & Beverage • Games • Gardening • Graphics • Hardware
Health & Fitness • Internet and the World Wide Web • Networking • Office Suites
Operating Systems • Personal Finance • Pets • Programming • Recreation • Sports
Spreadsheets • Teacher Resources • Test Prep • Word Processing

The IDG Books Worldwide logo is a registered trademark under exclusive license to IDG Books Worldwide, Inc., from International Data Group, Inc. Dummies.com and the ...For Dummies logo are trademarks, and Dummies Man, For Dummies, Dummieswear, and Dummies 101 are registered trademarks of IDG Books Worldwide, Inc. All other trademarks are the property of their respective owners.

IDG BOOKS WORLDWIDE
BOOK REGISTRATION

Register This Book and Win!

We want to hear from you!

Visit **http://my2cents.dummies.com** to register this book and tell us how you liked it!

✔ Get entered in our monthly prize giveaway.

✔ Give us feedback about this book — tell us what you like best, what you like least, or maybe what you'd like to ask the author and us to change!

✔ Let us know any other *For Dummies®* topics that interest you.

Your feedback helps us determine what books to publish, tells us what coverage to add as we revise our books, and lets us know whether we're meeting your needs as a *For Dummies* reader. You're our most valuable resource, and what you have to say is important to us!

Not on the Web yet? It's easy to get started with *Dummies 101®: The Internet For Windows® 98* or *The Internet For Dummies®* at local retailers everywhere.

Or let us know what you think by sending us a letter at the following address:

For Dummies Book Registration
Dummies Press
10475 Crosspoint Blvd.
Indianapolis, IN 46256

™

...FOR DUMMIES

**BESTSELLING
BOOK SERIES**